BEYOND REMEMBERING

BEYOND REMEMBERING

The collected poems
of
AL PURDY
selected and edited by
Al Purdy
&
Sam Solecki

HARBOUR PUBLISHING

Harbour Publishing
P.O. Box 219
Madeira Park, BC
Canada V0N 2H0

THE CANADA COUNCIL | LE CONSEIL DES ARTS
FOR THE ARTS | DU CANADA
SINCE 1957 | DEPUIS 1957

We acknowledge the financial support of the Government of Canada through the Book Publishing Industry Development Program for our publishing activities. We further acknowledge the support of the Canada Council for the Arts and the Province of British Columbia through the British Columbia Arts Council for our publishing program.

Cover design by Martin Nichols, Lionheart Graphics
Cover photograph by Frank O'Connor
Frontispiece photograph and photograph on page 179 by D'Arcy Glionna
Photograph on page 445 by Vanessa Solecki Nelson
Photograph on page 577 by Barry Peterson & Blaise Enright-Peterson
All other photos courtesy Eurithe Purdy
Edited for the house by Silas White
Proofreading by Patricia Wolfe

Canadian Cataloguing in Publication Data

Purdy, Al, 1918–2000.
  Beyond remembering

ISBN 1-55017-225-5

  I. Solecki, Sam, 1946– II. Title.
PS8531.U8A17 2000   C813'.54   C00-910768-1
PR9199.3.P8A17 2000

Printed in Canada

For Eurithe

BOOKS BY AL PURDY

POETRY

The Enchanted Echo (1944)
Pressed on Sand (1955)
Emu, Remember! (1956)
The Crafte So Long to Lerne (1959)
The Blur in Between: Poems 1960 – 61 (1962)
Poems for All the Annettes (1962)
The Cariboo Horses (1965)
North of Summer: Poems from Baffin Island (1967)
Wild Grape Wine (1968)
Love in a Burning Building (1970)
The Quest for Ouzo (1971)
Hiroshima Poems (1972)
Selected Poems (1972)
On the Bearpaw Sea (1973)
Sex and Death (1973)
In Search of Owen Roblin (1974)
The Poems of Al Purdy: A New Canadian Library Selection (1976)
Sundance at Dusk (1976)
A Handful of Earth (1977)
At Marsport Drugstore (1977)
Moths in the Iron Curtain (1977)
No Second Spring (1977)
Being Alive: Poems 1958 – 78 (1978)
The Stone Bird (1981)
Birdwatching at the Equator: The Galapagos Islands (1982)
Bursting into Song: An Al Purdy Omnibus (1982)
Piling Blood (1984)
The Collected Poems of Al Purdy (1986)
The Woman on the Shore (1990)
Naked With Summer in Your Mouth (1994)
Rooms for Rent in the Outer Planets (1996)
To Paris Never Again (1997)
The Man Who Outlived Himself (with Doug Beardsley, 1999)

OTHER

No Other Country (prose, 1977)
The Bukowski/Purdy Letters 1964 – 1974: A Decade of Dialogue (with Charles Bukowski, 1983)
Morning and It's Summer: A Memoir (1983)
The George Woodcock/Al Purdy Letters (edited by George Galt, 1987)
A Splinter in the Heart (novel, 1990)
Cougar Hunter (essay on Roderick Haig-Brown, 1993)
Margaret Laurence – Al Purdy: A Friendship in Letters (1993)
Reaching for the Beaufort Sea: An Autobiography (1993)
Starting from Ameliasburgh: The Collected Prose of Al Purdy (1995)
No One Else is Lawrence! (with Doug Beardsley, 1998)

EDITOR

The New Romans: Candid Canadian Opinions of the US (1968)
Fifteen Winds: A Selection of Modern Canadian Poems (1969)
Milton Acorn, *I've Tasted My Blood: Poems 1956–1968* (1969)
Storm Warning: The New Canadian Poets (1971)
Storm Warning 2: The New Canadian Poets (1976)
Andrew Suknaski, *Wood Mountain Poems* (1976)

CONTENTS

THE SEVENTIES

THE EIGHTIES

FOREWORD
by Margaret Atwood

Ibegan to read Al Purdy's poetry about the same time it changed from being odd and ungainly to being remarkable – in the early sixties. I was just into my twenties, writing a lot of poetry but not liking much of it; like most young poets then, I wanted to be published by Contact Press – a highly respected poet-run co-operative – and I read everything issued by it; and thus I read Purdy's *Poems for All the Annettes* in 1962, when it first came out.

I was somewhat frightened by it, and did not fully understand it. This was a new sort of voice for me, and an overpowering one, and a little too much like being backed into the corner of a seedy bar by a large, insistent, untidy drunk, who is waxing by turns both sentimental and obscene. For a young male poet of those days, this kind of energy and this approach – casual, slangy, subversive of recent poetic convention – could be liberating and inspirational, and some found in him an ersatz father figure. But for a young female poet – well, this was not the sort of father figure it would be altogether steadying to have.

Then, in 1965, *The Cariboo Horses* – Purdy's breakthrough book – came out, and I found that the drunk in the bar was also a major story-teller and mythmaker, though still wearing his offhand and indeed rather shabby disguise. This is poetry for the spoken voice par excellence – not an obviously rhetorical voice, but an anecdotal voice, the voice of the

Canadian vernacular. Yet not only that either, for no sooner has Purdy set up his own limits than he either transcends or subverts them. Purdy is always questioning, always probing, and among those things that he questions and probes are himself and his own poetic methods. In a Purdy poem, high diction can meet the scrawl on the washroom wall, and as in a collision between matter and anti-matter, both explode.

It would be folly to attempt to sum up Purdy's poetic universe: like Walt Whitman's, it's too vast for a précis. What interests him can be anything at all, but above all the wonder that anything at all can be interesting. He's always turning banality inside out. For me, he's above all an explorer – pushing into nameless areas of landscape, articulating the inarticulate, poking around in dusty corners of memory and discovering treasure there, digging up the bones and shards of a forgotten ancestral past. When he's not capering about and joking and scratching his head over the idiocy and pain and delight of being alive, he's composing lyric elegies for what is no longer alive, but has been – and, through his words, still is. For underneath that flapping overcoat and that tie with a mermaid on it and that pretence of shambling awkwardness – yes, it's a pretence, but only partly, for among other things Purdy is doing a true impersonation of himself – there's a skillful master-conjurer. Listen to the voice, and watch the hands at work: just hands, a bit grubby too, not doing anything remarkable, and you can't see how it's done, but suddenly, where a second ago there was only a broken vase, there's a fistful of brilliant flowers.

FOREWORD
by Michael Ondaatje

We were very young and he was hitting his stride – *Poems for All the Annettes, The Cariboo Horses*. There had been no poetry like it yet in this country. Souster and Acorn were similar, had prepared the way, but here was a voice with a "strolling" not "dancing" gait or metre, climbing over old fences in Cashel township... (And who ever wrote about "township lines" in poems before Al did?)

And with this art of walking he covered greater distances, more haphazardly, and with more intricacy. Cashel and Ameliasburg and Elzevir and Weslemkoon are names we can now put on a literary map alongside the Mississippi and The Strand. For a person of my generation, Al Purdy's poems mapped and named the landscape of Ontario, just as Leonard Cohen did with Montreal and its surroundings in *The Favourite Game*.

We were in our twenties (and I speak for my friends Tom Marshall and David Helwig, who were there with me) and we didn't have a single book to our names; we were studying or teaching at the university in Kingston.

. . . And Al and Eurithe simply invited us in. And why? Because we were poets! Not well-known writers or newspaper celebrities. Did Kipling ever do that?

Did D.H. Lawrence? Malcolm Lowry had done that for "Al– something or other" in Dollarton, years earlier.

These visits became essential to our lives. We weren't there for gossip, certainly not to discuss royalties and publishers. We were there to talk about poetry. Read poems aloud. Argue over them. Complain about prosody. We were there to listen to a recording he had of "The Bonnie Earl of Murray." And sometimes we saw Al's growing collection of signed books by other Canadian poets. (My favourite dedication among them was "To Awful Al from Perfect Peggy.")

All this changed our lives. It allowed us to take poetry seriously. This happened with and to numerous other young poets all over the country, right until the last days of Al Purdy's life. He wasn't just a "sensitive" man, he was a generous man.

Most of all we should celebrate his fervent, dogmatic desire to write poetry. A glass-blower makes money. A worm-picker has a more steady income. Al, a man who had the looks and manner of a brawler, wanted to be a poet. And what is great is that he was a bad poet for a long time and that didn't stop him. That's where the heroism comes in.

And when he became a good, and then a great poet, he never forgot the significance and importance of those bad poets – they were rather like those small homes and farms north of Belleville, "a little adjacent to where the world is," and about to sink into the earth. He had been there. It gave his work a central core of humbleness, strange word for Al. It resulted in the double take in his work, the point where he corrects himself.

"I have been stupid in a poem..."

As he was not ashamed to whisper in a poem – this in a time of mid-century bards. Al never came with bardic trappings.

"Who is he like?" you ask yourself. And in Canada there is no one.

I can't think of a single parallel in English literature. It almost seems a joke to attempt that. He was this self-taught poet from up the road. What a brave wonder.

So how do we respond to all that Al was and stood for?

The great Scottish poet Hugh MacDiarmid, who was pretty close to Al in some ways, had by the time of his death become the embodiment of what his country's culture was, and stood for, and stood against. Fellow Scottish poet Norman MacCaig recognized MacDiarmid's contribution by saying:

"Because of his death, this country should observe two minutes of pandemonium."

PREFACE

This is my last book. Sam Solecki is the editor, and now seems a good time to thank him, for that and many other reasons. And to thank Eurithe for many many reasons. I said to her a moment ago, "What does it feel like to live with someone who writes poems most of his life and yours?"

She said, "To me it feels normal. I can't compare it with anything else. It was a life."

Sure it was a life. But can't I wring even a modest superlative out of her like: "Al, it was wonderful! I loved every minute of it!" Couldn't she lie a little just to make me happy? I tell you, it's maddening to live with a woman who always has to tell the truth, as if it hurts her in the esophagus or eardrum or in her instep to exaggerate just a wee bit. I tell her shut up then, I got this very important document to write, outlining my Philosophy and World View of the Hereafter.

So I'm left alone to talk with a bunch of ghosts, at least people I can't see, potential readers, past readers, people who can't stand my stuff (no, they can't read anyway). But there are a few, I guess. And now I have a subject. I've reached age 80, and I started to write at 13. Now I hafta make an embarrassed confession: I feel the same way Eurithe does: I can't compare our lives with any others. (But I hate women who're always right like that.)

It was a life, she said. And I thought it was a pretty good one. We did what we wanted to do, went where we wanted to go. I wrote the way I

liked, and kidded myself some of it was pretty good. We were broke –
and I mean nearly penniless – a few times in earlier days. A few times,
for god's sake? Nearly always. There were periods when I was so
depressed I felt like suicide – having failed at everything I tried to do. But
we pulled out of it, with some difficulty. And those periods I called "The
Bad Times" seem to me now something like Triumph. "Don't you think
so, dear?"

"They were horrible. You should have committed suicide."

What are ya gonna do with a woman like that?

Anyway, yes, it was a life. I wouldn't have wanted any other.

AL PURDY
Sidney, BC / Ameliasburg, Ontario 1999

THE FIFTIES

AT EVERGREEN CEMETERY

The still grey face and withered body:
without resistance winter enters in,
as if she were a stone or fallen tree,
her temperature the same as the landscape's –
How she would have complained about that,
the indignity of finally being without heat,
an insult from the particular god she believed in,
and worse than the fall that killed her –
Now a thought flies into the cemetery
from Vancouver, another from Edmonton,
– and fade in the January day like fireflies.
I suppose relatives are a little slower
getting the evening meal because of that –
perhaps late for next day's appointments,
the tight schedule of seconds overturned,
everything set a little back or ahead,
the junctures of time moving and still:
settling finally into a new pattern,
by which lovers, hurrying towards each other
on streetcorners, do not fail to meet –
Myself, having the sense of something going
on without my knowledge, changes taking place
that I should be concerned with,
sit motionless in the black car behind the hearse,
waiting to re-enter a different world.

FROM THE CHIN P'ING MEI

Fifty men at arms with bows and lances
from the River Prefect. From the District Yamen
twenty more. Two hundred from General Chang.
The boom of drums, the clang of gongs –
She would have been frightened, my little one,
if she were alive and her palanquin,
passing through the South Gate at noonday,

had encountered the funeral procession
of a dead lady – she would have wept.

ON THE DECIPHERMENT OF "LINEAR B"
(by Michael Ventris and associates)

Grammatic structure first, then phonetic values:
Ventris mailing progress reports to philologists
for comment (by air across the Atlantic):
the endgame – all the dusty Cretan sibilants
hissing delightedly back to life on scholar tongues,
whispering possible gossip to the co-translators
– that turned out to be inventories,
amphorae in warehouses, wine long vanished,
dried to red dust in the guts of Mycenaean warriors;
listings of clergy reserves, military property:
"Horse vehicle, painted red, supplied with reins";
words, preserved like nothing machines make,
perfect, unflawed, the same.

We see them (dramatic as hell), the code-breakers,
in shirt sleeves, drinking gallons of coffee:
gowned Oxford dons, real estate brokers,
American academics – a linguistic orgy,
broken by twitterings of girlish excitement,
punctuated with cries of discovery.

It turns out Minos was maybe an expatriate
Greek, who said to hell with hiero-
glyphic symbols: brought in the smith Daedalus
(a bad mistake re Pasiphae's morals)
to promote Greek investment, Linear B and stud poker –
Well anyway, Ventris figured it out,
and everyone can sit down after work reading
comic books or Agamemnon's diaries now.

But Knossos did burn, its flaming windows
signalled the stars 3,000 years ago:
when men died foetal, rolled into blackened balls,
and women, abandoned by children and lovers,
fled to the palace upper rooms with skirts on fire:
and over the island a south wind blowing –

WHOEVER YOU ARE

If birds look in the window odd beings
look back and birds must stay birds.
If dogs gaze upward at yellow oblongs
of warmth, bark for admittance
to hot caves high above the street,
among the things with queer fur,
the dogs are turned to dogs, and longing
wags its tail and turns invisible.

Clouds must be clouds always, even if
they've not decided what to be at all,
and trees trees, stones stones, unnoticed,
the magic power of anything is gone.
But sometimes when the moonlight disappears,
with you in bed and nodding half awake,
I have not known exactly who you were,
and choked and could not speak your name . . .

WHERE THE MOMENT IS

I forget whether I ever loved you
in the past – when you enter the room
your climate is the mood
of living, the hinge of now,
in time the present tense.
Certainly you are the world

I am not done with,
until I dispense with words –
Yet neutral: something I say
will flash back like light
or shadow; you wait,
to be a stranger I've not met
or fondled or slept with.
The action begins and quickly
word, inflection, reaction fall
into this place the moment is,
like truth and just as variable.
I can predetermine your future,
and taste you becoming in my mouth,
a blank map to explore
in silence, a thought gone out
of me to make you be or say –
Eventually you back against
a wall and I or we may
suddenly find our mouths screaming
in anger or laughter
without meaning – and wince.
But the damned trouble is
I keep finding you before and after
my existence – in my absence
you expect or mourn without a sound.

LOVE SONG

I imagine you a bitch as bad and spiteful
As Jezebel – then confuse you with Judith's tears
Shining taller than Holofernes' glinting spears . . .
(When you sniff the acoustics of your nose are delightful.)

Five minutes ago I was young, five minutes ago
I loved a woman . . . But I grew old suddenly,
Immersed in literature and decadent philosophy . . .
(But I can be two men if I have to.)

I will seem to you like a man seen on the street
Several times, who unaccountably disappeared,
But was not missed or ever really here . . .
(Unlike the man delivering beer from Porlock's Grocery.)

Coleridge knew you and maybe Shelley,
Rhodomontade and hyperbole.
Rhetoric, metaphor, embroidery . . .
(Love is ambivalence and sex is a bully.)

Love is ambivalence and sex is a bully,
But I can be two men if I have to,
Unlike the man delivering beer from Porlock's Grocery . . .
(When you sniff the acoustics of your nose are delightful.)

GILGAMESH AND FRIEND

Eabani, or Enkidu, made by an itinerant goddess
From clay, hairy, perhaps human,
Destined to have carbuncles, goiter, fear of death –

Became friend of beasts, notable in that
He learned their language (played the flute?),
Was weaned from animals by a courtesan . . .

(How?) Joined Gilgamesh to initiate heroism
(First known ism?) in the Sumerian microcosm.
Killed bulls, wizards, monsters like Shumbaba

(Who had no genitals, thank goodness!) in a cedar forest,
Judiciously aided by Bel, Aruru, and Shamah.
Through the adolescent world these Sumerian tourists

Joyed in their senses. But Eabani died.
Girl-crazy Gilgamesh, trophy-hunter, fame-seeker,
Wept (got drunk?), troubled gods with sharp cries.

Sought Utanapishtim, the old ark navigator
From flood days, senile but certified immortal:
With snappy snarl asked him his recipe.

Denied. Gilgamesh, the tired folk hero,
Died, first speaking to late-comer Assur-
Bani-pal about a stone tablet to commemorate

Himself by: laid down among discarded jewellery,
Brazen spears, piled armor, heard desert jackals whine
(Grinned?), nipping heels of tearful concubines:

Felt numbness, emptying, first slow tremor
Of translation, became a story,
And went stammering into the centuries . . .

AT ROBLIN LAKE

Did anyone plan this,
set up the co-ordinates
of experiment to bring about
an ecology of near and distant
batrachian nightingales?
– Each with a frog in his throat,
rehearsing the old springtime pap
about the glories of copulation.
If not I'd be obliged if
the accident would unhappen.

The pike and bass are admirably silent
about such things, and keep their
erotic moments *a mensa et toro*
in cold water. After which I suppose
comes the non-judicial separation.
Which makes them somewhat misogynists?
In any case frogs are ignorant
about the delusion and snare women

represent – they brag and boast
epicene, while piscene culture doesn't.

This tangential backyard universe
I inhabit with sidereal aplomb,
tho troubled with midnight debate
by frog theologians, bogged
down in dialectics and original
sin of discursiveness
(the god of boredom at one remove,
discreetly subsidized on wooden plates) –
Next morning I make a shore-capture,
one frog like an emerald breathing,
hold the chill musical anti-body
a moment with breath held,
thinking of spores, spermatozoa, seed,
housed in this cold progenitor,
transmitting to some future species
what the wall said to Belshazzar.
And, wondering at myself, experiencing
for this bit of green costume jewellery
the beginnings of understanding,
the remoteness of alien love –

THE SIXTIES

POEM FOR ONE OF THE ANNETTES

Which one of you? – oh now
I recognize that tear-stained pro-
Semitic nose shaped wonderfully for
your man Murray's kisses but
he left didn't he?
      Oh Annette
           cry like hell
for Columbus Ohio and Taos New Mexico
where he is and you're not
                As if
the world had ended and
          it has –

Or the Anita with undressed hips that
could break a man in half in bed and
big unpainted Rubens breasts affixed to
          a living woman
swinging high over Montreal
             As if
the whole damn town was a whorehouse full
of literarily inclined millionaires with a yen
for your kind of dirty-story-book-love and
          it is –

Or Janine from Poland who's
a citizen of Canada knocked up
in Montreal by a Yank from
Columbus Ohio and
          abandoned and
the abortion took place in the Town of
Mount Royal and the foetus had
        no name –

Cry for your own bad judgement in
   loving him with good tears that
      will not
          fall

but stay
in the blue beginning of every evening when
factory watchmen are coming on duty and
silent lovers are visible as moths hovering on
streetcorners
                    in eccentric silver orbit
as permanent as any in
                    Maisonneuve's cynical metropolis –

Cry the common sickness with ordinary tears
                                        As if
they would flood the whole quasi-romantic town of
Montreal with the light of your darkness and
follow the gutters and sewers glowing down
thru sewage disposal plants by the river and
into the industrial waste of your dreams to
          the sea
                the shapeless mothering one-celled sea –

          Oh Anita, they do.

POSTSCRIPT [1962]

I say the stanza ends, but it never does,
there being something continual,
apart from the blaze of man, in a woman –
at least he somehow thinks there is.
After a parting grimly convivial
nostalgia comes like an old shaman,
crossing Côte des Neiges in the rush hour –
But she is far from here in another city,
smiles there, sleeps with another man and
bites in bed, likes sad music about
unfaithful lovers, old faces, burnt toast –
Nothing I do not recognize and love
again but recurs monotonously as tho
even this long silence was metrically

arranged and
           soon there will be words –
I say the stanza never ends
               and it never does.

ARCHAEOLOGY OF SNOW

Bawdy tale at first
           what happened
in the snow
what happens
           in bed or anywhere I said
                  oh Anna
        here –
here –   here –
    here –
        here –

But gone Anna
        next day gone
        gone next day
        just gone
to Melbourne Vienna or that place I forget
on De Bullion Street and get lost
looking and can't find any more and go home
Day after next day
           I found her
           heavy buttocks
           in the snow
printed there
           like a Cambrian trilobite
Except the girl was not there
but was there also somehow
veritable as proof of a lie
or truth of an illusion

I cut a stick and shoved it

into the snow beside her
to mark the spot
and stayed there beside her an hour
            (O hound
            of faithfulness)
studied the beautiful outline
(Helen of Illyria with the big behind)
inline   interior cross section
        outline   vivisected
        by prying blunt gradual grey day
(As I remember now it didn't snow for
quite a long stretch and there
was a spell of cold weather to
fracture two
            of the balls
of the pawnbroker on Craig Street if any and even
if there weren't it would have if there had been)
The beautiful outline
                    ah
                        exquisite as wind
life and art combined
blowing and pressing
its shape on water
like an invisible woman
    For a month's weeks
                    I went there
where she was and was and was
and kept being with no surcease
                    at all

But weather got warmer
icicles melted
            spring medicine dropped
on hot necks from downtown office buildings
        The snow that indicated Anna
was grey as grey and greyer went rotten as
an old man's wornout old underpants with
                            ragged crotch
or fairy castles in Spain with absentee landlords

I bent over her
                sniffing sadly
                for Anna
I said to myself sadly
                of course
she's done for and I'm a fool
                of course a fool
weakly watching her vanish
obsessively watching nothing
           But use your head man
                use
the dirty snow to
                        make repairs
fill in the melted places
fill in the flaws and stretch marks
patch the dints and dimples of
this impatient to depart
            eroded and almost erased mannequin woman
                  with snow
                  patient snow

Now she's still there
                silently still there
          sweetly still here
          a few more moments
          to hang in a private art gallery
          of permanent imaginings
No I say
          she's quite gone or will
be soon and it's hardly surprising seeing
that spring is coming and brooks
and water and earth are moving
                    moving
moving
         Yes
I say
      she's gone
             But
the snow itself wasn't her

                              nor any part of her
                              wasn't a woman
                              indicated one
                              pointed to one
and what the snow surrounds is not perishable
            SHE MUST BE STILL THERE
has to be there
only the snow is melted
the form is HERE
                        has to be
                        must be

As if we were all immortal
in some way I've not fathomed
as if all we were
has only changed its shape
as if all we are
co-exists in so many forms
we encounter the entire race
of men just by being
                        alive here
Ourselves amorous
            ourselves surly
                and immortal as hell
(each a valid self)
moving as Anna does in
                            the sub-
divisions of time was
the split fractions of time is
        And in the plumed fields of light
        are the shapely deeds of our flesh
        the lovely omniscience of women
We need to exist but once
in the green shadows
                        in the sunlit places
and there's no end of humans
            My god what an agony to be sub-divided like
            this and to be continuous and to be every-
            where like a bunch of children's blocks

Beyond Remembering

disappearing inside each other my god
and not being also migawd
also what grandeur

THE LISTENERS

"I might have married her once but
being an overnight guest of hers changed my mind –"
A big man who looked like a truck driver,
getting sober as you can get on beer,
and he suddenly burst out with that –
"What happened?" I said.
"Her old man was dying of something or
other in a room downstairs without
drugs and screamed most of the time –
I could see the line of light under her door,
and I kept wanting and then not wanting
her between yells. I'd hear the wind blow,
the woodwork creak, and listen some more and
think of the girl – then he'd scream."
The waiter came by with beer.
                                "Here," I said,
and paid him and grinned in the familiar friendly
roar of the jammed full tavern and talk boomed
in my ears –
                "Go on," I said.
"After midnight, me lying and listening,
hearing people asleep and some not asleep,
the sounds an old house makes to itself
for company, the nails and boards and bricks
holding together such a long time and knowing
so many things about people
                                then he'd scream and
I'd say to myself, 'Go on an die, go on an die –'
They must've had the windows open wide,
for the sound came in from outside too.
I'd hear the crickets and then he'd scream!

Finally I heard the girl scramble out of bed,
she came rushing into my room in a nightgown
and dragged me downstairs and outside,
holding my hand so hard she cut thru calluses,
holding my hand and running like hell
into the fields
                    into the fields . . .
Oh it was good, I thought, it was fine,
the silence and her wanting me and I –
But I looked and it wasn't wanting in her eyes,
not wanting at all in her grey eyes
                                        but waiting . . .
Migawd, what was she waiting for in that
                              wheat field?
What did she want to make me do or say or be
suddenly there in the moonlight?
Well (he said defiantly), I wouldn't."
Reassurance seemed in order when I
looked at the big sweating red face and said,
"Nothing happened: you didn't make love,
the old man didn't die, you went away unchanged –"
He looked at me and the room grew silent,
as if everyone had been listening to his story,
at closing time around the upside down tables,
everyone listened still
                    everyone listened –

FOR NORMA IN LIEU OF AN ORGASM

Five years without one?
         migawd girl that husband
         of yours is a sky-blue idiot!
What's it like my dear?
         I guess nobody knows
         what thunder's like or pain
or what fleshly couturier
         lures the modest shopgirl

into an ultimate nudity –
No one ever lived very long
  in the exaggerated zone
  and bomb-bursting place that
  fucking is
    or pushed a
  mathematic past a
  prepared landscape
  into flesh
in fact you
  are not to believe in
      pain
       sorrow
  or death at all
  make no travel preparations
  until you suddenly arrive there
        my dear
  unarmed on the wonderful battlefield . . .
Oh?
  well
   if words must suffice it's
  the werewolf metamorphosis
  in which animals and men
  transfer themselves painfully
  (then grow discontented
  with the moonlit landscape)
  and thick fur
  sprouts from Ivory breast and thigh
  wolf's head gleams white and somewhat human
And in the forest
  there is a rumour
    of love –

SPRING SONG

– philosophic musings from under an
old Pontiac while changing the oil and
observing a young lady in summer attire
on her way to the rural mail box –

You neanderthals with guns and bombs
stop exactly where you are
assassins wait in your own dark thoughts
and armies marching thru the rain
with rifles dragging in the mud halt
with one foot raised to take a step
teetering at the dark crossroads
consulting your maps of hell
stop exactly where you are

The world's pain is a little away from here
and the hawk's burst of speed that claws
a fish from its glass house is earlier
and later than now under a rejuvenated
Pontiac with frogs booming temporary
sonatas for mortals and Beethoven
crows thronging the June skies and
everything still
                    everything suddenly goddam still
the sun a hovering golden bird
                    nothing moves
                    soft clouds wait
like floating houses in the sky
and the storm beyond the horizon waits
planets stopped in their tracks
high over the village of Ameliasburg
                    as if forever was now
                    and the grass roots knew it all
– but they don't you know and here I am
                    with both hands high
under the skirts of the world
trying to figure it out too late for

someone breathed or sighed or spoke
and everything rearranged itself
from is to was the white moon tracks
her silver self across the purple night
replacing time with a celestial
hour glass halfway between a girl
and woman I forgot till she comes jiggling
back from the dark mailbox at last migawd
hosanna in the lowest mons Veneris I
will never get to change the goddam oil

THE QUARREL

Lying side by side
                    naked in darkness
bodies stiff with anger
                    tempered thoughts clashing
like swords in the room's corners —
a limited sort of agony
that doesn't kill you,
but could —
The moon sinks teeth in bedroom
chews at the curtainrod
lifting ocean tides of rage
drags both
              onetime lovers
into its twitching pattern,
self-conscious on Mare Imbrium . . .

(Mare Imbrium, my darling!
Running with great 30 foot strides
in the apogee and perigee of love,
throwing handfuls of pumice and sliding
down shale hills in a dream slalom
to Lacus Mortis and Lacus Somniorum,
where youth is a twinkle in the eye
of the absolute,

and pride an absolute
necessity for virgins . . .)

Self-conscious on Mare Imbrium?
Mad as hell in a bedroom
                in Ameliasburg Township!
Even as in the councils of the great
                (my darling)
and the consultations of the kings of earth
a small quarrel like ours can't be solved:
                and while that white body protrudes
                over on my side of the bed
                pride is damn difficult . . .

O RECRUITING SERGEANTS!

No, I'll not go with you to fight for
human freedom or power steering or
the sanctity of marriage in
Madrid and Troy and Detroit,
or join the freedom riders
on their gallant adventure
thru Alabama and Georgia –
I'm much too much
a bungling little mechanic and
dare not tinker among
the blind engineers of the universe
who work such cruelty and sorrow with
levers extending all the way down here,
and whose complaint dept. has
a dead switchboard –
        But to all you with burning barns,
lost causes and dishonoured flags,
washable skins and souls convulsed with
gallantry I say:
                Press on!
Mine is the cynicism no flag shall squander

(tho the ugly pregnant servant girl
in her last miscarried tormented ten minutes
((in the last reel or act or chapter))
turns out to have been my sister),
no lost cause claim casually
for its glorious dead;
no writhing murdered Christ
or bloody openmouthed Caesar
talked to death on the livingroom floor
inspires my soul to sob for any leader,
least of all yours –
Mine is the commonplace acceptance of good
or evil
      (a Persian at Marathon,
     a Turk at Lepanto),
the cynicism of
          the defeated majority that
wickedly survives
        virtue –

EVERGREEN CEMETERY

I guess it is ever green . . .
and what's sure if green isn't?
Me standing here in death's
ceded town
      in full summer
the dead down there unfreezing comfortably
the cold miserable rain untouching them
outnumbering all to hell the last newcomers:
1 human, 2 chipmunks, some squirrels –
Child me (subtract 30 years)
yelling down the rotting mausoleum vent:
      "Hoo-hoo – wake up!"
The dead inside silent
        silent now.

So – the swaggerers flaunt
over graves an appropriate green panache,
the braggarts delve into dumb roots,
and the lovers join an unemotional passion,
as earth shapes and reshapes itself
                              again and again.

But the dead are wholehearted about being dead,
no half measures no shilly-shallying:
they're committed, dedicated
                              to purposelessness.
And I get a grim glee from all the high-sounding
old aspirations and clichés ending in damp ground,
glee close to grief maybe, a hangman's gladness:
if that's being human it's best done with.

But it's too complicated to sum up
in telling phrase or easy pessimism,
syllogism or denouement . . .
I've seen this same graveyard sunlight
at a beach, its gold coins
mottled on a girl's flesh
and groped for them under a blanket:
I've seen these trees spilling down mountains
that I trudged up sweating,
and loved for their banners' brightness.

Well
        I've no business in this damn place,
not yet anyway with the taverns open,
tho my mother has:
inept christian that she was,
bumbling among the granite colossi
searching for her redeemer . . .
But I remember her savage grey face
before she died in a drugged fever,
and nurse telling me she'd stuffed her false teeth
up her rectum (in a pleased shocked voice):
                that sharpened elemental

grinning face
with empty jaws which
almost as I watched bit
                    hard on death.

Which reminds me I'd better hurry and get out
of here before the gates close.

MIND PROCESS RE A FAUCET

The faucet is cool green shadowed spring –
some stocky old water god with
knobby knees sits there making magic –

Or a grim sunburned Roman engineer
(came with the lease?) kneels in the flooded
kitchen to curse this damned aqueduct –

No such fantasy of metal and water,
not the unreasonable slim princess
crawling continuously from every drop and hiccuping –
But the flash-picture, the idea of faucet.

And I can't make it be
what it isn't by saying,
or take the shape of a word's being.

For multiple identity confuses anyway,
there must be a single total,
all water – torrents of god-stuff.

(Absurd delight in this sort of thing –
as if the sprawled mind was exercising,
asked its sybil self questions – grins derisively
behind the hand at its own shell game.)

Obviously the idea of faucet is its own function,
a lovesome sound (god wot?) dripping thru the night,
concentrating desperately on retaining its faucet shape:
Water, keep thinking WATER, you'll be all right!

Essence? analyse the metal constituents:
nickel-steel, imposed form – but I keep thinking
of mineral molecules before and after they got here,
the lyric rubble, mind that holds and joins –

Mind that gets bloody tired! – you too, reader,
need shock after shock – for myself continuous discovery,
else in the midst of somnolence: defeat after defeat.

Now relax in the cerebral split levels
of mind – and silence on the fourth floor
in an apt. where nothing works very well:

and round the city's misty hemisphere
lights come on like discordant signals,
answered by starry holes in black tissuepaper,
which makes no sense at all –
and the faucet drips.

RURAL HENHOUSE AT NIGHT

            In green dominions
of vanquished hawks and lost
territorial domain
of weasels duped electrically
and rats dispatched by science
these call girls
                  coaxed
by kilowatts' chicanery
to lay
        for more than 24 hours . . .

INDIAN SUMMER

In the big house with the heat turned off
lights flashed on for a night,
and crickets trapped in the wainscoting
chirped in drowsy sleep and
the high sky of the painted ceiling
turned blue again and bird-haunted:
and over and over the echoes rolled
from the little dog's excited ki-yi-ing –

Briefly briefly all things
          make the sounds
                    that are theirs –
the moon comes drifting
thru the hollow windy living room,
and the paint-flaked kitchen
(equipped with all the latest
          old-fashioned appliances)
is full of hunger and
          empty of all but need –
Words here are simpering imbeciles and
                    dare not hope
                    to break this silence –
Only the falling plaster does,
and the returning cold –

REMAINS OF AN INDIAN VILLAGE

Underfoot rotten boards, forest rubble, bones . . .
Animals were here after the plague,
after smallpox to make another ending:
for the tutelary gods of decay
acknowledge aid from any quarter . . .
Here the charging cotyledons of spring
press green forefingers
on femurs, vertebrae, and delicate

belled skulls of children;
the moon's waylaid light does not shrink
from bone relics and other beauties of nature . . .

Death is certainly absent now,
at least in the overwhelming sense
that it once walked at night in the village
and howled thru the mouths of dogs –
But everything fades
and wavers into something else,
the seasonal cycle and the planet's rhythm
vary imperceptibly into the other;
spirits of the dead are vanished,
only great trees remain,
and the birth certificate of cedars
specifies no memory of a village . . .

(And I have seen myself fade
from a woman's eyes
while I was standing there,
and the earth was aware of
me no longer –)
But I come here as part of the process
in the pale morning light,
thinking what has been thought by no one
for years of their absence,
in some way continuing them –
And I observe the children's shadows
running in this green light from
                              a distant star
into the near forest –
wood violets and trilliums of
a hundred years ago
blooming and vanishing –
the villages of the brown people
toppling and returning –
What moves and lives
        occupying the same space,

what touches what touched them
                    owes them . . .

Standing knee-deep in the joined earth
of their weightless bones,
in the archaeological sunlight,
the trembling voltage of summer,
in the sunken reservoirs of rain,
standing waist-deep in the criss-cross
rivers of shadows,
in the village of nightfall,
the hunters silent and women
bending over dark fires,
I hear their broken consonants . . .

NIGHT SONG FOR A WOMAN

A few times only, then away,
leaving absence akin to presence
in the changed look of
buildings
            an inch off centre –

All things enter
into me so softly I am
aware of them
                    not myself
the mind is sensuous
                    as the body
                    I am a sound
out of hearing past
Arcturus
            still moving outward

– if anyone were to listen
they'd know
            about humans

PAUSE

Uneasily the leaves fall at this season,
forgetting what to do or where to go;
the red amnesiacs of autumn
drifting thru the graveyard forest.

What they have forgotten they have forgotten:
what they meant to do instead of fall
is not in earth or time recoverable –
the fossils of intention, the shapes of rot.

THE OLD WOMAN AND THE MAYFLOWERS

The old woman went into a field for mayflowers
and couldn't get out –:
the cracked voice that prevailed
in a thousand backyard quarrels
broke in a bubble of saliva
that popped and ran down her cheek
like silver slime,
and her mouth held the shape of a cry;
the steel will that evicted
uncounted boys from her apple tree
turned out to be nothing more
than an appetite for trouble:
she bogged and died.
It was some sort of hag-tenderness
perhaps, that made her go there;
ill considered access of feeling
for beauty, or brain softening
after almost 80 years of bitchiness:
an era akin to the Peloponnesian Wars
for some chronicler of Ameliasburg Township.
She'd picked maybe a dozen mayflowers
before dying, and a goat ate them
out of her hand, leaving the stems

tight-clutched. We think it was Mueller's
goat. He called it Trixie.

THE MACHINES

He sweated vomit over those
                damn things
blood and oil on his hands
gave him a stupid dignity
like a bear smeared with garbage
The days fled into smoky weeks
and he learned to operate
one machine after another
learned them all
                how to gauge
the "spock" of a needle plunging
hard thru cloth beside his hand
adjusting the varied rhythms of flesh
with the balanced shifting stance of
a boxer anticipating
        his steel opponent and
walking backward all day long
pursued
        6 feet lengthways
and 4 feet 6 inches sideways
by a spastic hunchback detective
on rails urging him to confess
with metal jaws going "graff-graff"
every 2 seconds
        he managed to retain all 10
clever fingers and perhaps a soul
At the end all the submissive
hymning roar of machines praised him
for what he was
        took him for master and lord
mechanic of their metal destiny until
one afternoon he shoved a pipe-wrench

into closing jaws and heard them groan
out steel blood and shriek once
for their anthropomorphic god
                                    Fired
he went into the street laughing
picked up a woman near Main & Hastings
paid her $5 and went to
bed and sobbed himself
to sleep . . .

WINTER WALKING

Sometimes I see churches
like tons of light,
triangles and hexagons
sideways in air.
Sometimes an old house
holds me watching, still,
with no idea of time,
waiting for the grey shape
to reassemble in my mind,
and I carry it away
(translated back
to drawing board, concept,
mathematic and symbol);
I puzzle myself
with form and line
of an old house
that goes where man goes.
A train's violent anapest
(-- —! -- —!)
cries in my ears,
and leaves me a
breathless small boy.
What entered me trembling
was not the steel's dream.
And walking by,

in a pile of old snow
under a high wall
a patch of brilliant
yellow dog piss
glows, and joins
things in the mind.
Sometimes I stand still,
like a core at the centre
of my senses, hidden and still –
All the heavy people,
clouds and tangible buildings,
enter and pass thru me:
stand like a spell
of the wild gold sunlight,
knowing the ache stones have,
how mountains suffer,
and a wet blackbird feels
flying past in the rain.
This is the still centre,
an involvement in silences –

THE CARIBOO HORSES

At 100 Mile House the cowboys ride in rolling
stagey cigarettes with one hand reining
half-tame bronco rebels on a morning grey as stone
– so much like riding dangerous women
        with whiskey coloured eyes –
such women as once fell dead with their lovers
with fire in their heads and slippery froth on thighs
– Beaver or Carrier women maybe or
        Blackfoot squaws far past the edge of this valley
on the other side of those two toy mountain ranges
        from the sunfierce plains beyond

But only horses
        waiting in stables

hitched at taverns
                    standing at dawn
pastured outside the town with
jeeps and fords and chevys and
busy muttering stake trucks rushing
importantly over roads of man's devising
over the safe known roads of the ranchers
families and merchants of the town
                    On the high prairie
are only horse and rider
                    wind in dry grass
clopping in silence under the toy mountains
dropping sometimes and
                    lost in the dry grass
                    golden oranges of dung

Only horses
                    no stopwatch memories or palace ancestors
not Kiangs hauling undressed stone in the Nile Valley
and having stubborn Egyptian tantrums or
Onagers racing thru Hither Asia and
the last Quagga screaming in African highlands
                    lost relatives of these
                    whose hooves were thunder
the ghosts of horses battering thru the wind
whose names were the wind's common usage
whose life was the sun's
                    arriving here at chilly noon
                    in the gasoline smell of the
                    dust and waiting 15 minutes
                    at the grocer's

THANK GOD I'M NORMAL

From the west coast X writes,
"– someone at CBC is trying to block me."
In Toronto W says, "I want him to die,
if he'd just die –
then I'd have enough money to publish my poems."
Only the guy in Montreal says nothing,
having gotten all the awards going already.
Besides, he's so neurotic he's written
a handy literary guide to the bughouse.
From Calgary, "They won't publish my poems.
They're afraid of em, for I tell the truth.
And They can't stand Truth!"
From the Maritimes: We've got a tradition behind *us*!
(It's what they sit on.)
Me, I'm like all the rest: I wanta be famous!
But I'm not gonna be paranoiac
          I'm not I'm not I'm not I'm not I'm not –
Anyway, I don't know how to end this.
But the morning mail drops in the slot,
and a letter from the scholarship people says
"It is with regret that we inform you –"
          Why – why, the sonsabitches!

PERCY LAWSON

(Contract Negotiator – Vancouver Upholsterers' Union)

Sitting with Lawson in 1954
          sitting with Percy Lawson
ill at ease in the boss's panelled office
after work hours talking of nothing
talking of practically almost nothing
a lousy nickel raise that is
          haggling over a lousy nickel
and maybe besides the long and hourly
bearable toil of an almost lifetime

(East Indians: 35 years
       Canadians: 70 – figures approximate)
Listen in again in the boss's panelled office
       listen to Lawson
listen to Percy Lawson
– thinking of girls in the cutting room
afraid of the union
       afraid for their jobs and
thinking of me – afraid of Watt or
not afraid
       only wanting to be liked
and knowing for sure I'm not
Thinking of Lawson
       up from the coal mines
on the island and gotten fat
since talking and haggling and
being afraid of practically nothing
but death and his wife and damn near
       everything but not
not bosses
not Watt
And what's the contract news from Watt who
if I said what I thought he was would
sue me for damn near everything
would sue me right now in a poem and
get a judgement for one lying lyric
       I can't write
       (I'll be damned if I write)
in praise of Watt
in praise of
       practically nothing
But I listen to Percy Lawson
       haggling over a lousy nickel
listen to the sonuvubitch
       haggling over a lousy nickel
the twentieth part of a dollar that
       winks among the words
like a clean magician's coin
born from virginal nothing and not

mined or smelted and sweated and laboured for for
the twentieth part of a wasted hour back there
in the silvery guts of a labouring terribly useful lifetime
In a tactical pause between the chop
          of words Lawson turns
the little fat man probably dead now
          turns then and gives
me a gold-toothed grin

SONG OF THE IMPERMANENT HUSBAND

Oh I would
I would in a minute
if the cusswords and bitter anger couldn't –
if the either/or quarrel didn't –
and the fat around my middle wasn't –
if I was young if
                    I wasn't so damn sure
I couldn't find another maddening bitch
like you holding on for dear life to
all the different parts of me for
twenty or twenty
                    thousand years
I'd leave in the night like
a disgraced caviar salesman
                    descend the moonlight
stairs to Halifax
                    (uh – no – not Halifax)
well then Toronto
          ah
I guess not Toronto either/or
rain-soaked Vancouver down
                              down
                                        down
the dark stairs to
the South Seas' sunlit milky reefs and
          the jungle's green

                    unending bank account with
all the brown girls being brown
                    as they can be and all
the one-piece behinds stretched tight tonight
in small sarongs gawd not to be touched tho Oh
beautiful as an angel's ass
– without the genitals
And me
                    in Paris like a smudged Canadian postcard and
(dear me)
                    all the importuning white and lily girls
of rue Pigalle
                    and stroll
the sodden London streets and
                    find a sullen foggy woman who
enjoyed my odd colonial ways and send
a postcard back to you about my faithfulness and
talk about the lovely beastly English weather
I'd be the slimiest most uxorious wife deserter
                    my shrunk amoeba self absurd inside
a saffron girl's geography and
hating me between magnetic nipples
but
    fooling no one
in all the sad and much emancipated world
Why then I'll stay
                    at least for tea for
all the brownness is too brown and
all the whiteness too damned white
and I'm afraid
                    afraid of being
any other woman's man
who might be me
                    afraid
the unctuous and uneasy self I glimpse
sometimes might lose my faint and yapping cry
for being anything
                    was never quite what I intended
And you you

                    bitch no irritating
questions re love and permanence only
                    an unrolling lifetime here
between your rocking thighs

                    and the semblance of motion

MOUNTAIN LIONS IN STANLEY PARK

Canadian as the Winnipeg Gold-Eye or
the Calgary Eye-Opener and
regional in this province as Strontium 90 and
international as a boundary they
lived here before night's fuses were blown –

Remember the child?
                    He thought darkness had a nucleus
                                        something plotting
outside his range of vision something
                    that moved and shambled
                    laughed without logic
                    and drooled –
It's rather a comfort now
to see the caged cougar's
fierce eyes focused
                                        serious
                                        (non-idiotic) and
to be involved in the cougar's simple problems
(the snap of a bone in the head exchanging
                                        light for darkness)
and walking to the edge of this floodlit concrete
not stopping at all
on the edge of the great trees –

Running
where the wild tribes go
beyond boundaries

and desolate cities
naked hairless lost one
and sun-bright cougar
into the forest
toward our dark beginnings

Vancouver

MICE IN THE HOUSE

One of them scampers down the curtain
and up to my motionless feet –
I have the feeling watching that
representatives of two powerful races
are meeting here calmly as equals –
But the mouse will not be damn fool enough
               to go away and write a poem –

LU YU
   (AD 1125–1209)

On the day of Lu Yu's last sickness
a thin coffin was ready,
and two quilts to cover him,
and the gravediggers paid
                   their work done.
Then he started to write another poem
a short time before death,
about drinking wine again in the village –
He was working on the poem when they buried him,
so that half a line protruded from the earth
                   in wind and weather's hearing –
With sunlight touching the first young syllables,
the last ones flowering from a dark coffin:
          "marketplace the in/drink more One"

The first three words above ground
the last ones wine in the Red Dust.
Near the village of Shanyang
                    in Chekiang Province . . .

WINTER AT ROBLIN LAKE

Seeing the sky darken & the fields
turn brown & the lake lead-grey
as some enormous scrap of sheet metal
& wind grabs the world around the equator
I am most thankful then for knowing about
          the little gold hairs on your belly

IN SICKNESS

Fever and then chills
        body shaken and sweating thru the night
then yellow sunlight on the floor
                            so strange
I haven't had time to notice how light transforms
old paint that way
                  then tossing and turning
I get interested in the way my hand looks
scar on finger
slashed from glass
              when I was a child
and fever allows me to remember –
And the far twitter of a sparrow
fifty feet away in a cedar
tree and a dog howling to be
let in at some farmhouse
                  Fever and chills
                  oranges and lemons
                  say the bells of St. Clement's &

FeVeR aNd cHiLLs
and myself muttering thru the night
half asleep and tossing in darkness
– the darkness inside myself
full of coiling tubes & pumps & valves
my brain imprisoned atop this mindless factory
observing the faulty side effects of automation –
                    I am tucked away
                    in the blanket's corner
                    I am secreted
                    like a white candle
                    in the red darkness
                    I see the myth of God
                    is a kitchen chair
                    full of wormholes
                    and fall down and worship –
I moan peevishly for water and some hag brings it
and overwhelmed with my own intrepidity I lean
forward and drink and slobber and wonder
is that what affection
                    is a glass of water?
And stagger to the bathroom scales and
migawd I lost 8 pounds –

Morning and the birds sing and wind blows a little,
morning and it's summer – hour after hour
the sun shines hot and there's a patch of blue
leaning in the window: Oh bring me a big kettle
of elephant soup honey also a dozen great auk's
                              yellow eggs eh?
Don't say one word: just stand there with a broom
for 5 minutes while the house gets dirtier and dirtier,
just stand there all morning long and let me look at you.

SESTINA ON A TRAIN

I've always been going somewhere – Vancouver
or old age or somewhere ever since I can remember:
and this woman leaning over me, this madwoman,
while I was sleeping, whispering, "Do you take drugs?"
And the sight of her yellow-white teeth biting
the dark open wide and white eyes like marbles

children play with but no children play with marbles
like those – saying, "Do you take drugs?" And Vancouver
must be somewhere near this midnight I can't remember
where tho only the sister holding the madwoman,
fighting her: me saying stupidly, "No, no drugs."
She wanting to talk and sitting there biting

at something I couldn't see what the hell she was biting,
only her white eyes like aching terrible marbles
and mouth crying out, "I don't want to go to Vancouver!
Don't let them take me!" She didn't remember
the sad scared children, children of the madwoman
herself, recognized only me the stranger, asking what drugs

I took and wouldn't stop asking that. What such drugs
do besides closing those eyes and keeping those teeth from biting
that tongue into rags and soothing a forehead damp as marble's
cold stone couldn't be altogether bad eh? All the way to Vancouver
where I was going and thought I could remember
having lived once I comforted the madwoman

while the sister minded her frightened children: madwoman,
courtesan, mother, wife, in that order. Such drugs
as I know of don't cause this snapping and biting
at shadows or eyes like glaring lacustral marbles
and mouth crying, "Don't let them take me to Vancouver!"
And leaning her head on my shoulder's scared calm . . . I remember

now the promise I made and do not wish to remember
going somewhere and falling asleep on the train and the madwoman

shakes me softly awake again and, "Yes, I do take drugs,"
I say to her and myself: "I get high on hemp and peyote biting
at scraps of existence I've lost all the smoky limitless marbles
I found in my life once lost long before Vancouver –"

I've forgotten that child, his frantic scratching and biting
for something he wanted and lost – but it wasn't marbles.
I remember the Mountie waiting, then the conductor's "Vancouver
     next! Vancouver!"

NECROPSY OF LOVE

If it came about you died
it might be said I loved you:
love is an absolute as death is,
and neither bears false witness to the other –
But you remain alive.

No, I do not love you
        hate the word,
that private tyranny inside a public sound,
your freedom's yours and not my own:
but hold my separate madness like a sword,
and plunge it in your body all night long.

If death shall strip our bones of all but bones,
then here's the flesh and flesh that's drunken-sweet
as wine cups in deceptive lunar light:
reach up your hand and turn the moonlight off,
and maybe it was never there at all,
so never promise anything to me:
but reach across the darkness with your hand,
reach across the distance of tonight,
and touch the moving moment once again
        before you fall asleep –

COMPLAINT LODGED WITH LCBO
BY A CITIZEN OF UPPER RUMBELOW

I am driving thru town with a case
of beer in the back seat
with two empties in it
which is illegal see and
I notice this cop in the rear
view mirror following me on
a motorcycle and for
a minute I feel peculiar
At the stop street I carefully
STOP
      and the cop stops too not
to be caught that easy
and I see him watching how
I sit so I sit up straight as
"The Motorist" by Praxiteles
excavated by Henry Ford IV
from under a million traffic tickets
of dead Greeks speeding in Argos agora
or was it "Hermes" or "Pallas Athene"
and not "The Motorist" at all?
                  Anyway
there's that cop on my tail
and I signal a left turn
and he signals a left turn
I signal a right turn
and he signals a right turn
and I think what the hell
is this a game or something and
maybe didn't I brush my teeth
this morning and grin with all of them
in the rear view mirror and figure
out a hand signal for a ground loop
and inverted Immelmann plus
an unorthodox Christiania I learned
once on Parnassus which lofts
me among the treetops there encountering

God (hi pops) 50 feet above the
business section we stop to talk and
I ask him about that damned cop
of his and (haw) how I fooled him
But he's parked waiting
for me at the Presbyterian
steeple that got struck by lightning
like a blue cop-angel who's
a dead ringer for the prophet Isaiah
And I says "You didn't make the ground-loop
signal" and he says "It ain't in the book"
and I guess that's so it ain't so
I get fined fifteen bucks
for the booze
and let off with a warning
but just the same –

OLD ALEX

"85 years old, that miserable alcoholic
old bastard is never gonna die," the man said
where he got bed and board. But he did.
I'll say this for Alex's immortality tho:
if they dig him up in a thousand years,
and push a spigot into his belly why
his fierce cackle'll drive a nail in silence,
his laugh split cordwood and trees kowtow
like green butlers, the staggering world
get drunk and sober men run scared.

So you say: was I fond of him?
No – not exactly anyhow. Once
he told his sons and daughters to bugger off,
and then vomited on their memory. It'd be
like liking toadstools or a gun pointing at you –
He sat home three weeks drinking whiskey,
singing harsh songs and quoting verse and chapter

from the Bible: his mean and privileged piety
dying slowly: they rolled him onto a stretcher
like an old pig and prettied him with cosmetics,
sucked his blood out with a machine and
dumped him into the ground like garbage.

I don't mourn. Nobody does. Like mourning an ulcer.
Why commemorate disease in a poem then?
I don't know. But his hate was lovely,
given freely and without stint. His smallness
had the quality of making everyone else feel noble,
and thus fools. I search desperately
for good qualities, and end up crawling
inside that decaying head and wattled throat
to scream obscenities like papal blessings,
knowing now and again I'm at least God.
Well, who remembers a small purple and yellow bruise long?
But when he was here he was a sunset!

HOCKEY PLAYERS

What they worry about most is injuries
                broken arms and legs and
fractured skulls opening so doctors
can see such bloody beautiful things almost
not quite happening in the bone rooms
                as they happen outside
And the referee?
                He's right there on the ice
not out of sight among the roaring blue gods
of a game played for passionate stockbrokers
children wearing business suits
and a nation of television agnostics
who never agree with the referee and applaud
when he falls flat on his face

On a breakaway
the centreman carrying the puck
his wings trailing a little
                on both sides why
I've seen the aching glory of a resurrection
                in their eyes
                if they score
but crucifixion's agony to lose
– the game?

                We sit up there in the blues
bored and sleepy and suddenly three men
break down the ice in roaring feverish speed and
we stand up in our seats with such a rapid pouring
of delight exploding out of self to join them why
theirs and our orgasm is the rocket stipend
for skating thru the smoky end boards out
of sight and climbing up the appalachian highlands
and racing breast to breast across laurentian barrens
over hudson's diamond bay and down the treeless tundra where
auroras are tubercular and awesome and
stopping isn't feasible or possible or lawful
but we have to and we have to
                                laugh because we must and
stop to look at self and one another but
        our opponent's never geography
                        or distance why
            it's men
            – just men?

And how do the players feel about it
this combination of ballet and murder?
For years a Canadian specific
to salve the anguish of inferiority
by being good at something the Americans aren't
And what's the essence of a game like this
which takes a ten-year fragment of a man's life
replaced with love that lodges in his brain
            and substitutes for reason?

Besides the fear of injuries
is it the difficulty of ever really overtaking
a hard black rubber disc?
– Boys playing a boy's game in a permanent childhood
with a screaming coach who insists on winning
sports-writer-critics and the crowd gone mad?
– And the worrying wives wanting you to quit and
your aching body stretched on the rubbing table
thinking of money in owners' pockets that might be yours
the butt-slapping camaraderie and the self-indulgence
of allowing yourself to be a hero and knowing
everything ends in a pot-belly

Out on the ice can all these things be forgotten
in swift and skilled delight of speed?
– roaring out the endboards out the city
streets and high up where laconic winds
whisper litanies for a fevered hockey player
Or racing breast to breast and never stopping
over rooftops of the world and all together
sing the song of winning all together
sing the song of money all together

             (and out in the suburbs
there's the six-year-old kid
whose reflexes were all wrong
who always fell down and hurt himself and cried
and never learned to skate
             with his friends)

HOME-MADE BEER

I was justly annoyed 10 years ago
in Vancouver: making beer in a crock
under the kitchen table when this
next-door youngster playing with my own
kid managed to sit down in it and
emerged with one end malted –
With excessive moderation I yodelled
at him
       "Keep your ass out of my beer!"
       and the little monster fled –
Whereupon my wife appeared from the bathroom
where she had been brooding for days
over the injustice of being a woman and
attacked me with a broom –
With commendable savoir faire I broke
the broom across my knee (it hurt too) and
then she grabbed the breadknife and made
for me with fairly obvious intentions –
I tore open my shirt and told her calmly
with bared breast and a minimum of boredom
       "Go ahead! Strike! Go ahead!"
Icicles dropped from her fiery eyes as she
snarled
       "I wouldn't want to go to jail
       for killing a thing like you!"
I could see at once that she loved me
tho it was cleverly concealed –
For the next few weeks I had to distribute
the meals she prepared among neighbouring
dogs because of the rat poison and
addressed her as Missus Borgia –
That was a long time ago and while
at the time I deplored her lack of
self-control I find myself sentimental
about it now for it can never happen again –

Sept. 22, 1964: PS, I was wrong –

ONE RURAL WINTER

Trapped
         abandoned
                  marooned
like a city thief in a country jail
bitching about all the fresh air
the rural mail my only communication with outside
surrounded by nothing
                  but beautiful trees
                  and I hate beautiful trees
I'm lost beyond even the remote boundaries
of Ameliasburg
                  and I ask you
what could be more remote than a burg
named after a German dumpling named Amelia?
Why just close your eyes tight shut here
and you don't see little dots of light
                  – you see fresh cowpads
But it's winter now
                  beyond the economic wall
(I have two nickels a dime and quarter
and not a damn cent
in my pockets but a wife
who comes out at night when I'm asleep
and won't meet the burning stare
of my closed dreaming womanless eyes
not for two nickels a dime and quarter anyway)

                  In the backyard
phallic pieces of wood and stones embedded
in ice (notice the Freudian terminology please)
a failed writer I'm trapped forever
in the 3rd Post-Atomic Pre-Literate Glacial Period
(making witty remarks like "Cold out, ain't it Zeke?")
It's got so I'm even afraid to go outside
in order to experience the rich rural experience
that is part of our common Canadian heritage
I might catch my foot in a lateral moraine or something

and be trapped forever
                    in Ameliasburg Township

The earth is frozen
the beautiful trees are frozen
even the mailbox's metal nose is cold
and I'm getting a little chilly myself
living in a house I built one tropical summer
with Unemployment Insurance money
                    and a bad-tempered wife
But I got into this mess myself
and I ain't blamin the Class Struggle
besides things are gonna get better
in ten or twenty years I think

It does improve my character
                    no doubt of that
to walk half a mile to the outdoor shithouse
with the temperature at 40 below
But *Maclean's* Magazine is absorbing toilet tissue
and all the spiders and microbes and things
I trained last summer to sit up and chant
in unison Hallelujah What a Bum
                    to visiting imaginary females
from the neighbouring seminary
                    – are frozen stiff
But the place is warm and comfortable
despite the perfumed gale below
as long as you can keep your mind
                    on the beautiful girl
tacked on the wall who advises that
                    SPRING IS HERE
and I should have my crankcase flushed out
Then wiped and buttoned and zippered
I plunge back to the house
thru a white world of nothing
                    but snow
                              and the damn WIND
steals all my internal heat

it howls like a dog in my summer underwear
my heavy body is doped with wind and cold
                        and the house door
                        drags me into the hall
                        and the door knob
                        is a handle
I hold onto the sky with

ROBLIN'S MILLS

The mill was torn down last year
and stone's internal grey light
gives way to new green
a shading of surface colour
like the greenest apple of several
The spate of Marthas and Tabithas
            incessant Hirams and Josephs
is stemmed in the valley graveyard
where the censored quarrels of loving
and the hatred and by golly gusto
of a good crop of buckwheat and turnips
end naturally as an agreement between friends
            (in the sandy soil
that would grow nothing but weeds
or feed a few gaunt cattle) –
And the spring rain takes their bodies
a little deeper down each year
            and maybe the earliest settlers
some stern Martha or speechless Joseph
perhaps meet and mingle
            1,000 feet down –

And the story about the grist mill
rented in 1914 to a man named Taylor
by the last of the Roblin family
who demanded a share of the profits
that poured golden thru the flume

because the new miller knew his business:
       & the lighting alters
       here and now changes
to then and you can see
       how a bald man stood
sturdily indignant
       and spat on the floor
and stamped away so hard the flour
dust floated out from his clothes
like a white ghostly nimbus
around the red scorn
and the mill closed down –

       Those old ones
you can hear them on a rural party line
sometimes
       when the copper wires
sing before the number is dialed and
then your own words stall some distance
from the house you said them in
       lost in the 4th concession
       or dimension of wherever
       what happened still happens
       a lump in your throat
       an Adam's apple half
       a mile down the road
       permits their voices
       to join living voices
       and float by
       on the party line sometimes
       and you hang up then
       so long now –

THE COUNTRY NORTH OF BELLEVILLE

Bush land scrub land –
        Cashel Township and Wollaston
Elzevir McClure and Dungannon
green lands of Weslemkoon Lake
where a man might have some
        opinion of what beauty
is and none deny him
              for miles –

Yet this is the country of defeat
where Sisyphus rolls a big stone
year after year up the ancient hills
picnicking glaciers have left strewn
with centuries' rubble
              backbreaking days
              in the sun and rain
when realization seeps slow in the mind
without grandeur or self-deception in
              noble struggle
of being a fool –

A country of quiescence and still distance
a lean land
        not like the fat south
with inches of black soil on
        earth's round belly –
And where the farms are
        it's as if a man stuck
both thumbs in the stony earth and pulled

              it apart
              to make room
enough between the trees
for a wife
        and maybe some cows and
        room for some
of the more easily kept illusions –

And where the farms have gone back
to forest
                are only soft outlines
                shadowy differences –
Old fences drift vaguely among the trees
                a pile of moss-covered stones
gathered for some ghost purpose
has lost meaning under the meaningless sky
                – they are like cities under water
and the undulating green waves of time
                are laid on them –

This is the country of our defeat
                and yet
during the fall plowing a man
might stop and stand in a brown valley of the furrows
                and shade his eyes to watch for the same
                red patch mixed with gold
                that appears on the same
                spot in the hills
                year after year
                and grow old
plowing and plowing a ten-acre field until
the convolutions run parallel with his own brain –

And this is a country where the young
                leave quickly
unwilling to know what their fathers know
or think the words their mothers do not say –

Herschel Monteagle and Faraday
lakeland rockland and hill country
a little adjacent to where the world is
a little north of where the cities are and
sometime
we may go back there
                to the country of our defeat
Wollaston Elzevir and Dungannon
and Weslemkoon lake land

where the high townships of Cashel
                    McClure and Marmora once were –
But it's been a long time since
and we must enquire the way
                    of strangers –

COUNTRY SNOWPLOW

                    Tyrannosaurus
comes lumbering around the stalled
Quaternary glaciers to deliver his ancient
                    thundering manifesto
modified to suit the times –
                    Tyrannosaurus
roaming the bed clothes of earth –
Warm in the cold hutch rabbits endure
their scarcities
                    owls survive a dream
of pterodactyls –
                    SNOW
engendering in marsupial darkness
the fierce equations of light –
                              To rescue
the perishing
                    married woman expecting
strength from snowshovel husband
he knowing and searching the shapes of self
to seize the disparate ghost that strength is
baby about to be born or old man dying
without help
                    in diesel thunder
the transistor's and sick woman's bones
            dance
                    neuter together –
Others
            with all the resources of not-needing
(the white dust being merely white dust) hold

steadfast in the pouring
                    millrace of cold
marshal around them magazines
                    collections of postage stamps
and all the old absorbing hobbies of
                    getting and keeping and counting
barricade themselves in themselves and
wait
        indignant at the lateness of the hour –
                    Thunder dies
and in the monster's milky wake
                    come separate and severally
the chattering mammals –

WHAT IT WAS –

It was not exactly the inequalities
of schoolboy against bullying teacher
or later the fear fitting into a
strange conformity at a boarding school
or how cruelly alien boys were
– for at the time I searched out chinks
of reality in the high walls around
me and found perilous escape in books with
night flights west and sky causeways –
Later still I tore the loose membrane from
a third ear sharpening steadily now
I could never account for
and listening –

It was never either exactly when things
fell into place with a plop audible
in ordinary ears – so that at least I knew
what others thought about the general purpose
            of condoms and women
            ham and eggs
            religion and

the institution of marriage etcetera
and all the adjustments began
of deciding whether I really agreed with them
plus the dark intangibles like death and why why –
And making decisions by not making them
and the failure personally often
and the shame sometimes the shame
and again the listening –

Of course other problems exist here now
the necessity for patterns and pattern-makers
deciding which are certainties and which variables
(and very few of the former and mostly latter)
and always making mistakes
        and sometimes the brain and heart's failure
to know say
        this is the moment you'll always remember
        this is the wind-blown instant of time
        that swings you into the future
        oh heavy as the heavy cellar stones of the world
        but hammering on the gates of the sun
or merely a little older and bewildered about things
you didn't understand that perhaps meant nothing
        and fumbling to stay alive
        and always the listening –

THE VIPER'S MUSE

It is portentous and a thing of state
A writes to B
        A praiseth B's poem saying
"Canada hath need of thee in this hour she
is a fen"
      etcetera etcetera
                straightway
a second letter flieth fast to A i.e.
"Thou'rt the sweetest singer of our old

                unmusical colonial breed"
(which proveth that the pen
at least hath better manners than the sword say)
O A embarrasseth B
                    with untruth
B does not dare reply unkind
                    which is to say
he
    I mean that is B
                    he lieth in his teeth
But whoso turns as I this night to praise
another poet partly
                    partly prays
exaggeration isn't such a bloody crime
as outright lying is and was while
                    Ananias'
planet riseth silent gibbous yonder
                    over Parnassus

DEATH OF JOHN F. KENNEDY

Not for high office
the US presidency
as some Americans might feel
and certainly not for Camelot
that great lot of hot
                CRAP
– do I feel this peculiar loss
But he seemed the first of something
whatever it was
– tired old men swept away
on the garbage heap of history
Probably I'm wrong about him
he may even have been Doctor
Frankenstein about to unloose monsters
on an unsuspecting populace
a new apocalypse

today or tomorrow
It doesn't matter now
it didn't happen and doesn't
affect this ancient sorrow
I liked the man –

And thinking of his death and so many others:
how the mind empties of passion and speculation
how the population of the world is replaced
every hundred years the Caesars and streetcleaners
and fathers and mothers and painfully awkward
adolescents without furore and
no one escapes in the outcry only
pyramids and some broken bits of pottery
survive the long howl of a funeral oration
                    and out in the suburbs all the time
a mother of six
                    is quietly having another baby –

            And I mourn Kennedy
            the man everybody knows
– strangers who never met
connected by a dead man's compass points
and vectors penetrating now
                        like battery terminals
for which the power supply
jams under a heavy load of messages from
huntsmen falling asleep standing in snowstorms
in the 2d Ice Age forever and Sumerian shepherd
kings catching cold and dead of the sniffles and
messages from rock cairns in Transylvania
and exiles in a Roman province from Hyannisport
and Sierra Maestra and Crimea and silence:
for which the power supply
is an inflection of a subordinate clause
                on television
                a remembered grin –

FIDEL CASTRO IN REVOLUTIONARY SQUARE

He begins to speak
about guns and drums and sugar
production higher this year
(a million people listening)
about impossible peace
and war and I wonder
how it was
with that young student
years ago in Havana drinking
with friends silently the colour
of Cuban April on his face
from flowers and the red earth
outside fading in the gold afternoon
I wonder about that young student
and speculate the exact moment
he sprang to his feet
stuttering with earnestness:
>"Listen to me
>we're going to take over
>all of us here in this room
>the people here in this room
>and all the people
>we're going to take over the country"

The fragile intention flees
from face to face like fever
becomes a condition of existence
a thought to think when first
putting on your pants in the morning
and the faces gather around him
the whispering ghosts of justice
say to him "Fidel! Fidel!?"
and the high talk begins
And a stranger sits down then
shaken and sweating
not the same young student
not the same man
Ten years and three hours

later in 1964
the long speech ends
and it's "Fidel! Fidel!"
without any question at all
Everyone joins hands and sings together
a million voices and bodies
sway back and forth in the sunlight
and make some remark about being human
addressed to no one exactly
spoken to no imperialist
snarled at no invader
as natural as eating supper
that is able to touch the future
and fill an emptiness
and fills an emptiness in the future
Or else that's another illusion
something nice to believe in
and all of us need something
something to lift us from ourselves
a thing we touch that touches
a future we don't know
the continuity of people
a we/they and me/you concept
as saccharine as religion
to comfort a world of children
with proletarian lullabies
A million people move to the exits
under a sky empty of everything
returning to the fact of duration
and chicken hearts in nutritive solution
and glands living the good life
                    in a test tube
the great ambiguity the last cliché
And back at the shining Cadillac
we came in (Batista's old car)
under the side where I hadn't
noticed before the body
of a small dead animal

Cuba

LATE RISING AT ROBLIN LAKE

All hours the day begins one may
awake at dawn with bird cries
streaking light to sound to song
to coloured silence wake with
sun stream shuttle threading thru
curtain shadows dazzling eyes at
4 p.m. and 9 p.m. and 1 a.m. one May
awake inside a moving house earthbound
by heart-tick and clock-beat only all
one August afternoon once why
stumbling yawning nude to front
window there on the dock
            in noon fog lit
with his own slow self-strangeness
stood a tall blue heron

            and the day began with him

PEONIES BESIDE THE LAKE

We fed them potato peelings and rotten meat
we fed them fermented garbage for 5 years
while the stems sickened
            and leaves turned yellow
we fed them garden fertilizer and horseshit
begged from the only farmer with horses for miles
We gave what women have sometimes given
who have no sons and mourn their lost children
            in the menses of growing things
which bear no fruit and cannot be eaten
            except by tongues of the eyes
– or the gentleness of senility in very old women
who really do not know why something aches
inside them when a flower is born
as we are ignorant of our own motives

                    after such a long time waiting
to see how the new peonies shine
                    reddening the dull lake water

HELPING MY WIFE GET SUPPER

Something basically satisfying real and valid
about being a husband
brandishing a knife and cutting
up soggy tomatoes
                    not just red
but red all through
And there's something undeniably profound about
                    being red all through
like a cavalry charge in the salad
But I could get indignant at this lettuce
for allowing itself to be sliced
by somebody's husband like so much dead meat
                    not making a move
to defend itself just
lying there limply relying on being green
Not like the onion
                    which is not defenseless
                    for nobody makes friends with an onion
                    except another one
                    and then they don't trust each other
                    like two skunks
And the carrot's such a bright orange orange
it ought to be more than just a carrot
which anyway is a futile condition to be in
and it might be better not to be a carrot
if you could manage to get out of it
                    be warned beforehand
you were liable to be somebody's husband
                    but nobody ever is

MY GRANDFATHER TALKING – 30 YEARS AGO

Not now boy not now
some other time I'll tell ya
what it was like
the way it was
without no streets
or names of places here
nothin but moonlight boy
nothin but woods

Why ain't there woods no more?
I lived in the trees an
how far was anywhere was
as far as the trees went
ceptin cities
          an I never went

They put a road there
where the trees was
an a girl on the road
in a blue dress
an given a place to go
from I went
into the woods with her
it bein the best way
to go an never get there

Walk in the woods an not get lost
wherever the woods go
a house in the way
a wall in the way
a stone in the way
that got there quick as hell
an a man shouting Stop
but you don't dast stop
or everything would fall down
You low it's time boy
when you can't tell anyone

when there ain't none to tell
about whatever it was I was sayin
what I was talkin about
what I was thinkin of –?

METHOD FOR CALLING UP GHOSTS

Walking sometimes in the streets of the town
I live in and thinking of all the people who
lived here once and fill the space I fill –
If they'd painted white trails on the sidewalk
everywhere they went, it would be possible
to see them now.
                    Imagine them as line drawings,
and at once they become visible again,
people crossing the empty streets at midnight,
or during the rush hour
                    squeezed and overlapped by the living
before the lights change –
And this method must be used to think of them
or they disappear when you look
                    and no one is there.
This incident:
                    sitting with friends
in the chalet restaurant on top of Mount Royal
talking of a tree swaying back and forth in the wind,
leaving no silvery whip marks of its travelling self
                    or proof of passage.
                                        But we say
"That tree will always be there,
flogging the air forever."
Said in a commonplace tone it
doesn't sound exciting
                    but it is oh it is!
And something I've thought of every now and then:
how everything we do or say has an effect somewhere,
passes outward from itself in widening circles,

a sort of human magic by which
a word moves outside the nature of a word
as side effect of itself
                         the nature of a word being
that when it's been said it will always be said
– a recording exists in the main deep of sound.
And I think if there was a god somewhere
                    he'd be damn jealous.
It's a morbid idea perhaps,
if you don't think it's ridiculous:
so many line drawings of dead men,
so many white trails on downtown streets –
But I don't care much if it is for
it exalts me to think of those people
passing by tonight in the room where I sit writing,
on the roads that I will walk tomorrow
in the echoing rooms of yesterday –
And I think of the first space ship leaving earth,
going where men have never loved women,
                    traced out their lives there
                    in the marginless emptiness
until the pale death angel of earth
                    comes for us on the star ships –

THE OLD GIRL FRIEND

We made love in a parked cemetery
with youthful uneasiness
about the stationary dead
                         After marriage
I sat between them at a movie
holding hands with both
chuckling polygamous and evil
at this beginning of having enough of women
Now my laughter at all my selves
includes our meeting at 40
with somnolent gossip of middle-aged certainties tho

never now the goose girl wondering what came next
and which hand was which and where but never
why in a parked car while the dead talked
softly whatever the dead discuss
Never the goose girl now or gander lout
                    from
                    1940
who made a jewelled baldric from a sweat shirt
and simmering flesh imperishable as grass roots
and a silver bugle from a jalopy's horn
that kept going "Yippee Yippay"
all night long
in the catacombs of moonlight
among the tombs of tumescent corpses
until a dead spinster complained
she couldn't sleep
and the old caretaker
came

POSTSCRIPT [1965]

I say the stanza ends
            but it never does
there being something continual,
apart from the blaze of man, in a woman –
At least he somehow thinks there is.
After a parting grimly convivial
nostalgia comes like an old shaman,
you travel backward in time and finally
come to a place she never was to
some small town with desolate streets and
yourself inside yourself
            unable to get out or
a city sheerly grey with a child's ennui –
You come to a place she never was and
everything that happened happened
            without her:

tho blindly in darkness
          lovers were coming together
the gilled foetus formed
          the flippered thing
climbing the long climb up from animal
          changing from it to her and you
the bundle of instincts and appetites becoming
a small girl crying on her way home from school
pig-tailed teenager necking in parked cars
hearing about incest rape sodomy and Jesus
lover of your soul and body and
your strawberry innocence
          stereotypes and approximates
          of you you you
          in deep tombs of memory –

You travel backward in time and come
to the double rorschach bedsheet blot and
the silvery look she had in the bathtub and
the double standard of pain in the guts
of love that was always much less than freedom
          can never be freedom exactly –
And you come to the power struggle and quarrelling
          over the deed and title
of whatever shone thru your eyes at each other
whatever was given whatever was owed
the debt of flesh that is non-material
          and you come to the sweating
welded flesh in stormy bedsheet sea until
          morning comes
the shivering landlocked awakening comes
          that morning or later on –

(The snail has lost its shell and toothless lion
grumbles alone in dangerous country –
The rhino's horns have fallen along a trail
deep in dark woods crowded with big-game hunters –
The eagle has left its claws in the blood-red sky

Beyond Remembering

the antelopes have all gone lame and
the lover has no luck at all –)

You come to a place she never was
        or will be in time that circles
around behind and traps you here and now and you
        weep because you do not weep
        for each other
        but sentimentally
        and vicariously
in an absence of self you are hardly aware of
for all young things
the new and continually arriving hardly-able-to-stand things
        that live here
in the trees and the woods and the green fields of summer –

TRANSIENT

Riding the boxcars out of Winnipeg in a
morning after rain so close to
the violent sway of fields it's
like running and running
naked with summer in your mouth and
the guy behind you grunts and says
"Got a smoke?"

Being a boy scarcely a moment and you
hear the rumbling iron roadbed singing
under the wheels at night and a door jerking open
mile after dusty mile riding into Regina with
the dust storm crowding behind you and
a guy you hardly even spoke to
nudges your shoulder chummily and says
"Got a smoke?"

Riding into the Crow's Nest mountains with
your first beard itching and a

hundred hungry guys fanning out thru
the shabby whistlestops for handouts and
not even a sandwich for two hundred miles
only the high mountains and knowing
what it's like to be not quite a child any
more and listening to the tough men
talk of women and talk of the way things are
in 1937

Riding down in the spit-grey sea-level morning
thru dockyard streets and dingy dowager houses
with ocean a jump away and the sky beneath you
in puddles on Water Street and an old Indian woman
pushing her yawning scratching daughter
onto a balcony to yell at the boy-man passing
"Want some fun? – come on up" – and the girl just
come from riding the shrieking bedspring bronco
all the up and down night to a hitchpost morning
full of mother and dirt and lice and
   hardly the place for a princess
   of the Coast Salish
     (My dove my little one
tonight there will be wine and drunken suitors
from the logging camps to pin you down
in the outlying lands of sleep
where all roads lead back to the home-village
and water may be walked on)

Stand in the swaying boxcar doorway
moving east away from the sunset and
after a while the eyes digest a country and
the belly perceives a mapmaker's vision
in dust and dirt on the face and hands here
its smell drawn deep thru the nostrils down
to the lungs and spurts thru blood stream
campaigns in the lower intestine
   and chants love songs to the kidneys
After a while there is no arrival and
no departure possible any more

you are where you were always going
and the shape of home is under your fingernails
the borders of yourself grown into certainty
the identity of forests that were always nameless
the selfhood of rivers that are changing always
the nationality of riding freight trains thru the depression
over long green plains and high mountain country
with the best and worst of a love that's not to be spoken
and a guy right behind you says then
"Got a smoke?"
You give him one and stand in the boxcar doorway
or looking out the window of a Montreal apartment
or running the machines in a Vancouver factory
you stand there growing older

THE NORTH WEST PASSAGE

                   is found

needs no more searching
and for lack of anything better to do
waiting the plane's departure north from Frobisher
I lounge on the bed poring over place-names
on maps
            and baby it's cold outside
I amuse myself with the idea of
                        Martin Frobisher
"Admiral of the Ocean-Sea" who was
"hurte . . . in the Buttocke with an Arrowe"
running down the beach near here
to escape the blood-mad Skraelings hoping
to reach Mrs. Frobisher in time for tea
But Frobisher didn't make it either
in 1576
            and it's two hours until dinner
tho I'm not really very hungry just now
Locate Fury and Hecla

on the orange-coloured paper
north west of where I am on Baffin
and go rocking thru history
in search of dead sailors
suspended from Ariadne's quivering cord
and find them at the precise point
where the meter registers "alive"
when a living man remembers them
and the Minotaur's bull-roar
trembles in the northern lights
and a red needle flickers
on the playback device

Locate the *Terror* and *Erebus* that way
Franklin's ships preserved in ice
with no place-names for them
it'd be much too close to hell
and the big jets might take a wrong turn
skimming over the top of the world
or the ICBM computers make a quarter inch error
and destroy the illusion of paradise by mistake
and Capt. James' letter to the Emperor of Japan
suddenly gets delivered three centuries later
Or take the Ringnes boys
                    Ellef and Amund
heroic Norwegian brewers whose names
cling alcoholically to islands up there
or Boothia after an English gin distiller
Names like Ungava and Thule
                    the Beaufort Sea and Ellesmereland
places to drop cigarette butts in
while the big jets go popping over the horizon
to Moscow and you can snooze 5 minutes
before the stewardess brings dinner
or read the *New Yorker* with a double whiskey
and make it last a hundred miles
for it's a long time since Luke Foxe's cook
served "beer in small cans" to the sailors
and it didn't last one nautical mile

The North West Passage is found
and poor old Lady Franklin well
she doesn't answer the phone
tho once she traded her tears for ships
to scour the Arctic seas for her husband
but the *Terror* and *Erebus* sank long ago
and it's still half an hour before dinner
and there isn't much to do but write letters
and I can't think of anything more to say
about the North West Passage
but I'll think of something
maybe
a break-thru
to strawberries and ice cream for dinner

Frobisher Bay

ARCTIC RHODODENDRONS

They are small purple surprises
in the river's white racket
and after you've seen them
a number of times
in water-places
where their silence seems
related to river-thunder
you think of them as "noisy flowers"
Years ago
it may have been
that lovers came this way
stopped in the outdoor hotel
to watch the water floorshow
and lying prone together
where the purged green
boils to a white heart
and the shore trembles
like a stone song

with bodies touching
flowers were their conversation
and love the sound of a colour
that lasts two weeks in August
and then dies
except for the three or four
I pressed in this letter
and send whispering to you

Pangnirtung

ESKIMO GRAVEYARD

Walking in glacial litter
frost boils and boulder pavements
of an old river delta
where angry living water
changes its mind every half century
and takes a new direction
to the blue fiord
The Public Works guy I'm with
says you always find good gravel
for concrete near a graveyard
where digging is easy maybe
a footnote on human character
But wrapped in blankets
above ground a dead old woman
(for the last few weeks I'm told)
without a grave marker
And a hundred yards away
the Anglican missionary's grave
with whitewashed cross
that means equally nothing
The river's soft roar
drifts to my ears and changes
tone when the wind changes
ice debris melts at low tide

& the Public Works guy is mildly pleased
with the good gravel we found
for work on the schoolhouse
which won't have to be shipped in
from Montreal
and mosquitoes join happily
in our conversation   Then
he stops to consult
with the construction foreman

I walk on
toward the tents of The People
half a mile away
at one corner of the picture
Mothers with children on their backs
in the clean white parkas
they take such pride in
buying groceries at HBC
boys lounging under the store
in space where timber stilts
hold it above the permafrost
with two of them arm in arm
in the manner of Eskimo friends
After dinner
I walk down among the tents
and happen to think of the old woman
neither wholly among the dead
nor quite gone from the living
and wonder how often
a thought of hers enters the minds
of people she knew before
and what kind of flicker it is
as lights begin to come on
In nightlong twilight
and thoughts of me
occur to the mosquitoes
I keep walking
as if something ought to happen
(I don't know what)

with the sun stretching
a yellow band across the water
from headland to black headland
at high tide in the fiord
sealing in the settlement
as if there was no way out
and indeed there isn't
until the looping Cansos come
dropping thru the mountain doorway
That old woman?
It occurs to me
I might have been thinking
about human bookkeeping
debits and credits that is
or profit and loss
(and laugh at myself)
among the sealed white tents
like glowing swans
hoping
for a most improbable
birth

Pangnirtung

TREES AT THE ARCTIC CIRCLE
(Salix Cordifolia – Ground Willow)

They are 18 inches long
or even less
crawling under rocks
grovelling among the lichens
bending and curling to escape
making themselves small
finding new ways to hide
Coward trees
I am angry to see them
like this

not proud of what they are
bowing to weather instead
careful of themselves
worried about the sky
afraid of exposing their limbs
like a Victorian married couple

I call to mind great Douglas firs
I see tall maples waving green
and oaks like gods in autumn gold
the whole horizon jungle dark
and I crouched under that continual night
But these
even the dwarf shrubs of Ontario
mock them
Coward trees

And yet – and yet –
their seed pods glow
like delicate grey earrings
their leaves are veined and intricate
like tiny parkas
They have about three months
to make sure the species does not die
and that's how they spend their time
unbothered by any human opinion
just digging in here and now
sending their roots down down down
And you know it occurs to me
          about 2 feet under
those roots must touch permafrost
ice that remains ice forever
and they use it for their nourishment
they use death to remain alive

I see that I've been carried away
in my scorn of the dwarf trees
most foolish in my judgements
To take away the dignity

of any living thing
even tho it cannot understand
          the scornful words
is to make life itself trivial
and yourself the Pontifex Maximus
          of nullity
I have been stupid in a poem
I will not alter the poem
but let the stupidity remain permanent
as the trees are
in a poem
the dwarf trees of Baffin Island

                                        Pangnirtung

METRICS

Expecting to arrive at a crowded village
I land on a little rocky island
as a kind of star boarder
in charge of an Eskimo family
and English is not spoken here
At first I think it must be
the place I'm supposed to arrive at and
the facsimile I'd made beforehand didn't match
the real thing
          tho it has
      the same sky and the same sea
as the place in my head
Feeling unsure of myself
I take a fast count of the population
(14 Eskimos   1 white man   some dogs)
as a rational measure to make sure
I'm not a computer with built-in defects
          but a man
with heavy loneliness included
for which there seems no answer
And the brown children peer out

                    behind
             small
        snotty
      faces
with secret rules to their games
the hunter breaks out a torn spare tent
his wife sews with a hand machine
among stones and
                into
           it   an
        raise   east
      we   wind
while a blind husky bitch
sniffs at my heels
Now the pictures in my head
of what I'd expected things to be like
start to come true
                       bones everywhere
even inside the tent
that swells in wind like a heart
                   trying to break
loose from flesh and
pieces of animal carcass around
yellow blubber in cold sunlight
a white whale's body in shallow water
on the beach with blood
like smoke
           drifting
                     from the beast face
another island 200 yards away
covered with gaunt starving dogs
climbing the crags like goats apparently
left there for the Arctic summer
to survive or not survive
My lost feelings begin to simmer down
to a take-what-comes attitude
tho I set up the portable typewriter
on a cardboard box in the tent
for an "order of things"

I can stay outside
or join in case of desperation
            and eat some beans
and try to decide if all this is a poem
Brief Arctic twilight
            darkens the stone island
something neither day nor night begins
blue water loses what makes it alive
shadows aren't shadows but proxy things
            that represent things
and I wonder what I represent
(– some hustings of the soul?)
Here I'm alone as I've ever been in my life
a windup gramophone scratching out "You Are
My Sunshine"
            in the next tent
the sea crowded with invisible animals
the horizon full of vague white shapes
of icebergs in whispering lagoons where
Old Squaw ducks are going
                        "ouw-ouw-ouw"
And I think to the other side of that sound
I have to
            because it gathers everything
all the self-deception and phoniness
of my lifetime into an empty place
and the RUNNER IN THE SKIES
I invented
            as symbol of the human spirit
                crashes like a housefly
my only strength is blind will
                        to go on
I think to the other side of that sound
                    "ouw-ouw-ouw"
to the point where I know some damfool ducks
are having a ball out there
                    far out
                        there
where I can't join them

and really it isn't really it isn't
the echo of cosmic emptiness at all
(really it isn't!)
and start typing

Slaughter Beach (Brown's Harbour)

TENT RINGS

Stones in a circle
on an island in the Kikastan group
placed there long ago
to hold down the skirts
of caribou skin tents
All over the Arctic
these tent rings
going back thousands of years
in the land where nothing changes
The Dorset People of Baffin
nomads down the centuries
in hustling seawind
left them and journeyed on
Thule people of Greenland
and the wild Skraelings
of Norse legend
wanderers among the islands
in the Beaufort Sea
left such rings of stone
The radioactive detective
Carbon 14 provides no calendar
tho it dates horn scrapers
ivory spear heads
and bones of men
Here's another one
weathered granite boulders
from the Precambrian
before there was life at all
arranged here fifty years ago

or several thousand
In some sense I think of them
as still here in the circle
the small brown men
they lived so strongly
with such a gift of laughter
the morning sun touches
and glances off
their sparkling ghosts
To enter these tent rings
is mingling with the past
being in two places
having visions
hearing voices
sounding in your head
almost like madness
summoned by wizard angakoks
a thousand-year-old spell
relayed and handed down
a legacy
from dead to the living
Turning away from here
now in the future I suppose
the stones will be rectangular
even octagonal maybe
having the shape of canvas tents
that came from white traders
and some visitor
in the far future
(probably non-human)
will notice them
and not know whether
they belonged to the Innuit
the "men pre-eminently"
or white men
who were also visitors
and thought to be human

Kikastan Islands

STILL LIFE IN A TENT

(Or, Tenting tonight in the old camp ground)

In a cave hollowed out in the rain
near a pile of ghostly groceries
and some books
The wind comes
within two feet of where I'm lying
then stops
waiting
and the canvas bulges

I have a slight fever
temperature of maybe 100
nothing to speak of
but no medicine here
And I have a small fear that changes
shape and size
when I consider what might happen
(canoe trip by sea to Pang
among the waving kelp lines
that anchor somebody's world
maybe the seal towns
or Erewhon and Atlantis
with Jonahsie nursing the motor
smiling but irritated
at me for making him
miss the good hunting weather
and myself sick in the bilge)

Waves rumble and rant now
on the still listening beach
pounding motherless bergs
to death on rocks
stranding the big calves
at tidal ebb
A clump of yellow flowers
I noticed this afternoon
must be straining their roots

in the windy twilit night
hoping to hold onto
their few home-inches
(like comic yellow flags
of a 40-acre duchy
between Russia and China)
Oh misery me misery me
I am sick as hell
and so sorry for me
touch my forehead
and swallow carefully
expecting it to hurt
smoke a cigarette
drink some coffee
wish it were brandy
hope for morning
and the big wind howls
Now a berg splits
inside/outside the tent
a dry white noise
wet dogs drift in
and out of hearing
I lie there fevered and
float a single thought out
into a night tinted
with day flowers in my mind
then send a second one
to join the first
and my thoughts travel together
in fevered fantasy
north of summer
with ice become a thousand-foot wall
so photo-real it might be
me both here and there
staring up and up
a fevered little man
at that cold altar
where June July and August
are a brief tremor

on god's thermometer
My blood burns and burns
with bells of systole and diastole
tolling over the northland
while I strike cross-capillary
with ham sandwich and thermos
to find the court of the Seal-King
where trader and blind explorer
fumbled along the kelp lines
to reach their graves in a blizzard
or came at last to drown

Here I am again
back from the court of the Seal-King
lying in bed with fever
and I'm so glad to be here
no matter what happens
– riding the wind to Pang
or being bored at Frobisher
(waiting for clearing weather)
I'm so glad to be here
with the chance that comes but once
to any man in his lifetime
to travel deep in himself
to meet himself as a stranger
at the northern end of the world
Now the bullying wind blows faster
the yellow flags rush seaward
the stones cry out like people
as my fever suddenly goes
and the huskies bark like hell
the huskies bark like hell

In a cave hollowed out in the rain
near a pile of ghostly groceries
and some books
morning soon

Kikastan Islands

WHEN I SAT DOWN TO PLAY THE PIANO

He cometh forth hurriedly from his tent
and looketh for a quiet sequestered vale
he carrieth a roll of violet toilet tissue
and a forerunner goeth ahead to do him honour
yclept a snotty-nosed Eskimo kid
He findeth a quiet glade among great stones
squatteth forthwith and undoeth trousers
Irrational Man by Wm. Barrett in hand
while the other dismisseth mosquitoes
and beginneth the most natural of natural functions
buttocks balanced above the boulders
Then
      dogs[1]
         Dogs[3]
            DOGS[12]
               all shapes and sizes
all colours and religious persuasion
a plague of dogs rushing in
having been attracted by the philosophic climate
and being wishful to learn about existential dogs
and denial of the self with regard to bitches
But let's call a spade a shovel
therefore there I am I am I think that is
surrounded by a dozen dozen fierce Eskimo dogs
with an inexplicable (to me) appetite
for human excrement
              Dear Ann Landers
what would you do?
              Dear Galloping Gourmet
what would *you* do
              in a case like this?
Well I'll tell you
NOT A DAMN THING
You just squat there cursing hopelessly
while the kid throws stones
and tries to keep them off and out from under

as a big black husky dashes in
swift as an enemy submarine
white teeth snapping at the anus
I shriek
        and shriek
        (the kid laughs)
        and hold onto my pants
        sans dignity
        sans intellect
        sans Wm. Barrett
        and damn near sans anus
Stand firm little Eskimo kid
it giveth candy if I had any
it giveth a dime in lieu of same
STAND FIRM
Oh avatar of Olympian excellence
noble Eskimo youth do your stuff
Zeus in the Arctic dog pound
Montcalm at Quebec
Horatius at the bridge
Leonidas at Thermopylae
Custer's last stand at Little Big Horn
"KEEP THEM DAMN DOGS OFF
YOU MISERABLE LITTLE BRAT!"

Afterwards
Achilles retreateth without honour
unzippered and sullen
and sulketh in his tent till next time appointed
his anus shrinketh
he escheweth all forms of laxative and physick meanwhile
and prayeth for constipation
addresseth himself to the Eskimo brat miscalled
        "Lo tho I walk thru the valley of
            the shadowy kennels
      in the land of permanent ice cream
          I will fear no huskies
          for thou art with me

and slingeth thy stones forever and ever
                thou veritable David
                                        Amen"

PS Next time I'm gonna take a gun

                                        Kikastan Islands

WHAT CAN'T BE SAID

The Ladies Auxiliary of Baffin Island
(Kikastan Eskimo Chapter)
comes to visit me every day
They gossip about what's exciting
killer whales out in the harbour
rumored exodus of penguins from Toronto
whether mother love prevents child neurosis
relatives at Ungava having to learn French
and ice exploding bad language in Eskimo
I keep busy serving tea
and don't understand a word
One lady extracts a big floppy breast
from her low-cut evening gown
and shoves it all in her kid's mouth
he bubbles like a milk shake
when we run short of milk for tea
I pantomime using hers
then we sing "You Are My Sunshine"
in English and Eskimo at once
with Purdy as guest conductor
They grin at me
I grin back
and we sit there like a bunch of monkeys
about as phony as you can get
I in my small corner of the tent
they in the rest of it
while the dogs howl outside

and harbour ice keeps exploding
Later when it gets colder
one of the ladies
gives me a big piece
of canvas to throw over the tent
and sews it on securely
to keep me warm at night
– What can I say?

Kikastan Islands

DEAD SEAL

He looks like a fat little old man
an "Old Bill" sort of face
both wise and senile at the same time
with an anxious to please expression
              in fact a clown
which is belied on account of the dark slow worm
of blood crawling down his forehead
that precludes laughter
or being anything but a dead animal
tho perhaps part of a fur coat

Often I want to pet something
that looks like this
(and been warned the Eskimo dogs are dangerous)
which appeals to me on common ground i.e.
they unsure of what being an animal consists of
I equally unsure of what a human being is supposed to be
(despite the legal and moral injunctions that say
              "Thou Shalt Not"
nobody says or is likely to say with real conviction
              "Thou Shalt – go ahead and Shalt"
              or "shall" as the case may be)
On the other hand it would be ridiculous
to pat the head of a dead seal

touch the wet blood that streams back from the boat
a feather of smoky brown in the water widening
into a crude trailing isosceles triangle
with mathematically impossible fish
re-tracing the seal's ghost past not
knowing they're involved in anything

And here he is now
                    casually taking a nap
with flippers like futile baby hands
and clown look of just pretending
            I shan't wake him
for it would be disgusting to touch the blood
and it's unnecessary to prove anything
even to myself
                    Then change my mind
                    "I (damn well) Shalt"
– reach out as if the head were electric
with a death-taboo invisibly attached
dark and dank-cold with the hair on it
sticky where the bullet touched
                            less gently
smooth elsewhere like an intimate part
            of the human body
that must be touched with delight in living
not curiosity and defiance of breaking rules
– But I am no hunter
            of any kind
go back to the tent
            to sit for a few minutes
inside the white canvas blindfold and wonder
what got into me?

                                    Kikastan Islands

HBC POST

Here Eskimos come with sealskins,
the bread and butter of the Arctic,
a rare polar bear, some fox maybe –
They bring in a bundle of furs
and throw it on the floor,
then look at the post manager:
$7 is the price for a good ring seal,
$14 for the glossy patterned harp seal:
but many have bullet holes
or other imperfections –
The HBC man inspects the furs,
decides on a fair price and notes it down,
hands the slip of paper
with an offered amount to the hunter.
Then a slight pause,
his optimistic estimate meets
the concrete fact of the money they're worth.
No bargaining at all. But the manager talks
to the hunter in his own language,
explains the reasons behind his price,
picks out a fault here and another there,
and the transaction ends with acceptance,
and another hunter is waiting.
But in the Eskimo's mind I have seen
clothes for the whole family,
new rifles with telescopic sights,
100-pound sacks of flour and groceries,
shining marine engines, clean white tents,
stacked up dream-high in his mind
                come tumbling down –

Pangnirtung

THE SCULPTORS

Going thru cases and cases
of Eskimo sculpture
returned from Frobisher
because they said it wasn't
good enough for sale to
T. Eaton Co. Ltd.
Getting itchy excelsior packing
inside my shirt and searching
for one good carving
one piece that says "I AM"
to keep a southern promise
One 6-inch walrus (tusk broken)
cribbage board (ivory inlay gone)
dog that has to be labelled dog
polar bear (badly crippled)
what might be a seal (minus flipper)
and I'm getting tired of this
looking for something
not knowing what it is
But I guess they got tired too
looking for rabbit or bear
with blisters from carving tools
dime-sized and inflating
into quarters on their fingers
waiting
for walrus or white whale
under the ice floes to
flop alive on their laps
with twitching animal faces
unready to taste the
shoe blacking carvers use
for stone polish
I'm a little ashamed of myself
for being impatient with them
but there must be something
there must be something
one piece that glows
one slap-happy idiot seal

alien to the whole seal-nation
one anthropomorphic walrus
singing Hallelujah I'm a Bum
in a whiskey baritone
But they're all flawed
broken
      bent
          misshapen
failed animals
with vital parts missing
And I have a sudden vision
of the carvers themselves
in this broken sculpture
as if the time & the place & me
had clicked into brief alignment
and a switch pulled
so that I can see and feel
what it was like to be them
the tb out-patients
failed hunters
who make a noise at the wrong time
or think of something else
at the trigger moment
and shine their eyes
into a continual tomorrow
the losers and failures
who never do anything right
and never will
the unlucky ones
always on the verge
of a tremendous discovery
who finally fail to deceive
even themselves as time begins
to hover around them
the old the old the old
who carve in their own image
of maimed animals
And I'd like to buy every damn case

Pangnirtung

AT THE MOVIES

The setting is really unreal
about 150 Eskimos and whites
jammed into a Nissen hut to
watch Gary Cooper and Burt Lancaster
in a technicolor western shootemup
Eskimos don't understand the dialogue
at all but they like the action
and when noble Gary is in danger
or sinister Lancaster acts menacing
a tide of emotion sweeps the hot little hut
and kids crawling on the floor are quiet
sensing what their parents feel
that something tremendously important is happening
When the Anglican minister changes reels
(his blond head glinting as he administers
spiritual unction to his flock)
cigarettes are lit and everyone talks and
a kid crawls under my legs grinning bashfully
Jim Kilabuk says something I can't quite hear
a baby cries in the pouch on his mother's back
and is joggled gently
It's hot and stuffy as hell in the theatre
doors have to be opened
the odour of white and Eskimo
making a point for air conditioning
Lights go out and Gary Cooper rides again
the forces of evil are finally defeated
only the virtuous bullet kills
violence neutralizes violence
like a mustard plaster
(tho I kinda like the bad guy)
the way it always does in American movies
with an obvious moral a clear-cut denouement
Outside the fiord looks like poured blue milk
mountains like bookmarks under a cold sky
islands are moonscapes
where this story happens

It's 11 p.m.
some of the hunters visit their boats
where dead caribou drain into bilgewater
and the rest of the moviegoers go
home to tents on the beach or prefab houses
and dogs howl to make everything regional
But the point I'd hoped to separate
from all these factual things stubbornly
resists me and I walk home slowly feeling stupid
rejecting the obvious
threading my way between stones in the mud
with the beginnings of a headache.

Pangnirtung

WASHDAY

An oil drum full
of greasy water simmering
all morning with
a blubber fire
underneath
Two women dip
water into plastic tubs
then scrub by hand
with store detergent
I stand and watch
then join the scrubbing
myself
for no reason or any
I can think of
and work at the clothes
seriously as hell
And Leah laughs
her smooth broad face
convulsed with it
a small saliva bubble

blown from her lips
and even Regally
so much darker and quiet
concedes a smile
I think then
even without knowing
the language at all
it's possible to speak
to them
            dark hair falling
in Leah's eyes as
she laughs and brushes
it back giving me
washday instruction
the baby asleep
on her back
Regally impatient
at this foolery
her standing darkness
looms over me like speech
disapprovingly
They chatter about it
in Eskimo
and I try to figure out
what they're saying
remembering I read somewhere
how they add syllable to
syllable so
that a sentence
is just one long word
that keeps being added to
or something like that
Leah still smiling
over the crazy visitor
who wants to wash her clothes
brown eyes and
deep dimples in cheeks
she keeps talking
Suddenly I

feel I'm picked up
with surprised vertigo
and held
between those lips
as she adds my name
to the weightless sounds
breathed out
some of the "me" I am
removed
the walled self
defenses down
altered
I'm given to the air
then back to myself
like a gift from her
On impulse
I say
        "Leah"
and stop then
but she looks at me
queerly
And wind promenades
among the tents
and big white clouds
wander westward
and the dogs
shit around us

Kikastan Islands

WHAT DO THE BIRDS THINK?

Are they exiles here from the rest of the world?
Déjà vu past egg and atom
from the yellow Sahara-ocean
or farmlands in Ontario
a witness   hanging   painted

in the rural blue
while a plowman half a mile down
in the dark field with a snoring tractor
moves in circular sleep?
Or exiles from the apple country
where Macs and Spies plop soft
on wet ground in slow autumn days
with the rotten tangy odour
of cider rising on moon-wept nights?
Have they lists and a summary
of things elsewhere and
remember the crimson racket
encountering tropic strangers
or nests of an old absence
lined with a downy part of themselves
far south?
And being south do they think sometimes
of the rain and mists of Baffin
and long migrations wingtip to wingtip
a mile high
and mate to mate in the lift and tremble
of windy muscles pushing them
pushing them where?
And do they ever
an arrow leader pointing the way
touch wearily down on ships passing?
– "Rest here a while and go on!"
(Forgotten in the hurry
of their streaming generations
another captain
called Noah
& Bjarni Herjolfsson
in horned helmet
and the sweeps' silver lifting
to a luring Hyperborean ocean
or whaling ships' myopic stumbling
from dull wave to dull wave and the
paint of the bright over-the-horizon-gazing
woman flaked with salt)

How are we kept here
by what bonds
are we always exiles
a chirping roar in the silence
of foxes and watery romp of walrus
in the long sea lands
or perched on rubbery muskeg
like blue teacups
or lost brown mittens
by what agency of restlessness
in the driftwood heart?
Until on a day the eggs hatch
and the young are trained to endurance
ice rattles the shroud of summer
the flight plans sent
the log book sand is scribbled on
"Goodbye – we are going – Hurry"
and mounting a shaft of sunlight
or the mizzen mast of the sky
they climb and go
And that is the way it is?
Except perhaps I wonder
do they ever
remember down there in the southland
Cumberland Sound
and the white places
of Baffin
that I will remember
soon?

Pangnirtung

THE COUNTRY OF THE YOUNG

A.Y. Jackson for instance
83 years old
halfway up a mountain
standing in a patch of snow
to paint a picture that says
"Look here
You've never seen this country
it's not the way you thought it was
Look again"
And boozy traders
lost in a dream of money
crews of homesick seamen
moored to a China-vision
hunting the North West Passage
they didn't see it either
The colours I mean
for they're not bright Gauguin
or blazing Vincent
not even Bruegel's *Hunters in the Snow*
where you can get lost
and found in five minutes
– but the original colour-matrix
that after a giant's heartbeat
lighted the maple forests
in the country south
You have to stoop a little
bend over and then look up
– dull orange on a cliff face
that says iron deposits
olive leaves of the ground willow
with grey silver catkins
minute wild flower beacons
sea blue as the world's eye –
And you can't be looking for something else
money or a night's lodging on earth
a stepping stone to death maybe
or you'll never find the place

hear an old man's voice
in the country of the young
that says
    "Look here –"

Pangnirtung

NEWS REPORTS AT AMELIASBURG

In the night of my sleep at embassies
in Hong Kong and Cairo and humid oil capitals
of Arab republics in New York and Moscow
in London and Paris in Accra and Rome
the people say no
philosophers search for new absolutes
hopheads pry into their negative psyches
Bedouins march thru stoplights of sand dunes
pickets circle round factories with banners
black non-violence reaches invisible barriers
at houses abandoned by wealthy distillers
rocks break the glass and death discolours the gutters
battalions of students are shouting their slogans
and the centuries roll onward like mass-produced coffins
to carry the world wherever the world may be going

At Delphi the Oracle gives odds on war and Leonidas
turns aside from the pass at Thermopylae
to attack the Americans
Hannibal drives his elephants into Toronto
Cleopatra and Antony have signed a treaty with Caesar
to burn down Chicago and destroy Los Angeles studios
Alexander turns from the gates of the Ganges
and moves with his generals and phalanx to bulldoze
    the Kremlin
while the eunuch priests conspire in Assyria
to defoliate the Vietnamese rice fields of bananas
At night in our own bodies comes a small dark whisper
relayed here from the beginning of human time

where ancient hunters confer with stones and tree-spirits
their campfires throwing enormous shadows on the forest
and witch-doctors dance in our blood forever

Only behind the centuries is something near silence
before the glaciers turned into ice cubes
before there was man
no young students to ponder old questions
of right and wrong and be sure that life is no bargain
but more important than sleep is
the windows are breaking around me

The groundhog pushes a stone to the mouth of his burrow
the goldfinch repairs his nest with a patchwork of sunset
the fox removes his teeth to a glass for safekeeping
squirrels retire to a rotten tree and the damn thing blossoms
pike in the monocle eye of the lake have switched off
                the planets
I have unbuckled my sword and lie there beside them
the sun has gone down in my village.

HOUSE GUEST

For two months we quarrelled over socialism   poetry   how to
                boil water
doing the dishes   carpentry   Russian steel production figures and
                whether
you could believe them and whether Toronto Leafs would take it all
that year and maybe hockey was rather like a good jazz combo
never knowing what came next
Listening
how the new house built with salvaged old lumber
bent a little in the wind and dreamt of the trees it came from
the time it was travelling thru
and the world of snow moving all night in its blowing sleep
while we discussed ultimate responsibility for a pile of dirty dishes
Jews in the Negev   the Bible as mythic literature   Peking Man

and in early morning looking outside to see the pink shapes of wind
printed on snow and a red sun tumbling upward almost touching the
          house
and fretwork tracks of rabbits outside where the window light
          had lain
last night an audience
watching in wonderment the odd human argument
that uses words instead of teeth
and got bored and went away
Of course there was wild grape wine and a stove full of Douglas fir
(railway salvage) and lake ice cracking its knuckles in hard Ontario
          weather
and working with saw and hammer at the house all winter afternoon
disagreeing about how to pound nails
arguing vehemently over how to make good coffee
Marcus Aurelius   Spartacus   Plato and François Villon
And it used to frustrate him terribly
that even when I was wrong he couldn't prove it
and when I agreed with him he was always suspicious
and thought he must be wrong because I said he was right
Every night the house shook from his snoring
a great motor driving us on into daylight
and the vibration was terrible
Every morning I'd get up and say "Look at the nails –
you snored them out half an inch in the night –"
He'd believe me at first and look and get mad and glare
and stare angrily out the window while I watched 10 minutes of
          irritation
drain from his eyes onto fields and farms and miles and miles of
          snow
We quarrelled over how dour I was in early morning
and how cheerful he was for counterpoint
and I argued that a million years of evolution
from snarling apeman have to be traversed before noon
and the desirability of murder in a case like his
and whether the Etruscans were really Semites
the Celtic invasion of Britain   European languages   Roman law
we argued about white being white (prove it dammit)   &
          cockroaches

bedbugs in Montreal   separatism   Nietzsche   Iroquois
         horsebreakers on the prairie
death of the individual and the ultimate destiny of man
and one night we quarrelled over how to cook eggs
In the morning driving to town we hardly spoke
and water poured downhill outside all day for it was spring
when we were gone with frogs mentioning lyrically
Russian steel production figures on Roblin Lake which were almost
         nil
I left him hitchhiking on #2 Highway to Montreal
and I guess I was wrong about those eggs

AT THE QUINTE HOTEL

I am drinking
I am drinking beer with yellow flowers
in underground sunlight
and you can see that I am a sensitive man
And I notice that the bartender is a sensitive man too
so I tell him about his beer
I tell him the beer he draws
is half fart and half horse piss
and all wonderful yellow flowers
But the bartender is not quite
so sensitive as I supposed he was
the way he looks at me now
and does not appreciate my exquisite analogy
Over in one corner two guys
are quietly making love
in the brief prelude to infinity
Opposite them a peculiar fight
enables the drinkers to lay aside
their comic books and watch with interest
as I watch with interest
A wiry little man slugs another guy
then tracks him bleeding into the toilet
and slugs him to the floor again

with ugly red flowers on the tile
three minutes later he roosters over
to the table where his drunk friend sits
with another friend and slugs both
of em ass-over-electric-kettle
so I have to walk around
on my way for a piss
Now I am a sensitive man
so I say to him mildly as hell
"You shouldn'ta knocked over that good beer
with them beautiful flowers in it"
So he says to me "Come on"
So I Come On
like a rabbit with weak kidneys I guess
like a yellow streak charging
on flower power I suppose
& knock the shit outa him & sit on him
(he is just a little guy)
and say reprovingly
"Violence will get you nowhere this time chum
Now you take me
I am a sensitive man
and would you believe I write poems?"
But I could see the doubt in his upside down face
in fact in all the faces
"What kinda poems?"
"Flower poems"
"So tell us a poem"
I got off the little guy but reluctantly
for he was comfortable
and told them this poem
They crowded around me with tears
in their eyes and wrung my hands feelingly
for my pockets for
it was a heart-warming moment for Literature
and moved by the demonstrable effect
of great Art and the brotherhood of people I remarked
"– the poem oughta be worth some beer"
It was a mistake of terminology

for silence came
and it was brought home to me in the tavern
that poems will not really buy beer or flowers
or a goddam thing
and I was sad
for I am a sensitive man

NOTES ON A FICTIONAL CHARACTER

With cobwebs between elbows and knees,
I say that I hate violence:
there have been street fights;
two wills glaring eye to eye arm
wrestling –;
hours struggling for my soul or hers
with a woman in a taxi;
whacked and bloody and beaten in a poolroom,
playing pool with the winner and winning,
then the walk home, and fall down like a broken chair,
that kind of pride.
All violence,
the inner silent implacable defiance
of money or god or damn near anything:
but it was useful once
to the middle-aged man with belly and ballpoint
getting drunk on words but sobering ah sobering.
Remember the factory manager Arthur Watt,
big, charming smile, attractive personality,
who worked alongside his crew,
to increase production,
wearing a white shirt and tailored trousers:
one day Watt and four others
pulled against three of us across a table,
hauling the cover onto a mattress
much too big for the cover, with ropes,
a workday job delightfully turned to a tug-o-war:
me, digging up more strength than I had,
aimed it at Watt especially,

yanked the bastard toward me,
dragged an extra ten pounds of myself
from the guts and yanked
the boss till his head banged wood with
both arms stretched toward me on the table praying
to Allah there is no god but Allah
                        W. Purdy . . .
The trick was to keep an absolutely straight face,
no expression whatever hold
the chortle to a goddam whimper
of pure joy that started in the balls
and raced 90-miles-per-hour to the angels' antennae
where it sang sweet songs to female cherubs
emerging in the factory dust as a deprecating tsk-tsk,
a normal cigarette cough,
successfully dishonestly solicitous.
As a matter of course he hated me,
which I accepted modestly as my just due:
I've drawn it after me down the years,
that sobbing violence,
ropes to the mattress past like cobwebs
that break with a sudden movement or gentle smile:
or, tough as steel hawsers,
the ropes drag me inch by inch
to the other side of the table,
where the factory manager waits
his unruly workman with a gun,
to watch with amazed eyes
while I write this poem,
like blossoming thistle.

THE WINEMAKER'S BEAT-ÉTUDE

I am picking wild grapes last year
in a field
            dragging down great lianas of vine
tearing at 20 feet of heavy infinite purple

having a veritable tug-o-war with Bacchus
who grins at me delightedly in the high branches
of one of those stepchild appletrees
unloved by anything but tent caterpillars
and ghosts of old settlers
become such strangers here
I am thinking what the grapes are thinking
become part of their purple mentality
that is
        I am satisfied with the sun and
eventual fermenting bubble-talk together
then transformed and glinting with coloured lights in
        a GREAT JEROBOAM
that booms inside from the land beyond the world
In fact
I am satisfied with my own shortcomings letting
myself happen then
              I'm surrounded by Cows
black and white ones with tails
At first I'm uncertain how to advise them
in mild protest or frank manly invective
then realize that the cows are right
it's me that's the trespasser
         Of course they are curious
perhaps wish to see me perform
        I moo off key
        I bark like a man
        laugh like a dog
        and talk like God
        hoping
they'll go away so Bacchus and I can get on with it
Then I get logical thinking if there was ever a
feminine principle cows are it and why not but
what would so many females want?
I address them like Brigham Young hastily
"No, that's out! I won't do it!
           Absolutely not!"
Contentment steals back among all this femininity
thinking cows are together so much they must be nearly

all lesbians fondling each other's dugs by moonlight why
Sappho's own star-reaching soul shines inward and outward
from the soft Aegean islands in these eyes and
I am dissolved like a salt lick instantly oh
        Sodium chloride!
        Prophylactic acid!
        Gamma particles (in suspension)!
        Aftershave lotion!
        Rubbing alcohol!
                suddenly
I become the whole damn feminine principle so
happily noticing little tendrils of affection steal
out from each to each unshy honest encompassing
golden calves in Israel and slum babies in Canada and
a millionaire's brat left squalling on the toilet seat in
Rockefeller Center
        Oh my sisters
        I give purple milk!

DETAIL

The ruined stone house
has an old apple tree
left there by the farmer
whatever else he took with him
It bears fruit every year
gone wild and wormy
with small bitter apples
nobody eats
even children know better
I passed that way on the road
to Trenton twice a month
all winter long
noticing how the apples clung
in spite of hurricane winds
sometimes with caps of snow
little golden bells

And perhaps none of the other
travellers looked that way
but I make no parable of them
they were there and that's all
For some reason I must remember
and think of the leafless tree
and its fermented fruit
one week in late January
when wind blew down the sun
and earth shook like a cold room
no one could live in
with zero weather
soundless golden bells
alone in the storm

THE BEACH AT VARADERO

These multi-coloured people
– the brown and black ones
and a lobster redman
in the sun at Varadero
bulging from the human blue-
print standing in breakers
for waves to slam against
a long way ago
from the rock farm I was
born on a long way
from Varadero was my grandfather
building stone fences
between clearings
to measure time with
and hewing white pineflesh
into cathedrals like barns
big enough for a farmer
to turn outside in the summer
large enough for a man
to know without saying

what trees already know
far from the royal palms
far from the dusty *latifundia*
and the red earth of Cuba
with little lizards darting
from islands of shadow
into seas of sunlight
far from the yellow sand
the son of my father
letting himself be knocked down
by senseless water
only an object
a temporary barrier
to the marching breakers
in a water valley
in a fragment of time
an hour before dinner
on the beach at Varadero
an Ontario farmer's son
in a far country
thinking of my fathers

Varadero, Cuba

DREAM OF HAVANA

Talking to Red Chinese sailors
with a Cuban interpreter
at the bar in a dark night club
and so hot the air is thick
you have to move sideways
and backward to go forward
Outside on the waterfront
anti-aircraft guns point to the sky
searchlights swing like jumpy nerves
awaiting the Roman invasion
a grey American warship

cruises beyond the 12-mile limit
an international ghost
waiting for buttons to be pushed
In the Sierra Maestras
tanks rumble over mountain roads
and knock down ripe coconuts
Here in Havana Fidel
finds another friend's apartment
and settles down for the night
while his potential assassin
dials information
What world is this I've come to?
I don't believe it
not for a moment
and my thoughts exit
sideways and backward
to childhood and a lost dog
tantrums and broken toys
trouble enough
mothers in long ago doorways
calling children home at night
for bedtime stories
while the Red Chinese sailors
mumble in my ear
and I drink white rum
to the sound of trombones

Havana, Cuba

HOMBRE

– Met briefly in Havana
among the million Cubans waiting
Fidel's speech on May Day 1964
under a million merciless suns
He came around and shook hands
with the foreign visitors
a guy who looked like a service station attendant

in his olive drab fatigues and beret
but with the beard and black cigar
the resemblance ended
– the Argentine doctor and freedom fighter
Che Guevara
And I remember thinking the North Vietnamese ladies
looked especially flower-like beside him
I remember his grip particularly
firm but perfunctory
half politician and half revolutionary
for he had many hands to shake that day

Later he disappeared from Cuba
and there were rumours of quarrels
between himself and Castro
and US newspapers asked nervously
"Where is Che Guevara?"
Then Havana Radio reported Guevara
had joined guerrillas in "a South American country"
but the US expressed some small doubt
about the reliability of Havana Radio
while I thought of him – shaking hands

Back home in Canada I remembered Guevara
along with structural details of Cuban girls
the Grand Hotel at Camaguey with roosters
yammering into my early morning sleep
an all-night walk in Havana streets with a friend
a mad jeep-ride over the Sierra Maestras
where sea-raiders attacked a coastal sugar mill
and Playa Giron which is the "Bay of Pigs"
where the dead men have stopped caring
and alligators hiss in the late afternoon
Again May Day in Havana 1964
with a red blaze of flowers and banners
and Castro talking solemnly to his nation
a million people holding hands and singing
strange to think of this in Canada
And I remember Che Guevara

a man who made dreams something
he could hold in his hands both hands
saying "Hiya" or whatever they say in Spanish
to the flower-like Vietnamese ladies
cigar tilted into his own trademark
of the day when rebels swarmed out
of Oriente Province down from the mountains

"Where is Che Guevara?" is answered:
deep in Bolivian jungles leading his guerrillas
from cave to cave with scarlet cockatoos screaming
the Internationale around his shoulders
smoking a black cigar and wearing a beret
(like a student in Paris on a Guggenheim)
his men crawling under hundred-foot trees
where giant snakes mate in masses of roots
and men with infected wounds moan for water
while Guevara leads his men into an ambush
and out again just like in the movies
but the good guy loses and the bad guys always win
and the band plays the Star-Spangled Banner
Well it is over
Guevara is dead now and whether the world
is any closer to freedom because
of Che's enormous dream is not to be known
the bearded Argentine doctor who translated
that dream to a handshake among Bolivian peasants
and gave himself away free to those who wanted him
his total self and didn't keep any
I remember the news reports from Bolivia
how he was wounded   captured   executed   cremated
but first they cut off his fingers
for fingerprint identification later
in case questions should be asked
and I remember his quick hard handshake
in Havana among the tiny Vietnamese ladies
and seem to hold ghostlike in my own hand
five bloody fingers
of Che Guevara

SHOESHINE BOYS ON THE AVENIDA JUAREZ

These, I suppose, are the underdogs
people are always talking about.
But they're alive:
for a genuine underdog is dead,
or else it's a matter of days or weeks
until stigmata appear on his face.
If I knew Spanish I could talk to them,
as it is I ought to be feeling guilty
– but the hell with that!
In this context they're happier than I am,
which is a different thing than wearing
a necktie which may enhance contentment tho
by being a handy convertible hangman's noose.
Later in the year I'll catch up on happiness
from an almost 100% reservoir of the stuff
available day to day in each man's life –

In the meantime I get my shoes shined
(pay 1 peso and 20 centavos – 9^1/2 cents).
Then I get my shoes shined again
by the next "boy" on the Avenida Juarez.
And the first boy is kinda mad
he thinks I think he didn't do a good job.
The third shoeshine boy is middle aged,
with fat cheeks and a moustache.
He seems to think I am very funny,
his moustache quivers and he laughs at me.
Looking back I see the first and second boys
think I am nuts too; but they grin.
And when I get my twentieth shine,
far away down the Avenida Juaroz
past Alameda Park all the way to Sanborn's
House of Tiles, I see the brown shoeshine
boys grinning. But my face is serious,
for I've badly needed all twenty shines.
Tho I've given no tips,
tho my socks are getting a little dirty,

tho I'm getting a little sick of the idea,
a little sick of myself for thinking of it,
a little disgusted at being such a phony:
but the palimpsest of almost new black shoes
has twenty grinning portraits I'm taking back
to Canada on Tuesday morning (via CPA).
All the way down the Avenida Juarez
I see the grins go echoing farther and farther,
from mirror to mirror and mind to memory:
tho the first is beginning to forget the reason
he grinned (maybe a sick wife is more important),
and the fourteenth has seen thru me,
and looks cynical and dislikes me,
and thinks I'm a phony. I think he's right.
And all down the Avenida Juarez
the grins have faded out completely,
and probably only I shall remember
(and the CIA man twenty steps behind me)
being crazy as hell one morning,
and writing a poem about it,
and writing about writing a poem about it,
and making it into the echo of a poem,
the echo of a grin on the Avenida Juarez,
the echo of being alive once,
the echo of dying on the Avenida Juarez.

What really happened: there was just one shine:
the guy put on quite a sideshow,
panting a little to convince
me he was doing a good job
because I was a Norte Americano,
then got chased away by the cop on the beat
on accounta overcharging me 1 peso (8 cents) –
Or else he had no license to shine
my shoes anyhow anyway
the grins were pretty cynical
on the Avenida Juarez.
And the 90-year-old Indian
woman suckling her baby

and selling lottery tickets
sitting on the Commercial Bank
steps
        grinned
                and was told to move
along on accounta the cop
mistook it for happiness;
the fake Greek sculpture
with lipstick on their rumps
in Alameda Park pseudo
grinned
                and grins were pretty cynical
on the Avenida Juarez –
As cynical and sad as yours maybe
after reading a poem sad and cynical as this one
about having 20 phantom shoeshines,
a poem that isn't about anything really:
and it gets so
you just can't trust nobody eh?

                                        Mexico City

WATCHING TRAINS

Indian boys at Nakina and Sioux Lookout
from tent towns in the bush
and blueberry shacks by a railway siding
($1.50 a basket in bargain summer)
with schoolmarm passenger distributing
replicas of the new Canadian flag
Boys with their mouths open
some missing part supplied by trains
Thought will not come to them nor speech
they have no words for department stores
or pictographs for elevators going fifty
miles an hour into the sky
They watch the train

dumbfound as newfallen snow
        blank eyes and blank minds
that do not follow down the whispering rails
or think of anything
until the train goes
and birds dispute the ownership of silence

Hours or miles
later in the snowbush
with summer gone
they hear a diesel hoot
like blood that shrieks inside their toenails
trains
inside their inward eye
from all directions bearing down on them
from deadfalls under scrub cedar
and burned pine skeletons
and traplines where the red-eyed weasel
snarls in a wire noose
and foxes gnaw their forelegs
free from steel
the trains
converge from snowhung poplar coverts
mooseyards and small creeks
their bubble music choked with ice
the diesels vector in
And rails run down the day's horizon
a white eye slants on hogback hills
thru midnight zero Pullmans pass
and spike their echoes to the trees . . .

Trains
        things
                thought itself
no capital letters tattooed presto
on people
like Mr. Tecumseh and Mr. Hiawatha
or Joe Something
faces are faces

The skulls contain
pictures of things
woodsmoke messages
the melted circle of snow
around living trees
old loved rifles
the price of blueberries
people
happening memories
maybe death
and trains
trains
And will see them like small glory
among snarling dogs and chewed bones in the snow
as wind invades the tarpaper mansions
till June and the bush raspberries come

SHOPPING AT LOBLAWS

Nearly trapped her at the turnstile
for the fur jacket she wore
reaching out one hand
where the chrome cage held
quarry amounting to 100 pounds or so
Hesitated
then followed her down the aisle
with a wire baby buggy among the bananas
and citrus fruits her little behind
waggling both syllables in unison
unseizable past the eggs and cheese
guaranteed fresh and edible thinking
of her trapped in that turnstile
her anger resurrecting undead
meat electrocuting popcorn and
that would be some sort of beginning which
is always chaos known survivors say
But the Campbell's Soup distracts

me and 7 ounces of pacific salmon flip
their lids and gravitate ceilingwards also
canned corn beef attached locketwise
under a matron's brisket flops like Lazarus
makes like a quadruped galloping shoplifter
down aisles of cornflakes and cereal seed
germinating from memory
inside wax paper
Chaos again I guess is beginning
even for middle-aged windowshoppers
tho ending in definite order with
everything wrapped and packaged and
instinct roped tight and the sub-
conscious caged hot in white bone
turnstile
But me Neanderthal
I snarl happily
at rival buggy drivers and forget turn signals
run down an old-age pensioner in drugs and
sundries pursue the waggling
fanny to quality stationery my
quarry two shoppers in front but
I cut them off at instant coffee oh
the cut-rate jello
almost eludes at the cashier and
I reach out one trembling hand-wish to
touch
both packages
"Excuse me miss you uh dropped your camisole"
Me Neanderthal me
Itus Pickupus Emasculus Promiscuous
Her eyes look past me at some river bottom
full of unpackaged molluscs and slugs and snails
For someone the cashier rings up $14.98
for me she rings up a package of cigarettes
(I receive one pink stamp)
The packaged buttocks swirl thru
turnstile unhindered & conjure
a hautboy

opt for a buick
head for a duplex (or equivalent)
I lope to the tavern intending
to repackage myself better
or worse as "alcoholic" with
flesh coloured label outside
dow or red cap
Well it might have been *amor*
or some rare emotional disorder
doctors have no cure for anyway
but the fur piece
looked well worth trapping

POEM FOR EDA

She wears glasses
and has a slightly intellectual expression
as if she'd intended to read a book

        – then decided against it

FURTHER DEPONENT SAITH NOT

I am trapped in an old house
full of paint brushes and hammers
saws and spirit levels and things
which I am supposed to use
for some constructive purpose
but I take a drink of rye instead
and test the canned fruit for fermentation
in the cellar
whose rafters I am supposed to jack up
with a house jack
          and indeed do jack up
with a house jack

And god goes whooping thru the timbers
and shakes hands with all the door knobs
mistaking them for businessmen
and US Steel closes at 1984
but I prefer Seagram's 83
which stays open all the time
And there are 16 King James Bibles
and 12 hymn books in that cellar
without a word of a lie
and moved by some tender religious impulse
I sing "Throw Out the Lifeline"
to the dead who once lived
in this 100-year-old house
and were all music lovers
And somebody knocks at the door
and I figure it must be a bill collector
and I figure there must be a town out there
for there to be bill collectors
in any event he's unwelcome
In any case I have the Seagram's
and saws and hammers and paint brushes
and climb the walls to an attic
and sing from the roof at god
having belched loudly to secure his attention
sing "Show Me the Way to Go Home"
but he ignores the melodious sounds
And nails get bent and glass painted
and dead feelings hurt and it's a long time
till death a long way from birth in this house
I once lived in where I sat writing and drinking
rye and the ghosts of all the Purdys who ever lived
make hissing sounds out loud and cuss me good
But it's no use
I absolutely refuse to contribute to Foreign Missionaries
I got the Seagram's
and it seems like I've never been
anywhere else but here
So I hammer a nail vindictively
it bends

I clean a window energetically
it breaks
and I cut my finger on the damn glass
Anyway I got the Seagram's
      – no by god I haven't
           someone drank it the bastard
The fridge motor buzzes and drones
silence grimaces to itself
the walls creak and mutter like imbeciles
and there is someone at the door

      THERE IS SOMEONE AT THE DOOR

who wishes to deliver my death certificate
and a pleasing floral tribute for shut-ins
also my marriage certificate and birth ditto
title deed in fee simple for one used lawn mower
absolution for your sins absolutely
      Bring out your dead and come yourself
        I am not at home
          I am not at home

ATTEMPT

Man's sole gesture of defiance
at a hostile or indifferent universe
is standing outside at night
after the requisite number of beers
and with a graceful enormous parabola
trying to piss on the stars
failing magnificently

LOVE AT ROBLIN LAKE

My ambition as I remember and
I always remember was always
to make love vulgarly and immensely
       as the vulgar elephant doth
          & immense reptiles did
       in the open air openly
       sweating and grunting together
       and going
          "BOING   BOING   BOING"
                      making
every lunge a hole in the great dark
for summer cottagers to fall into at a later date
and hear inside faintly (like in a football
stadium when the home team loses)
ourselves still softly
       going
          "boing   boing   boing"
       as the vulgar elephant doth
          & immense reptiles did
in the star-filled places of earth
that I remember we left behind long ago
and forgotten everything after
on our journey into the dark

DARK LANDSCAPE

For a week the flies have been terrible
not medium-size houseflies
but heavy foreboding buzzard-creatures
dive-bombing thru clouds of insecticide
knocking dishes from shelves
and body checking the furniture
Lying awake in darkness I hear them
blundering thru night's frontiers
frantic about something

antennae picking up signals outside the house
as if there was a point to existence
other than personal
as if they registered a protest
No sun or wind on the grey lake
all morning and thru the long afternoon
summer cottagers gone
a pair of tall elms
dead long since from Dutch elm disease
are indistinguishable from other trees
their small bones leafless
Well I've no doubt weather
does influence human mood and
when it rains people are seldom optimists
in middle age the body itself
slows to contemplate nothingness
seasonal metrics stagger and jerk to a halt
mandolins in grass roots end
winter is coming
I sit stupefied
waiting . . .

Across the sky a flight of geese
goes sweeping to the continental vanishing point
sends a honking cry down here now
fading to an almost inaudible mockery
as they reach towards lands of the sun
All this brings on an opposite reaction
and I laugh I must laugh
it's too pat too trite and too goddam soon
too easy to turn down the music and wait
or alternatively
brush reality aside with physical action?
But "to live a life is not to cross a field"?
Is it then to cross many fields
wear blinkers and cultivate a cheerful outlook?
With brain relinquished the body takes over?
And I laugh and span the continent with a letter
write a dozen letters to Vancouver

Vancouver   Montreal   and Toronto
drink a glass of wine and knock the bottle over
down the dregs and stain my guts with purple
think about a girl who couldn't love me
(oh impossible and inconceivable to love you
as she passionately mentioned) and I laugh
and think – for life to have a meaning
or even several meanings well it's funny
tho one of them is getting rather drunken
in the afterbirth of youth and maybe wine and
maybe spring comes on forever spring goes on forever
said Aladdin to the jinn jinn gin

And maybe down below the lowest floorboards
where the dead flies buzz and blunder
a girl will whisper maybe yes I do
yes I do you euphemistic bastard
me as shouldn't me as oughtn't on accounta
you don't take women serious as you really
ought to do you
don't take livin serious
                Yes I do yes I do
tho I'm gettin rather elderly for crossin fields in winter
is serious as anything and hemispheres take longer
and elms are dying momently as I say this to you
        and flies are something terrible
        and mushroom clouds likewise
        and there's them that die of livin
        and there's them that joy in dyin
        and there's agony and screamin
        and all I have is laughter
        all I have is wine and laughter
        and the spring came on forever
        the spring comes on forever
                Yes I do

                                        Roblin Lake

INTERRUPTION

When the new house was built
callers came:
black squirrels on the roof every morning
between sleep and wakefulness,
and a voice saying "Hello dead man."
A chipmunk looks in the window
and I look out,
the small face and the large one
waver together in glass,
but neither moves
while the leaves turn into shadows.
Orioles, robins and red-winged blackbirds
are crayons that colour the air;
something sad and old
cries down in the swamp.
Moonlight in the living room,
a row of mice single file
route marching across the empty lunar plain
until they touch one of my thoughts
and jump back frightened,
but I don't wake up.
Pike in the lake pass and re-pass the windows
with clouds in their mouth.
For 20 minutes every night
the sun slaps a red paint brush
over dinner dishes and leftovers,
but we keep washing it off.
Birds can't take a shortcut home
they have to fly around the new house;
and cedars grow pale green candles
to light their way thru the dark.
Already the house is old:
a drowned chipmunk (the same one?)
in the rain barrel this morning,
dead robins in the roof overhang,
and the mice are terrified –
We have set traps,

and must always remember
to avoid them ourselves.

MY '48 PONTIAC

All winter long it wouldn't start
standing in the yard covered with snow
I'd go out at 10 below zero and coax
and say
        "Where's your pride?"
and kick it disgustedly
Finally snow covered everything
but television aerials and the world was
a place nobody came to
so white it couldn't be looked at
before nothing was something
But the old Pontiac lay there
affirming its identity
like some prehistoric vegetarian
stupidly unaware of snow
waiting for Tyrannosaurus Rex
to come along and bite off its fenders
"You no good American Pontiac you
(I'd say)
you're a disgrace to General Motors"
then go out and hitch up the dog team
When June hurried by it still wouldn't start
only stop
and the wreckers hauled it away

Now and then I go to visit my old friend
at Bud's Auto Wreckers
being sentimental about rubber and metal
I think it's glad to see me
and wags both tail lights
a true heart thumping eagerly
under the torn seat covers

I sit behind the wheel
on a parched August afternoon
and we drive thru a glitter of broken glass
among suicides and automotive murders
mangled chryslers and volkswagens
metal twisted into a look
of fierce helplessness
reversed violence in hunchback shapes
and containing it still
waiting to explode outward

We drive between dismantled buicks and
studebakers and one stuckup old cadillac
driven to Bud's by a doddering chauffeur
who used to play poker with Roman chariot drivers
and a silent crumpled grey plymouth
with bloodstains on the instrument panel
where a girl died
a '41 de soto with all the chrome gone
still excited from drag races
and quivering blondes whose bottoms it liked

My last visit was by moonlight and flashlight
to Bud's Auto Wreckers
where the old Pontiac waited
I turned the speedometer back to 5,000 miles
changed the oil
polished the headlights to look at death
adjusted the rear view mirror to look at life
gave it back its ownership card
and went away
puzzled by things

ROBLIN'S MILLS [II]

The wheels stopped
and the murmur of voices
behind the flume's tremble
stopped
  and the wind-high ships
that sailed from Rednersville
to the sunrise ports of Europe
are delayed somewhere
in a toddling breeze
The black millpond
turns an unreflecting eye
to look inward
like an idiot child
locked in the basement
when strangers come
whizzing past on the highway
above the dark green valley
a hundred yards below
The mill space is empty
even stones are gone
where hands were shaken
and walls enclosed laughter
saved up and brought here
from the hot fields
where all stories
are rolled into one
And white dust floating
above the watery mumble
and bright human sounds
to shimmer among the pollen
where bees dance now
Of all these things
no outline remains
no shadow on the soft air
no bent place in the heat glimmer
where the heavy walls pressed
And some of those who vanished

lost children of the time
kept after school
left alone in a graveyard
who may not change
or ever grow six inches
in one hot summer
or turn where the great herons
graze the sky's low silver
– stand between the hours
in a rotting village
near the weed-grown eye
that looks into itself
deep in the black crystal
that holds and contains
the substance of shadows
manner and custom
              of the inarticulate
departures and morning rumours
gestures and almost touchings
announcements and arrivals
gossip of someone's marriage
when a girl or tired farm woman
whose body suddenly blushes
beneath a faded house dress
with white expressionless face
turns to her awkward husband
to remind him of something else
The black millpond
                        holds them
movings and reachings and fragments
the gear and tackle of living
under the water eye
all things laid aside
              discarded
                        forgotten
but they had their being once
and left a place to stand on

WILDERNESS GOTHIC

Across Roblin Lake, two shores away,
they are sheathing the church spire
with new metal. Someone hangs in the sky
over there from a piece of rope,
hammering and fitting God's belly-scratcher,
working his way up along the spire
until there's nothing left to nail on –

Perhaps the workman's faith reaches beyond:
touches intangibles, wrestles with Jacob,
replacing rotten timber with pine thews,
pounds hard in the blue cave of the sky,
contends heroically with difficult problems of
gravity, sky navigation and mythopoeia,
his volunteer time and labour donated to God,
minus sick benefits of course on a non-union job –

Fields around are yellowing into harvest,
nestling and fingerling are sky and water borne,
death is yodelling quiet in green woodlots,
and bodies of three young birds have disappeared
in the sub-surface of the new county highway –

That picture is incomplete, part left out
that might alter the whole Dürer landscape:
gothic ancestors peer from medieval sky,
dour faces trapped in photograph albums escaping
to clop down iron roads with matched greys:
work-sodden wives groping inside their flesh
for what keeps moving and changing and flashing
beyond and past the long frozen Victorian day.
A sign of fire and brimstone? A two-headed calf
born in the barn last night? A sharp female agony?
An age and a faith moving into transition,
the dinner cold and new-baked bread a failure,
deep woods shiver and water drops hang pendant,
double-yolked eggs and the house creaks a little –

Something is about to happen. Leaves are still.
Two shores away, a man hammering in the sky.
Perhaps he will fall.

BOUNDARIES

In all these southern counties
                    with English names
York   Dufferin   Hastings   Northumberland
                    stood the great trees
          gone for a hundred years now
and the mannered expressionless urban names
                    mark the boundaries
insert themselves like worn silver shillings
          in mouths of city people
          to spend on tiny vistas
                    in parking lots
                                fenced backyards

Far north the still-rich vulgarity
                    to match
a man-breaking country
          "The Torngat Mountains"
                    east of nowhere
westerly
          "Telegraph Creek"
                "100 Mile House"
northerly
                "Arctic Red River"
                    "Tuktoyaktuk"
Nobody speaks those names without feeling
the tongue touch rank bear-steak
or prickling devil's club
and remembers mountain land
                    the iron north
beyond the last streetlight
drowned in snow

teeth chatter over mere pronunciation
biting the stammered name
to pieces held there a moment
in a man's cold mouth
the edge of our loneliness

LAMENT FOR THE DORSETS
(Eskimos extinct in the 14th century AD)

Animal bones and some mossy tent rings
scrapers and spearheads   carved ivory swans
all that remains of the Dorset giants
who drove the Vikings back to their long ships
talked to spirits of earth and water
– a picture of terrifying old men,
so large they broke the backs of bears
so small they lurk behind bone rafters
in the brain of modern hunters
among good thoughts and warm things
and come out at night
to spit on the stars

The big men with clever fingers
who had no dogs and hauled their sleds
over the frozen northern oceans
awkward giants
                  killers of seal
they couldn't compete with little men
who came from the west with dogs
Or else in a warm climatic cycle
the seals went back to cold waters
and the puzzled Dorsets scratched their heads
with hairy thumbs around 1350 AD
– couldn't figure it out
went around saying to each other
plaintively
                  "What's wrong? What happened?

Where are the seals gone?"
And died

Twentieth-century people
apartment dwellers
executives of neon death
warmakers with things that explode
– they have never imagined us in their future
how could we imagine them in the past
squatting among the moving glaciers
six hundred years ago
with glowing lamps?
As remote or nearly
as the trilobites and swamps
when coal became
or the last great reptile hissed
at a mammal the size of a mouse
that squeaked and fled

Did they ever realize at all
what was happening to them?
Some old hunter with one lame leg
a bear had chewed
sitting in a caribou-skin tent
– the last Dorset?
Let's say his name was Kudluk
and watch him sitting there
carving 2-inch ivory swans
for a dead grand-daughter
taking them out of his mind
the places in his mind
where pictures are
He selects a sharp stone tool
to gouge a parallel pattern of lines
on both sides of the swan
holding it with his left hand
bearing down and transmitting
his body's weight
from brain to arm and right hand

and one of his thoughts
turns to ivory
The carving is laid aside
in beginning darkness
at the end of hunger
and after a while wind
blows down the tent and snow
begins to cover him

After 600 years
the ivory thought
is still warm

THE RUNNERS

*"It was when Leif was with King Olaf Tryggvason, and he
bade him proclaim Christianity to Greenland, that the king
gave him two Gaels; the man's name was Haki, and the
woman's Haekia. The King advised Leif to have recourse to
these people, if he should stand in need of fleetness, for they
were swifter than deer. Erick and Leif had tendered
Karlsefni the services of this couple. Now when they had
sailed past Marvel-Strands (to the New World) they put the
Gaels ashore, and directed them to run to the southward,
and investigate the nature of the country, and return again
before the end of the third half-day."*

(from *Erick the Red's Saga*)

Brother, the wind of this place is cold,
and hills under our feet tremble,
the forests are making magic against us –
I think the land knows we are here,
I think the land knows we are strangers.
Let us stay close to our friend the sea,
or cunning dwarves at the roots of darkness
shall seize and drag us down –

Sister, we must share our strength between us,
until the heat of our bodies makes a single flame:
while the moon sees only one shadow
and the sun knows only our double heartbeat,
and the rain does not come between –

Brother, I am afraid of this dark place,
I am hungry for the home islands,
and wind blowing the waves to coloured spray,
I am sick for the sun –

Sister, we must not think those thoughts again,
for three half-days have gone by,
and we must return to the ship.
If we are away longer,
the Northmen will beat us with thongs,
until we cry for death –
Why do you stare at nothing?

Brother, a cold wind touched me,
tho I stand in your arms' circle:
perhaps the Northmen's runes have found us,
the runes they carve on wood and stone.
I am afraid of this dark land,
ground mist that makes us half ghosts,
and another silence inside silence . . .
But there are berries and fish here,
and small animals by the sea's edge
that crouch and tremble and listen . . .
If we join our thoughts to the silence,
if our trails join the animal trails,
and the sun remembers what the moon forgets . . .
Brother, it comes to me now,
the long ship must sail without us,
we stay here –

Sister, we should die slowly,
the beasts would gnaw at our bodies,
the rains whiten our bones.

The Northmen's runes are strong magic,
the runes would track us down,
tho we keep on running
past the Land of Flat Stones
over the Marvel-Strands
beyond the country of great trees . . .
Tho we ran to the edge of the world,
our masters would track us down –

Brother, take my hand in your hand,
this part of ourselves between us
while we run together,
over the stones of the sea-coast,
this much of ourselves is our own:
while rain cries out against us,
and darkness swallows the evening,
and morning moves into stillness,
and mist climbs to our throats,
while we are running,
while we are running –

Sister –

THE ROAD TO NEWFOUNDLAND

My foot has pushed a fire ahead of me
for a thousand miles
my arms' response to hills and stones
has stated parallel green curves
deep in my unknown country
the clatter of gravel on fenders registers
on a ghostly player piano
inside my head with harsh fraying music
I'm lost to reality
but turn the steering wheel a quarter
inch to avoid a bug on the road
A long time's way here since stone

age man carried the fire-germ
in a moss-lined basket
from camp to camp
and prayed to it
as I shall solemnly hold Henry Ford
and all his descendants accountable
to the 24,000-mile guarantee
Well there are many miles left
before it expires and several
more to the next rest
stop and I kick the fire
ahead of me with one foot
even harder than before
hearing the sound of burning
forests muffled in steel
toppling buildings
history accelerating
racing up and down
hills with my flesh grown captive
of a steel extension of myself
hauling down the sun and stars
for mileposts going nowhere fast
wanting speed and more Speed
– Stop
at a calm lake
embossed with 2-inch waves
sit there a few minutes
without getting out of the car
my heart a hammering drum
among the trees' and grass roots'
August diminuendo
watching the composed landscape
the sun where it's supposed to be
in its deliberate dance thru space
then drive steadily north
with the captive fire
in cool evening
towards the next camp

OVER THE HILLS IN THE RAIN, MY DEAR

We are walking back from the Viking site,
dating ten centuries ago
(it must be about four miles),
and rain beats on us,
soaks our clothes,
runs into our shoes,
makes white pleats in our skin,
turns hair into decayed seaweed:
and I think sourly that drowning
on land is a helluva slow way to die.
I walk faster than my wife,
then have to stop and wait for her:
"It isn't much farther,"
I say encouragingly
and note that our married life
is about to end in violence,
judging from her expressionless expression.
Again I slop into the lead,
then wait in the mud till she catches up,
thinking, okay, I'll say something complimentary:
"You sure are a sexy lookin mermaid dear!"
That don't go down so good either,
and she glares at me like a female vampire
resisting temptation badly:
at which point I've forgotten
all about the rain,
trying to manufacture
a verbal comfort station,
a waterproof two-seater.
We squelch miserably into camp
about half an hour later,
strip down like white shrivelled slugs,
waving snail horns at each other,
cold sexless antennae
assessing the other ridiculous creature –
And I begin to realize
one can't use a grin like a bandaid

or antidote for reality,
at least not all the time:
and maybe it hurts my vanity
to know she feels sorry for me,
she's sorry for *me*,
and I don't know why:
but to be a fool
is sometimes
my own good luck.

L'Anse aux Meadows, Newfoundland

PRIVATE PROPERTY

Not the Stone Age or Bronze or small
excitement of finding an arrowhead
that once stopped a deer mid-stride
to breathe a blood bubble
Just a pile of rocks
of an old house foundation
stone furniture fallen inward
(overlaid with wornout tires and tin cans)
of an early 19th-century (?) farmhouse
– but in the space I happen to occupy
a thousand things happened
or just one
with me at the moving end
Under the hot sun
I rummage in the earth
as if it were a clothes closet
poke a stick into crevices
shove rocks aside and dirty my hands
move a half-buried rotten timber
(a snake flickers his tongue at me)
underneath in the earth
what's left of an iron latch
that doesn't stop anyone
a hundred-year-old bone

come sizzling grease from an oven
with teeth-marks of dogs
and a little piece of blue china
from someone's dinner set
I hear a voice down there
"Enoch, you clean that up!
I never saw such a boy to break things."
A blond freckly boy maybe
gathers the coloured fragments
under the eyes of his angry mother
for a knife-edge moment of grief
that slams his door to the future
I hear a voice above me
"What you doin there?
This is private property!"
and that voice is the one last detail
needed to slam the rusty iron latch
and freeze me into a boy's grief
that twists the world to a halt
But then I notice another detail
cowshit on someone's boots up there
a man wearing faded overalls
and say "Sorry, I was just curious,
wondering about the people who lived here –"
I walk to the road
among stones and blue thistles and sky
and slow suspicious stare of the farmer
(one metal button gone from his bib)
and the family underground
going on and on

ABOUT BEING A MEMBER OF OUR ARMED FORCES

Remember the early days of the phony war
when men were zombies and women were CWACs
and they used wooden rifles on the firing range?
Well I was the sort of soldier you couldn't trust

with a wooden rifle
and when they gave me a wooden bayonet
life was fraught with peril for my brave comrades
including the sergeant-instructor
I wasn't exactly a soldier tho
only a humble airman
who kept getting demoted
                                    and demoted
                                                and demoted
to the point where I finally saluted civilians
And when they trustingly gave me a Sten gun
Vancouver should have trembled in its sleep
for after I fired a whole clip of bullets
at some wild ducks under Burrard Bridge
(on guard duty at midnight)
they didn't fly away for five minutes
trying to decide if there was any danger
Not that the war was funny
I took it and myself quite seriously
the way a squirrel in a treadmill does
too close to tears for tragedy
too far from the banana peel for laughter
and I didn't blame anyone for being there
that wars happened wasn't anybody's fault then

Now I think it is

SERGEANT JACKSON

In the long grass lying
there in 1944
hating that sergeant for thinking
three stripes made him so superior
he could get away with anything
peering thru tall grass at him
hoping his face might alter
flush or grow pale

and he'd double over with agony
from the force in my eyes
VOODOO thoughts
of an RCAF airman
– trying to make the self-important
bastard throw up his dinner
contract any ailment untrivial
like a permanent dose of clap
or imaginary fleas
approx. the size of rats
A big eagle circling the sun
with eyes a golden snare
looped round the green valley
snow peaks overhead
dust blowing across the airfield
the Skeena sailing past
railway tracks heading for Rupert
48-hour-pass cancelled
myself stuck there forever
where even Japs would be welcome
but they have more sense
and no woman for miles
and no woman for centuries
All this a long time ago:
I remember grass tickling my chin
mountains near and high and far away
axe blows smashing at silence
Indian canoes on the Skeena
totem poles and some friends
nothing is lost
That sergeant?
I convince no one now
even myself
that I hated him
but my hate was holy and beautiful then
and life got damned interesting
a sword was laid across the month of August
it worked like 100 proof booze
and made the landscape glow

Beyond Remembering

black runways where the planes landed
writhed like snakes in the heat haze
but no one else noticed
how the edges of things sharpened
and quivered like fine gold lettering
on pages of cracked parchment
and the crummy barracks lit up
during poker games
and left that time photographed
in the dumb compartments of memory
where love was slowly becoming possible

AUTUMN

Old men in poolrooms
watching kids shoot snooker
retired brakies haunting
sad railway yards
yearning for their old jobs
bald-headed profs emeritus
bothering computers
with senile statistics
homesick for laboratories
one-armed ex-soldiers lonesome
for the old excitement of gunfire
and fear that empties the bowels
but is strangely attractive
in retrospect

Old Willys
Stars and Durants and Whippets
rust quiet
in wreckers' yards humiliated
by automatic transmissions
and bent insignia of General Motors
harrows with broken teeth gnash the
dust of sheds

enigmatic butter churns and three-legged
chairs join the
big-busted dress dummies in attics
shushing the spiders

It is the time of death
and the fear of never
having lived at all
crazes the young
when pigs that escaped slaughter
eat dozens of fermented
apples and charge drunken thru
empty woods
and huntsmen somewhere else
are learning the trade

SKELETON BY AN OLD CEDAR

Now the bird's bones are little wires
that thrummed the air and
ants and other insects
negotiate the girders
and small wingbones
that slipped between raindrops
and hemispheres
are wrestled to earth
by nothing
but death
which had no form and shape
in the bird's mind
but came just as the wingtips
circled round this cedar
to meet from another direction
the black speck of his mate
(flightwind opening grey
down on her throat
like a silver pulse)

Circling the ragged cedar here
he came
      but never meeting her
four farms away
down by the county road instead
encountering some violence
that left no trace here
encountering a concept
beyond animal understanding
over the darkening pasturelands
that stops all meetings
and halts all travellers
      halfway home

"OLD MAN MAD ABOUT PAINTING"

From impulse challenge or defiance
Hokusai raised a great fifty-foot
framework of bamboo and red tissuepaper
higher than medium-sized pagodas
and painted his thoughts on the thing
along with mountain landscapes
releasing the slow drip-drip of water
in the mind shrieking Eureka at the stars
          in Japanese of course
           the wind
came by to wreck his paper canvas
during the Hour of the Rat
Everyone thought Hokusai was a damn fool
the rickshaw boys made wisecracks
and the charcoal burners razzed him
the beggars made faces behind his back
the saki drinkers kept right on drinking
the money lenders said he was a bad risk
and small boys continued the countdown
          one-two-three-four before
the monster painting slowly toppled

down in the dust
It kind of cheers me
during my own Hour of Despond
when I've failed at everything
scribbling poems on the reverse side
of cost schedules scrounged from garbage
to think of Hokusai in bleak poverty
before he painted a still-life of all Nippon
in the encyclopaedic *Mangwa Sketches*
and *Thirty-Six Views of Mount Fujiyama*
to think of that earlier idiotic painting
reared on momentary impulse
nobody understood but Hokusai himself
And sometimes I can actually see
the monster fifty-foot tick-tock
of paper visibly falling into the dust
without money value or the least permanence
but the fractional god of now defeated
perceptibly merges with forever
I am beginning to understand a little
about the reverse side of mountains

DEATH OF A YOUNG POET

A boy whose poems
        remained still
part of his personal being
even when written and dropped
into a public mailbox
And when some faceless man
rejected them I suppose it was
as if pins were stuck
        in a voodoo doll
on the other side of a continent
That mediocrity must be faced
and Furies are ridiculous editors
with snuffling noses and

bent-backward honesty
      he knew
Tho great thoughts were beyond him
in desolate back alleys of a city
and thundering caesuras begun
in the tick of ended pulse
his life's income taxed
and non-refundable
I grow old in the city rain
among garbage cans and broken bottles
and smell of a cat's afterbirth
and dogshit in gutters
lost somewhere
in my own decaying body

Only the written extensions
of myself are alive
somewhere else and I move
softly as a grave robber
bending no blade of grass
beneath the sidewalk
touching no live thing
and walking forever
in that curious dead light
the sun gives after it has gone down
My face is a shining grave marker
in the black rain
among the tombs
of my friends
      He was 27
he will remain 27
      a long time

THE DRUNK TANK

A man keeps hammering at the door
(he is so noisy it makes my ears ache),
yelling monotonously, "Let me outa here!"
A caged light bulb floats on the ceiling,
where a dung fly circles round and round,
and there is a greasy brown mattress,
too small for the bolted-down steel bunk,
and a high barred window permitting
fungus darkness to creep in the room's corners.
The man keeps hammering at the door
until a guard comes:
"I just happen to know the mayor in this town,"
he tells the guard,
"and it's gonna be too bad for you
if you keep me locked up here."
The guard laughs and turns away.
"It's no use," I tell my cell mate.
"Just wait until morning.
Then we'll be up in magistrate's court,
and being drunk isn't a very serious –"
"Who are you?" the man asks me.
"I don't know you –"
"I'm your friend," I say to him,
"and I've been your friend a long time.
Don't you remember?"
"I don't know you at all!" he screams.
"Stay away from me!"
"If that's the way you feel about it," I say,
and suddenly I'm not so sure as I was
– memory is a funny thing isn't it?
"Please sit down and wait until morning,"
I say to him reasonably –
Don't you think that was the right thing to say?
But he turns his back and hammers on the door:
"Guard! Guard! I want a cell by myself!
You've put a crazy man in here with me!"
He is so noisy.

And I watch him pounding on the black steel door,
a patch of sweat spreading on his back,
and his bald spot glistening –
He looks at me over his shoulder,
terrified:
and I spread my hands flat to show him
I have nothing but good intentions.
"Stay away from me! Stay away!"
He backs off into a corner shaking,
while I sit down on the bunk
to wait for morning.
And I think:
this is my friend,
I know it is my friend,
and I say to him,
"Aren't you my friend?"
But there he is at the door again,
he is so noisy . . .

JOE BARR

In a grey town of seven-week days
during an eternal childhood
where I was so miserable sometimes
at being me that I roamed lonely
over the reeking town garbage dump
unable to talk to anyone
locked in my own body
captive of the motionless sun
in an eternal childhood

Old Joe went there too
happy as a young dog
pushing the garbage with his stick
grinning like a split orange
telling himself stories all day
the doors of his prison opening

into rooms he couldn't remember
places he couldn't stay
the river providing a green sidewalk
that bore his mind's feet lightly
his days like scraps of colour
and the night birds always teaching
him songs that because of his stutter
he never learned to sing

I could have learned from Joe myself
but I never did
not even when gangs of children
followed him down the street
chanting "aw-aw-aw" in mockery
children have for idiots
In a town that looked like a hole
torn in blue clouds
where I made-believe myself
into a moonlit grasshopper
and leaped the shadowed boundaries
that bore my mind's feet lightly
forty years ago
In the grey town of memory
the garbage dump is a prison
where people stand like stones
the birds are stuffed and mounted
a motionless sun still hangs there
where Joe is a scrap of crimson
when the sun at last goes down

THE SEVENTIES

POEM

You are ill and so I lead you away
and put you to bed in the dark room
– you lie breathing softly and I hold your hand
feeling the fingertips relax as sleep comes

You will not sleep more than a few hours
and the illness is less serious than my anger or cruelty
and the dark bedroom is like a foretaste of other darknesses
to come later which all of us must endure alone
but here I am permitted to be with you

After a while in sleep your fingers clutch tightly
and I know that whatever may be happening
the fear coiled in dreams or the bright trespass of pain
there is nothing at all I can do except hold your hand
and not go away

MARRIED MAN'S SONG

When he makes love to the young girl
what does the middle-aged long-married
man say to himself and the girl?
– that lovers live and desk clerks perish?

When neons flash the girl into light and shadow
the room vanishes and all those others
guests who checked out long ago
are smiling
and only the darkness of her may be touched
only the whiteness looked at
she stands above him as a stone goddess
weeping tears and honey
she is half his age and far older
and how can a man tell his wife this?

Later they'll meet in all politeness
not quite strangers but never friends
and hands touched elsewhere may shake together
with brush of fingers and casual eyes
and the cleanser cleans to magic whiteness
and love survives in the worst cologne
(but not girls' bodies that turn black leather)
for all believe in the admen's lies

In rare cases among the legions of married men
such moments of shining have never happened
and whether to praise such men for their steadfast virtue
or condemn them as fools for living without magic
answer can hardly be given

There are rooms for rent in the outer planets
and neons blaze in Floral Sask
we live with death but it's life we die with
in the blossoming earth where springs the rose
In house and highway in town and country
what's given is paid for blood gifts are sold
the stars' white fingers unscrew the light bulbs
the bill is due and the desk clerk wakes
outside our door the steps are quiet
light comes and goes from a ghostly sun
where only the darkness may be remembered
and the rest is gone

IDIOT'S SONG

Give me peace from you
allow me to go on
and be what I was before you
if there was ever that time

But talk to me talk to me
or die soon before I do

I'll come where your body is
tho it answers nothing

But don't die
stay with me in the same world
or I'm lost and desolate
for here the light and dark
that touches you touches me
that you are here at all
delays my own death
an instant longer

JOINT ACCOUNT

The myth includes Canada,
inside the brain's small country:
my backyard is the Rocky Mountain trench
– wading all summer in glacier meltwater,
hunters with flint axes stumble south –
I take deed and title to ancient badlands
of Alberta around Red Deer:
and dinosaurs peer into Calgary office buildings –
Dead Beothucks of Newfoundland track down my blood;
Dorsets on the whale-coloured Beaufort Sea
carve my brain into small ivory fossils
that show what it was like to be alive
before the skin tents blew down –

The slope of mountain breast and the wind's words,
the moon's white breathing – these are hers:
her eyes' black flashing are the continent's anger
– my letters fall to silence at her land's white foot,
and waves have washed away her answer –
In the long body of the land I saw your own,
the mountain peaks,
the night of stars,
the words I did not speak,

and you did not,
that yet were spoken –

But reality is an overdrawn bank account,
my myths and cheques both bounce,
the creditors close in;
and all the dead men,
chanting hymns,
tunnel towards me underground.

AT THE ATHENIAN MARKET

You can see Sparta on bright days
the air so clear they say
you can see old cities
in the billowy upper air
spinning like coins
before the rains turned them
sideways into dust

In the clear air Argos
old cities beyond the islands
and you may see so far
it is lonely there
in the massed light ahead
that holds the world
in its bubble

At the marketplace
an old woman selling
bright oranges
and washing them each is
involved with converging lines
of light Phidias the sculptor
laboured over half an hour
ago coming together
on copper and bronze

ornaments from ancient cities
glinting on throats
of living girls
once become mineral stains
in tombs the blood of oranges
and earth shines with many colours
fading gently
on soft breasts

Rain loves them
they are loved by the sea
also as they slowly turn
in the sun turn slowly
those long ago girls
and yet so close to here
the currents of air are
disturbed like a drapery
in the room where we were born
before these Greek cities
before the sea was named
before us all

Greece

REMEMBERING HIROSHIMA

In the darkness is no certitude
that morning will ever come
in dawn spreading pink from the east
is no guarantee that light will follow
nor that human justice is more than a name
or the guilty will ever acknowledge guilt
All these opinions arrived at in years past
by men whose wisdom consisted of saying things
they knew might be admired but not practised
arrived at by others whose wisdom was silence
And yet I expect the morning

always I expect the sunlight
and search for justice in my own mind
abstracted from mercy and kindness and truth
but also involved in the human situation
and search for it in myself
with a kind of unbearable priggishness
I detest in other people
and yet the I/we of ourselves must judge
must say here is the road
if it turns out wrong take another
must say these are the murderers
identify them and name their names
must say these are the men of worth
and publish belief like personal fact
must say all this in the absence of any god
having taken a gleam inside the mind
having grown an opinion like rings on a tree
having praised quietly the non-god of justice
having known inside the non-god of love
and make a new god from all these human things
Self-righteous and priggish of course
because whatever is most important
sad and noble or obscene and terrible
ends in the mouth of clowns
But it's all any man can offer the world
a part of himself not even original
the strength he uses to say it
the time spent writing it down
the will and the force of solemnity
are his life tho his life ends tomorrow
and it will and he's wrong

Ameliasburg

ON THE BEARPAW SEA

1

A sea splitting the continent eighty
million years ago from the Gulf
of Mexico to the modern Arctic
and five hundred miles wide
– this being in late afternoon
of the day of the great dinosaurs

At the edge of the Bearpaw Sea
in swamps and steamy marshes
uncounted thousands of them
both flesh-eaters and vegetarians
one preying on the other
– monsters covered with scaly armour
small reptiles resembling ostriches
"Triceratops" like mobile homes
all vegetarians
the world their tossed salad

By contrast consider the carnivores
and their principal sub-species of horror
"Gorgosaurus" some thirty feet long
without enemies
but certainly no friends
legs like oversized fence posts
and enough teeth to masticate
an office building glass and all
Then one particular vegetarian
duckbill dinosaur
                        and let's
call him "Albert" for the
sake of reference without
any comic intention

Witness Albert
eighty million years ago

twenty-five feet long with a bun
of flesh like a prehistoric hair-do
perched atop his head and face
a creature no human has ever seen alive
– But there's Albert
VERITABLY ALIVE
calmly chewing luscious green salad
on the west shore of the Bearpaw Sea
which later became Alberta
– his body nearly immersed in water
nightmare head
stoking the great furnace of his belly
using only a few hundred molars
of his estimated eighteen hundred teeth

Albert probably had a personality
as most animals have – even humans
let's say gentle and perhaps patient
possessing some kind of love life
his table manners terrible
but likely he was more or less contented
under blue sky and bright yellow sun

This one particular day
the sun a flaming fireball
Albert chewing tender marine plants
at the sea's edge
his tiny brain half asleep
a truly cow-like dinosaur
unsuspecting if not quite trusting
the treacherous world's appearance
he plods slowly in shallow water
near the dangerous shore reaching
for prehistoric salad

On this memorable day becoming nervous
unaccountably so
sensing in the peculiar silence
something not quite right:

therefore Albert decides to exit
and make for safety in deep water
but too late
there's Gorgosaurus
red jaws gaping
and grabs Albert by the tail
(of course nobody is crazy
enough to attack a dinosaur
except another dinosaur)
teeth grinding that tail to hamburger

And I guess all this does seem comic
makes Albert a Disneyland character
back in the Cretaceous period
before a sense of humour even existed
However
the sober fossil record shows
that Albert's tail bones were broken
vertebrae crushed
and of course the blood and bellowing
attracted other carnivores before Albert
escaped with only the dignity
pain allowed him to keep
leaving a mouthful of himself
with Gorgosaurus romping and
slavering on the prehistoric shoreline

In the future/past Albert grew cautious
stayed well clear of anything
that moved with his good disposition ruined
broken tail aching continually
unable to swim quickly any longer
his diet become the tough sea weeds
growing far out in deeper water
As a result of which
Albert's digestion gave him trouble
during the long prehistoric weeks
before his tail healed
as it did heal tho misshapen and awkward

– and sometimes he made a mooing
unhappy sound to himself
that no one else heard

A long time later when Albert died
the primary reason was his shattered tail
– then moon-tides swept his rotting body
back to stinking marshes
by the stagnant watery shore
where flesh-eaters tore it apart
raising their great devil heads
in the calm star-filled evening
like holes poked in reality

Tiny mammals stayed in caves
or trees or whatever they were
as Gorgosaurus feasted and hungered
feasted again and hungered again
and earth a slow brown-green blanket
formed itself around Albert's skeleton
near the end of the Age of Dinosaurs
while the world plunged through space
as if it had somewhere else to go

2

Inside a glass case in "Dinosaur Valley"
a few miles from Brooks, Alberta
the bones of a duckbill dinosaur with broken tail:
that's Albert in 1971 AD

Curious sightseers surrounding the display-case
staring intently at Albert
in a landscape of buttes and hoodoos
a scene torn direct from creation
brown clay and eroded sandstone
grey "bentonite" ash from volcanoes
whose fires spewed over the Bearpaw Sea
before the earth's crust folded west of here

giving birth to the Rocky Mountains
the ash making a watertight seal for bones
– being alive in such a landscape
is like staring directly at a grey weathered skull

I am of course inside that glass case
irritated at the stupid expressions
then switch to the outside again
rubbing shoulders with farmers and housewives
feeling as if part of the earth had died
here and only the forlorn sagebrush
makes a mourning sound in the wind
– and I feel like a cosmic triviality
which is exactly what I am

In geologic terms it was eighty million
years ago before the Oldman and Belly
Rivers swung green loops thru wheatfields
among steamy swamps and ghost moss hanging
these great beasts fought and made love
their stockpiled semen in a few square miles
of dead earth here enough to depopulate Toronto
their momentary plug-ugly love-making
raising whole plateaus of sub-soil
post-coital threshings almost deciding
one-celled creatures not to divide
but stay virtuously single and celebrate
celibate freedom from in-laws
another million years or so
then reassess the situation
perhaps take a poll
of echinoderms brachiopods and trilobites

The sky so blue things must have trembled
and sunsets burned at the world-edge
– tiny three-toed horses without riders
and stone listened to stone
wondering whether to take a chance
or else remain stone forever

birds like red bonfires plunge thru trees
flying reptiles flap leathery wings
attack water reflections of themselves
which are not less unreal than they are

It is silent by the Bearpaw Sea
one listens in the mind's projection
in the brain's pre-programmed bone caves
and zip backward from womb to womb
and mouth to mouth with pelvic passwords
body cramped on the long laborious
road back half-terrified the smiling
kid brother you once knew ten centuries
back might be a monster and hence
LISTENING
how a scream rivets pain to sound
from something long dead that is again dying
– but not a tragedy
for tragedy is a human concept

The age of the great dinosaurs
lasted near two hundred million years
enough to drown all our human empires
in a pile of soggy kleenex
on the spiral nebula Augustus B

These boxcar heaps of flesh outside our era
beyond what I am able to understand
as a dog may seem to partly understand
something from the way its tail wags
In the same way if there was a God or gods
I would be unable to understand them as well
and being an earthman how may I understand the earth?
Which is to say
dinosaurs are "other" and alien to me
I suppose they might have felt deprivation
but not loss as such
absence but not grief
(altho how can I even be sure of that?)

suitable as the earth's ghost animals
and the strange fossils of ghosts

Even in their eating and mating and dying
all common points of contact – dinosaurs
do not resemble aunts or pets or teddy bears
are electrodes in the mind
and only as they once moved and we still
move thru waking depths of sleep
from birth to death is it possible
to consider them as part of nature

Now gawking among the gawking
sightseers inside and outside the glass
case a soldier's wife and one fat farmer
asking inane questions not inane to them
and the park warden proud of his coiled knowledge
my own wonderment as intense as theirs
I think of this death-like soil
where chemicals and amino acids
combined coalesced altered sprang to life
the same formulae implicit still
never written down but never forgotten
quickening warm blood and slowing cold
that leaped from slimy swamps
blossoming
at the sea's edge this strange thing
life I can only speculate about

I stand outside this glass case a caul
for the twenty-five foot duck-bill
dinosaur whom I've named Albert
thus opening him to human feelings
who have so little for their own kind
– his tail chewed by another unnamed reptile
but healed in the Mesozoic swamps
until he died later for unknown reasons
and his rotting body became garbage
decayed meat for carrion-eaters

entombed here for his deathtime
ending in a glass case tho not quite ending
the fossil pattern remains:
bones replaced by earth minerals
his component parts disassembled
gone crying into the earth in search of themselves
and in some strange way indestructible
in the sense that something that once existed
has its being still undeniably and forever

And the swaying ship the world is
sets course with her second-class murderous
passengers into that precarious
future I can neither see nor understand
But for the moment here is Albert
and here am I at the identical moment
which I think might indicate management
of the universe if I thought at all
the puzzle pieces of things were deliberate

And seeing the light in my own head as important
from some unknown viewpoint
but obviously brief
seeing various other things human
things fixed fast here slowly
embedded in lifetime and deathtime like "love"
also important taken in its wider meaning meaning
even a disappearing fossil like Albert
has a human handle attached
in a backward extension of our dual gender:
inane farmer – poet – and soldier's wife outside
the glass case in "Dinosaur Valley" inside
the "Oldman and Belly Rivers formation"
sun disappearing moon rising
the earth a dustmote before my dustmote eyes
and yet this place in the reeling universe
so fixed and certain I would know
it instantly returning here
after a thousand years

And what may have seemed comic
about the great patient reptile
with wounded tail who once lived and moved
in the exact space I move in now
(every step invades his ghostly bivouac)
has lost any possible humour for me
even a beast's pain scarcely less real
than the strange grief of being alive

In my mind the healed wound
becomes a kind of bridge
the scar tissue extending
across aeons of time
and I a mammal witness
a bright thread connecting my brain
to savage brains in the Bearpaw Sea
– a bridge without an ending

TOURIST ITINERARY

North of Kirkland Lake raspberries are red earrings
in heat like a tropic summer
but even in August nights are cold
trees shrink a little past the height of land
that slopes down the arctic watershed
Driving north
a bear crosses the road
at his private pedestrian crossing
the first animal we've seen
and almost ask for his autograph
Then Cochrane and the train to Moosonee
over the soft spongy trappers' country
crossing and re-crossing the Abitibi
until it joins the big Moose
our elderly train jogging the river valley
past rocks like the heads of queens
Indians with closed faces at Moose Factory

huge wood piles and shabby houses
selling bannock and toy boats for a living
knowing it isn't a very good one
knowing it's the best there is
I add another piece of mosaic
to the coloured memory inside
I know what the place looks like
tasted the food and touched the land
which is as much as any of us can do
following a road map in the mind
a memory of the place we came from
and the way we are always returning

MELODRAMA

Sometimes a reasonless panic
that I am trapped in Africa
the aeroplanes I travel in all crash
my body breaks down
the globe stops turning
leaves me here
stranded
halfway round the world
in a country so racist cold
palm trees drip icicles
I'm being too clever about it of course
but this place chills the blood
my senses taste the deep sickness
arrived here from the cave
a time before humans
I have naturally convinced myself
that something is about to happen
and will I interpret anything that does
as expected and normal
murmur aha to myself
or just go somewhere and get drunk?
The country scares hell outa me

remembering my own bad times
when I drank my own poison
and chewed my own heart
and stopped
for reasons I can't explain
except that I'm me and no one else
Here in Johannesburg
I listen to screams on night streets
crashing glass and hopeless anger
– sixteen murders
in Soweto the black suburb
over this last weekend
And yet it isn't violence
that's so frightening
but when daylight comes the perfectly calm
expressions of both blacks and whites
will resume
each so aware of the other
that to lose death would be a deprivation
and to lose hatred produce a blank place
in the mind like bone cancer removed
and nothing left there but nothing
Whatever the definition of obscenity
and cartography of guilt
I've always wanted to avoid making
because knowing is sharing it
these things emerge in the spirit
on the streets of Johannesburg an evil
I've stretched out my hand towards
and entered with my body

FLYING OVER AFRICA

It's kinda picturesque

Africa of the rain forests the storybook country
of Rider Haggard and Joseph Conrad

and breast-beating gorillas ignorant of English
lions like yellow Cadillacs
racing after springbok in the hot grasslands
where heat waves stitch chevrons of shadows
King Solomon's Mines and Kilimanjaro
Great Zimbabwe and the Congo's dark river soul
Tarzan and the jewels of Opar
"Fingerprints prove you Greystoke"
says Edgar Rice Burroughs under the bedclothes
with me but the flashlight goes dead
and the child is left alone with a stewardess
with nice legs saying "Please fasten your seat belt sir"
and my ears pop from being born

The Transvaal, on the high veld

150 years ago the Voortrekkers
headed north from Cape Colony
in search of new free land
and Bantu emigrating south for new land
were about to meet at Blood River
intruders and newcomers both
considered unwelcome by resident animals
– did the grass quiver expecting footsteps
the sun halt on its graven track
and some old prophet
nobody paid any attention to
froth at the mouth predicting
Lux toilet soap and Ford motor cars
ascend the mountains escalated in fire
and shriek the world was coming to an end
of its five billion year guarantee?
And sunset flickered over hacked bodies
bathed in a welter of blood
after the black and white battle
and clouds were windjammers of gold
– if somebody looked at clouds just before
dying and made the necessary image-connection
do golden ships then still sail the seas

of earth in the foundering world
of a dead man's brain pan?

      Trying to get used to it

On Johannesburg streets the sun batters
punch-drunk strangers in all directions
with bright clubs
but after two weeks of grim depression
I feel more or less physically content
despite Europeans Only signs on the urinals
separate store entrances for blacks
in this country so like the American South
intensified and gone sour with white fear
so strong you can smell it
oozing from bed sheets and clean shirts
ex-Europeans trapped with blacks
in a double dance of terror
But at least my depression stops
slums and hunger and injustice empty
out of me propelled by the sun
– and yet despite physical well-being
in this city of slavery and murder,
my face is stiffened by two weeks of heat
I can't smile
or perhaps only imagine that
At the hotel another meeting of black and white
the Bantu houseboy Solomon
and I drink brandy in my room
and talk about nothing exactly
– but there is some relief from talking
some feeling of striking a small flaw
into the monolithic apartheid maze
of laws and making them less efficient
weakening the superstructure
by omitting a comma
adding an insubordinate clause
from just one drink with Solomon –
he sitting on the bed alert and waiting

for his master's voice to come storming up
the stairwell and elevator shaft
me thinking Solomon was not so wise
to be born black in this country
and the brandy-thought makes me smile
– his black face with sunny highlights
both blacker and whiter than mine
doubly brightens and doubly darkens
his voice a musical colour
I mean so rounded and labial and curving
it wraps around furniture
for instance and sings on flat surfaces
I imagine on the yellow Kalahari
Desert it would slumber
across the sand to water
like a stringed wind instrument
join the whisper of deep springs
bubbling up from the sand – and I laugh
at my brandy-fancy and we are comfortable
together or so I wistfully imagine
while the great monolithic
many tentacled tongues of the law
beyond my window jabber in legalese
traffic mutters and the day darkens

THE JACKHAMMER SYNDROME

Once I wanted things so badly
they tended to heat up while I looked at them
glowing cherry red and disappeared
thus it was common on the streets
of my hometown twenty
years ago to hear young ladies utter
cries of dismay as their coiffures started
smoking and they vanished like rainbows
while I stared fixed and lasciviously
They say if you wish hard enough long

enough you'll get what you wish for
I maintain the opposite or nearly
one alternates wanting and not-wanting
at unpredictable intervals which
might be called the jackhammer syndrome
For example
I play pool with my brother-in-law
and nearly always lose at first
until finally I don't give a damn
then start to win
The balls jostle in genetic pairs
drop dead
true in side pockets and caroms click
like new false teeth in orbit with a steak
I play like a blind mathematician
give the ball underspin curves
straight from my draughtsman brain
and realize I'm winning by god winning
fifty mounted horsemen in the red desert
draw swords and swear fealty
my spaceship darts with unerring skill
among excreta of constipated planets
which turn out to be radium in fact
I can do anything
and encounter myself in the past thinking
of hide-and-seek and run-sheep-run
in my old hometown
where the kid was pretty funny
He will not know me now no
one does there
among those dream-circumstances
but patches of emotion hover still
on the streets where I lost all my battles
But I retain the memory of winning
close to my vest as a belly button
which is one advantage of total recall
and totally recall swimming
across a river meeting a girl halfway
along the wet footpath and going

on together to the other
side for an hour doing
nothing dizzily balanced
on the moment managing
to outwit myself carefully
not looking at her .
There are moments of such elation
in a man's life it's like being struck
alive on the street by the first
god one meets at an intersection
whom one must believe in a second
time after twenty years of atheism
You press the stomach of your business
suit flat and stride on into the sunset
pretending to be serious

DEPRESSION IN NAMU, BC

The eagle's passage sings there
crossing the sky on a high wire
salmon leap to find their other selves
black bear amble to breakfast at the river
the sun floats thru a blue notch in the hills

There was never a time
I did not know about such a place
to match the imagined place in my mind
– but I have lived too long somewhere else
and beauty bores me without the slight ache
of ugliness that makes me want to change things
knowing it's impossible

ARCTIC ROMANCE

Seldom thought of except when newspaper articles
tingle the blood with excess of chauvinism
or "Flyer Survives 9 Days in the Arctic"
and "Geologist Discovers Iron on Baffin"
There like an unused part of the brain
outside the campfire of consciousness
great beasts roam in the moonlight
bears dance all summer on the ice floes
some mystery of ourselves in the huge land masses
And the caribou always the caribou
their shaggy armies seen from aeroplanes
a native population like the Eskimo
cause for pride of a self-deprecating nature
Pride also that the national boundaries
loop far enough north for confirmed TV-watchers
to consider themselves basically outdoorsmen
hardy explorers condemned to be wage-earners
armchair adventurers thru no fault of their own
There is perhaps some wistfulness included
in all this also enough truth in the myth-making
to furnish subject-matter for non-lyric poets
as unwritten choreography of a nation
with no inclination to dance outside a campfire
circle which now very late on a dark night suddenly
must learn to

EASTBOUND FROM VANCOUVER

I certainly am a jet age
man technology's end
product courtesy Air Canada
and the US board of directors
Our DC-8 paws the ground
trembling hard then
a thousand jet white horses

break loose from the corral
another thousand broncs
pour in from open range
and we stampede down the black runway
leap at the sky
in an exaltation of worms
(flying makes me chortle
to be human almost
I can forgive myself for being
born naked without money)
But I'm really a flying chicken
figure I'll get it sure
this time and bound to die
in five minutes enjoy
every last second of the countdown
that leads to a fowl death
Then above the clouds by god
my wonder evaporates
for another big jet pops
out of the east west
bound and we pass each
other at a combined speed
of 1,500 m.p.h. say
And clear as your father's
and appalled mother's face
at first sight of the new
baby I see the horse
and buggy we become pass by
on the mind's radar
screen
       clop
          clop
             clopping
thru the backwoods clouds
Something about the human brain
I don't understand suddenly
I am a stone age man
sitting glumly on a boulder
which is pure gold like as not

having conceived half
a wheel can't complete
the rest of the circle
and a block I can't tackle
pulls down the stars

A GRACEFUL LITTLE VERSE

I'd run into you sometimes
perhaps talking with other people
and your voice would change
when you spoke
– among nervous smiles
sensible enthusiasms
in unremarkable kitchens
you
Elsewhere
in treetops the wind whirs up there
pools of silence cling to old buildings
over the blue soil of water
waves walk like whispering armies
a distant sound that might be joy
could be sorrow next door
There are times I listen
to electric motors
starting up beyond the darkness
or furniture without special significance
creaking like bones in the bodies of strangers
silent deployment of grammar and syntax in the poem
your breath makes trembling under a blouse
reverse braille of your steps in the grass
disappearing in the untranslatable universe

DEAD MARCH FOR SERGEANT MacLEOD

*(Seventy years old, wounded and returning to England from
Quebec with the corpse of General Wolfe in 1759)*

The sea outside is the river
St. Lawrence and the boxed corpse
once General Wolfe and the wide mouth
of the gulf is a womb of death and the lap
lap lap of water is memory memory
of drums and guns the smoking guns
outside Quebec the dead are shovelled
and buried each with a lithograph
in his head and heart and brain
of the last thought the last glass
of wine the last woman the last
small lead ball growing and growing
and becoming smaller being nothing
And what about you General   sir
in a coffin in the hold of the *Royal
William* draped in a flag does Gray's
"Elegy" still seem very important now
to you in your pine box at any rate
what about God whose existence is not
beyond doubt puttering around
in a workshop jammed with hypotheses
you with your weak body and chinless
face fixed fast with its last commands
like stones shied back from nowhere?
And you Sergeant MacLeod
are there wars ready
and waiting for you to arrive adrenalin
stored in your head musket balls
firing indiscriminate pop pop pop?
Old killer on the battlefields of Europe
old amputator of arms and legs and daylight
staring at Wolfe's corpse admiringly
what do you say Sergeant
any advice for new recruits now
and how do you speak to Generals even

if they're dead and don't hear a word
only the waves outside going lap lap lap
idiot music idiot questions idiot God?
— rockabye Skye baby rockabye home
inside the wooden walls of the womb of things
where we have been where we are going
when we are not —

WARTIME AIR BASE

At 6:30 a.m. the siren screams
penetrating hospital and barracks
naked women like white dolls
fall out of dreams from windows
men drown into daylight
the guard changes at 8 o'clock
No crashes now for two weeks
and the dead men are not dead
Five miles up in overcast
the base is hardly visible
things wait between before and after
armies march and counter-march
but are seen to be standing still
in an old photograph
On the planet's surface blue uniforms
cross in front of the camera
then disappear forever
Airmen in coveralls flip an up-yours
salute at the C.O.'s car passing
Harvard trainers galumph the clouds
Fairey Battles whistle on the runway
cheerful as steam kettles
Hurricanes blast towed targets
they turn to confetti
Ten miles up you can't see the base
but there's nobody there to not-see
Nineteen days without a crash

the dying men are still alive
The chaplain talks about sin on Sunday
what he really talks about is life
Women in uniforms are not de-sexed
but camp followers who caught up
Berlin   London   Dresden and those places
are only dream towns
The parade ground bakes in noon sun
control tower voices stop
everybody half asleep
nobody a.w.o.l.
the dead men move slowly
toward what they think is choice
it is one of those moments
when a towel in somebody's bathroom
might fall unnoticed
or a leaf drift down
lacking any reason to stay on the tree
Ten miles up there is nothing
unless you can imagine a face
that pays no attention to you
it looks the other way

PICTURE LAYOUT IN *LIFE* MAGAZINE
(May 8, 1970)

The Cambodian war in six pages:
the latest foreign war for US consumption
temple bells silent in Angkor Wat:
and thrown into the Mekong River
clothes ripped and torn
bodies of three dead Vietnamese

On the home front:
pretty cutout dresses in the next four pages
of the US President's three little Nixon women
smiling about their new wardrobe

paper dolls for nice American children
to clip with blunt scissors
and paste over the bodies of the dead Vietnamese

THE HORSEMAN OF AGAWA

(Indian rock-painting under the cliffs of Lake Superior)

It's spring and the steel platforms tourists usually stand on
are not installed yet so we take our chances
but I have to abandon my beer and use both hands for safety
We clamber down rocks unsteady as children
reach slanting stone ledges under the hundred-foot walls
my wife skipping ahead so nimbly I'm jealous of her
and say "Wait for me, dammit" but she won't
then take my shoes off and go barefoot

She sees the painting first and calls "Here!"
her face flattens and dissolves into no expression
I balance myself beside her on the tilted ledge
that slides off into deep water and the rock hurts my feet
but I feel the same way she does as the rock horseman canters
by two feet from my nose forever or nearly
The painted horseman rides over four moons (or suns) on his trail
whose meaning must be a four-day journey somewhere
the red iron oxide faded from Lake Superior storms
and maybe two hundred years since the Ojibway artist
          stood there
balanced above water like us
and drew with his fingers on the stone canvas
with fish eggs or bear grease to make the painting permanent
pitting fish eggs and bear grease against eternity
which is kind of ludicrous or kind of beautiful I guess

I have too many thoughts about the horseman
I might select one and say this is a signpost this painting
(in fact I've just done that)
a human-as-having-babies signpost

but also dammit part of the spirit
a thought taken out from inside the head and carefully left here
like saying I love you to stone
I think that after the Ojibway are all dead
and all the bombs in the white world have fizzed into harmlessness
the ghost of one inept hunter who always got lost
and separated from his friends because he had a lousy sense
          of direction
that man can come here to get his bearings calling out
to his horse his dog or himself because he's alone
in the fog in the night in the rain in his mind and say
"My friends where are you?"
and the rock walls will seize his voice
and break it into a million amplified pieces of echoes
that will find the ghosts of his friends in the tombs of their dust

But I mistrust the mind-quality that tempts me
to embroider and exaggerate things
                              I just watch my wife's face
she is quiet as she generally is because I do most of the talking
it is forty years old and has felt the pain of children
the pettiness of day-to-day living and getting thousands of meals
but standing on the rock face of Lake Superior
it is not lessened in any way
with a stillness of depth that reaches where I can't follow
all other thoughts laid aside in her brain
on her face I see the Ojibway horseman painting the rock with
          red fingers
and he speaks to her as I could not
in pictures without handles of words
into feeling into being here by direct transmission
from the stranded Ojibway horseman
And I change it all back into words again for that's the best I can do
but they only point the way we came from for who knows where
          we are
under the tall stone cliffs with water dripping down on us
or returned from a long journey and calling out to our friends

But the rock blazes into light when we leave the place

or else the sun shines somewhere else and I didn't notice it
and my secret knowing is knowing what she knows
and can't say and I can only indicate
reclaim my half-empty beer and drink it and tie my shoes
follow her up the tangled rocks past the warning sign for strangers
and wait till she turns around

TEMPORIZING IN THE ETERNAL CITY

Beatrice if I forget you
at the Borghese Palace let my heart
forget its transplant
from Canada but remember the stone dress
you wore and the sandal
that may have been unfastened
for hundreds of years
the sense of bones inside marble
a woman content to be there
and I more transient than she is
great beauty like great ugliness
survives the unremarkable

But it kept irritating me to do the same things
all the other tourists were doing
altho when I used the *pissoir*
it was a relief
At the Trevi Fountain I'm still fascinated
by magnified underwater measurements of women
and more than those
by all that's been written about the fountain
I want to mingle my own comments
with those of snotty 18th century Englishmen
on the Grand Tour
and fuck-up their memoirs
but can't think of anything
only a waterfall lost in the Canadian bush
which has had nothing written about it

except when autumn leaves drifting on the foam
are crimson letters

Strange to feel the difference
between Greeks and Italians
Athenians and Romans
Romans seem on their way somewhere all the time
Greeks have just returned
maybe the difference in quality of flotsam and jetsam
Scipio Africanus and Pericles
and I'm quite sure that one of these days
among such marvellous copies of Zeus and Jupiter
they're gonna excavate a primitive cash register

The women of course were women
I haven't yet seen any that weren't
which doesn't mean lack of appreciation
merely that when you take the gilding off a lily
all you really have is some gilding

I find an unopened copy of my own book
at a place near the Spanish Steps
and have this amazed feeling of not being unique here
Rather pettishly
I bought the only copy of myself in all Rome
thus denying Canadian culture to the Romans
an act they'd appreciate if they knew better

The saddest thing of all tho
was this US outfit trying to sell me
a Florida lot – a Florida lot in Rome! –
feeding me a good dinner first
and after the sales pitch I still said no
It saddened me to disappoint the super-hucksters
but at least they were disappointed at the Hilton

At the Borghese Palace:
I am an intruder here
on someone else's grief

who let himself in when no one was looking
And think of Beatrice
– how the air prints her name
as if the room contained a magnetic field
but even in ignorance of her name
there would still be something crouching here
joining the cadences of eternity

All around the bustle and clatter of new Rome
a tremendous weight of triviality
the solemnity of living and dying
hustlers and princesses   caesars and panhandlers
what's important lost but still slightly apparent
the past turned inside out
protrudes slightly into the present
and disappears before you can touch it
Which I suppose is why I reach out my hand toward Beatrice
And this marble mnemonic of someone who must have thought her
            important
for reasons the folded stone cannot explain
as if I had loved her painfully as well
she or some other

Italy

HANDS

At Acayucan we stopped
to water and feed
the engine's horses
            then walked the streets drowned
in sun
At the Super Mercado we said "Leche?"
meaning milk but there was no milk
except what the Indian women
in the marketplace supplied for babies
from their own bodies   unpasteurized

Little lizards darted up a ceiba tree
small hands and fingers like darning needles
attached to their one-tree forest
And I thought we should go back to the car
for heat made me *dizzy*
      so my wife took my hand walking
On the way back we passed the police station
and attached prison
      from each barred window a man
reached out imploring us for money
faces streaked with sweat and eyes coals
the hands reaching out and following us
thru dusty alleys of thatched huts and dogshit
and out to the high hill roads
over the narrow-waisted isthmus of Mexico
a woman made of red earth and flowers
a dream out of mind from the spoiled towns
and vultures patrolling the wind's four quarters
the hands followed us
down the long road to Coatzacoalcos

Mexico

IN THE CAVES

The grey hairy mountain shrieked
and gouts of blood splashed over our bodies
the way the sun looks when it is angry
I remember
that and the spear I never found
and search for in blood-wet grass
By then the bloody mountain was opened up
an old woman plunged inside with a knife
and dragged out the huge quivering heart
licking the blood around her lips
The people danced and chanted their song
to the mountain spirit that it might forgive them

then we tore even the bones apart for marrow
and there was nothing
Except when the spears struck
I felt the spears
and my own had missed its mark
I felt the red string of a shriek
leave my body and rise into the sky
The old men had never told me of this
but I think it is magic
how the spears strike inside me
again and again
I am no longer hungry
and have gone a little apart
to think about these things

It is useless
and the old men lose patience with me
I never learned to be a hunter
even the stones I throw at rabbits miss
bow strings scrape my fingers raw
and once the spear hurled at a mule deer
glanced off an old woman's shins
when she appeared unexpectedly
All that summer she cursed me
squatting at the cooking fire
I waited between shadows and light
not daring to come closer or go farther away
and the hunters roared with laughter
After the mountain shrieked
I forgot those things
and searching for my lost spear
there was something else
I have not found
not in a short career of making lopsided arrowheads
or scrapers that won't scrape
or chewing skins with the old women
choking over bad-tasting fur
I have not found the good feeling
that comes from doing anything well

for always I remember the shriek
Of course the rabbit dying makes his own sound
bright fish darken to death on the stones
the bear bites off spears and roars
running deer with an arrow in their sides
tumble down and cry
as a child does in sleep
But not as the mammoth shrieked
and stopped what it was doing and waited
for a message to return from the place it went
and waiting fell and falling became
an empty place in the grasslands

I have stopped being a boy
hair grows on my face but not quite man-hair
a fuzz yellow as willows in spring
the young women turn their heads
when I pass by and whisper together
a mixture of pity and scorn
for I am a poor hunter
in fact I am not a hunter at all
and not a very good craftsman either
and remain alive on sufferance
and dig in the ground for roots
and snatch scraps of meat from the fire
Sometimes in the emptiness around me
I have traced with a stick
in soft earth the shriek
beginning with the grey mountain body
tusks lifting to girdle the sky
eyes small red drops of blood
and to show those eyes in the dirt
I used blood from my wrist
Children came to laugh
but sometimes not to laugh
– one long-legged grey-eyed boy
watching the mammoth in the earth
watching the mammoth watching me
suddenly embarrassed for not laughing

and running into the woods
staying there a long time

In my head still I hear the mammoth shriek
that is perhaps my own sickness
but the Old Man cannot make it stop
with rattles and bone charms
to drive out the sickness
So I have come here
to caves at the edge of the higher mountains
where my people fear to come
bringing a few scraps of food
and a gourd full of water
animal fat to feed a weak flame
and scratch with flint at the soft rock face
and the red earth itself for blood
and the stone helps with its own shape
And the strong thing out of myself
makes the mammoth into another mammoth
who trumpets silently for me
from porous stone
And I do not know why
whether because I cannot hunt with the others
and they laugh
or because the things I have done are useless
as I may be useless
but there is something here I must follow
into myself to find
outside myself in the mammoth
beyond the scorn of my people
who are still my people
my own pain and theirs
joining the shriek that does not end
that is inside me now
The shriek flows back into the mammoth
returning from sky and stars
finds the cave and its dark entrance
brushes by where I stand on tip-toes
to scratch the mountain body on stone

moves past me into the body itself
toward a meaning I do not know
and perhaps should not
At the cave-mouth some children
afraid but very curious
the grey-eyed boy with food
watching me solemnly
for I have been here all night
and it is morning again

FLAT TIRE IN THE DESERT

It is nothing serious
cars go by now and then
making small tire marks in my head
– while I fumble at the bumper jack
drag out the spare
block one wheel with a stone
another with the flat itself
feeling damned irritated
at things for not behaving themselves
which my wife finds necessary to forgive
as if I were more than 50% responsible
for both flat tire and bad temper
Well the sun burns down and I slave away
no wind or hardly any
a vulture circles overhead
appears to give me special attention
and I feel a slight additional resentment
Cactus and mountains are all around
the sky goes up millions of miles
there is nothing here
but a man and a woman with a red Ford
and things are not at all serious
But I feel inside a kind of vacuum
that must have existed before creation
and after

a stillness not of death
but without memory or anticipation
I glance at my watch
to make sure it's going
and the cars have stopped
there is nothing
Of course
all this was just briefly
the feeling that nothing at all matters
and you particularly wouldn't be missed
and my hostility
might be the difficulty of admitting it
just briefly
before I turned the ignition key
and the car hesitated like a baby
that didn't want to be born
then roared into life
with my wife conspicuously silent
as she sometimes is
I say "Well?"
feeling defensive under
the sky a malignant neutral

Mexico

THE BATTLEFIELD AT BATOCHE

Over the earthworks among slim cottonwood trees
wind whistles a wind tune
I think it has nothing to do with living or dead men
or the price of groceries
it is only wind
And walking in the wooded dish-shaped hollow
that served to protect generals and staff
officers from sniper fire
I hear a different kind of murmur
– no more than that at least not definitely

the sort of thing you do hear
every now and then in a city never
questioning because it's so ordinary
but not so ordinary here
I ask my wife "Do you hear anything?"
She smiles "Your imagination again?"
"All right then don't you wish you had one?"
"If I did I'd burn your supper . . ."
the sort of thing she says to annoy me
the unanswerable kind of remark
that needs time to think about
I take my time watching the green curve
of the South Saskatchewan River below
a man riding an inch-long machine a mile distant
that makes dark waves cutting the yellow wheat
I wonder if Gunner Phillips heard the sound
on the day of May 12 in 1885
before the bullet knocked him down
the stairs he spent twenty years climbing?
Did Letendre with his muzzle-loader
clamped under one arm stuffing gun powder
down the barrel and jamming in a bullet
stop remembering great itchy beasts
pushing against log palisades at night
and running the buffalo at Grand Coteau
the Sioux screaming insults from a safe distance
at men from the White Horse Plain?
– all this in dream pantomime
with that sound and nothing else?
And old Ouellette age 90
his hearing almost gone anyway
wiping off river mist from his rifle
listening –?
Under my feet grass makes small noises
a bright-eyed creature I can't identify
is curious about me
and chitters because it's August
In May the annoyed general eats his lunch
on the cliffs ordering "a reconnaissance in force"

which his officers misinterpret as "attack in force"
Midlanders   Winnipeg Rifles   Grenadiers
move out from their own positions
and burst into the Métis rifle pits
with Captain Howard from Connecticut
a demonstrator for the Colt Firearms Company
of Hartford demonstrating
death at 500 rounds a minute
with the borrowed Gatling gun
But it isn't the sound I hear now
not the dead shifting positions underground
to dodge bullets stopped in mid-earth
here a little way under the black soil
where wheat yellow as a girl's hair blossoms
the Métis nation was born and died
as the last buffalo stumbles to his knees
and felt cold briefly while his great wool
blanket was ripped from bloody shoulders

It is for Parenteau and Desjarlais
Ah-si-we-in of the Woods Cree
for Laframboise and old Ouellette
and dark girls left alone
that such words as mine are spoken
and perhaps also for Gunner Phillips
in his grave above the South Saskatchewan
but most for myself
And I say to my wife, "Do you hear nothing?"
"I hear the poem you're writing" she says
"I knew you were going to say that" I say

In evening listening
to the duplicate rain-sound on the roof
of our camped trailer it seems
that I was wrong about my motives
and the dark girls mourning at Batoche
the dead men in shallow rifle pits
these mean something
the rain speaks to them

the seasons pass
just outside their hearing
but what they died for has faded away
and become something quite different
past justice and injustice
beyond old Ouellette and his youngest grandson
with the larking dog chasing a rabbit
green grass growing
rain falling
on the road cars passing by
Like the child I am/was I say "Me too"
camped on the battlefield of Batoche
just slightly visible in August
me an extension of anything that ever happened
a shadow behind the future
the bullets aimed at me
by Gunner Phillips and old man Ouellette
85 years ago
whispering across the fields of eternity

THE BEAVERS OF RENFREW

By day
chain saws stencil the silence in my head
black quotes appear on the red brain
Across glacial birthmarks old Jake
Loney is cutting his winter wood,
tongue drowned in a chaw of tobacco –
The belly button pond at one
end of the farm brims
full its cockleshell three acres:
– tonight the beavers are back,
and work their swing shift
under the moon.
Sometimes at low earthen dams
where the pouring spillway empties,
they stand upright in a pride of being,

holding rainbow trout like silver thoughts,
or pale gold Indian girls
arriving here intact from bone cameras
ten thousand ancestors ago,
before letting them spin down the moonlight
rapids as mortal lures
for drowned fishermen –
Among the beaver lodges
I stand unable to sleep,
but cannot stay awake
while poplar and birch fall around me.
I am not mistaken for a tree,
but almost totally ignored,
pissed on by mistake occasionally –
Standing here long enough,
seeing the gentle bodies moving
close to what they truly are,
I wonder what screwed-up philosophy,
what claim to a god's indulgence
made men decide their own importance?
And what is great music and art
but an alibi for murderers?
Perhaps in the far-off beginnings
of things they made a pact with men,
dammed the oceans for us,
chewed a hole in the big log bridge
wedged between Kamchatka and Alaska,
tore open the Mediterranean,
parted the Red Sea for Moses,
drowned Atlantis and the myth
of original sin
in the great salt womb of the sea –
And why?
Because they pitied men.
To the wet animal shivering in a tree
they said
  "Come on down –
      It's all right."
And he shinnied down with hairless

purple behind pointed east for heat,
tail between hind legs,
humbly standing on all fours,
touching his forelock muttering,
"Yessir yessir thank'ee kindly,"
but not knowing how to speak yet of course –
Beaver looked at this dripping creature
a miserable biological dead end:
but every failure has flashes of genius
exploding out of imminent death
and the man listened
to an agreement of the water beings
and land beings together
which men have forgotten since:
the secret of staying completely still,
allowing ourselves to catch up
with the shadow just ahead of us
we have lost,
when the young world was a cloudy room
drifting thru morning stillness –
But the rest of it
I have forgotten,
and the gentle beaver will not remind us:
standing upright at their earthen dams
holding the moonlit reins of water,
at peace with themselves –

"Why not make a left turn in
time and just stay here,"
I said next day to old Jake Loney,
"instead of going on to the planets?"
The chain saw bucked in his hands,
chewing out chunks of pine that toppled
and scarred the air with green absence.
Far off a beaver tail slapped water,
a bird looked for the tree that was gone –
Old Jake's cheek bulged its chaw of tobacco –
"Well, why not?" I said argumentatively,
before he could spit,

"Why not?"
And the log bridge across the Bering
burst with a roar around
me again nothing but water,
brown water –
                    "Why not?"

WILF McKENZIE

The red combine eats yellow
wheat a grumbling metal stomach
cropping the wide Saskatchewan plain
its appetite scarcely diminished
by stones
or a rabbit's spurt of panic

The knives and forks and spoons flash
bright silver in the roiled sunshine
fascinated I hold onto the railing
while a fifty-foot local storm
rides like a noonday ghost
over the scratchy planet's surface

I shout questions at old Wilf
as we ride the businesslike monster
ask the price of wheat and other prices
being alive for instance
me an interviewer asking me questions
expecting no surprise and I'm not
until he says "I'd rather be a farmer
and dead broke than work at anything else . . ."
I don't know exactly why I'm surprised
but I am by this passionate extravagance
exploding out of a dour transplanted Scot

Then Miriam comes for the wheat
we pour it onto the truck thru a long spout
she goes and we keep circling
Wilf quotes the Bible at me
me the agnostic me literary plastic man
but I listen respectfully and I am respectful
and envious too but with no sudden
vision of the loaves and fishes
illumining blue boredom and yellow monotony
hard work a muscular dystrophy of the spirit
making questions ultimate easy answers
being interchangeable with dollars at any bank
near the suitably fertile desert
where old Wilf McKenzie and his red combine
glimpse God in the full womb of granaries
and I too near the end of my life
in momentary strength or weakness
perfectly contented in Saskatchewan

EXCESS OF HAVING

Things do not stay where they are
I found that out soberly
driving to Belleville for groceries
while long summer country unrolled
like a flashing green light
to vision's end beginning
with fields that moved I mean
moved apart from the car's perspective
and numbered green squares on county
maps dived into my eyes
Always remembering this happened
sometimes rarely I stand
waving or whispering or blossoming
Always I've known that forests moved
at night taking their animals with them
because the child wanted to believe that

and I knew rivers lifted from black beds
to wind at night over a silver country
seen only with the third eye
to strand one astonished 80
-year-old fly fisherman
in the moon mountains at dawn
on earth clutching a half-empty
bottle of hundred-proof beer
Until now I hadn't quite
realized nobody owns anything
tho crazy men have said so all along
but I didn't believe them
literally no one owns anything
and that includes themselves
After I am dead and hence
buried the world will be turned
outside in
and the grave full of women
or at least one

THE TIME OF YOUR LIFE

Childhood – when toads and frogs rain down the sky,
and night is velvety as under the skirts
of a goddess, where it's always summer –
In winter water pours from gardenhose,
and turns to ice in town backyards;
coal shovels clear a hockey rink for boys
to play war, mothers watch anxiously:
King Arthur's court, with Eaton's catalogue
for breastplate, a hockey stick for lance –

The later legend has a big-league scout
sitting in smoky small-town rinks,
watching the local flash, signing him
to a contract for those fabulous arenas
where heroes remain boyish forever

and women they sleep with are always their wives,
while money grins green and freckles fade –

Begin before the beginning:
shortly after birth, even before school,
with ice luckily thick or drowning thin:
the painted backdrop of snow and dingy houses
fades, only the shouting children are real:
and sometimes on hard-crusted winter snow
I've seen the game escape its limits,
and leap the width and breadth of things,
become a mad chase going nowhere, out
past dangerous places where the current
nibbles cheese holes – out to the wide wide bay:
where iceboats leave their tracks to race with birds,
and fishing shanties are lost castles beyond the town,
and slow clouds loom ahead like giant goalies –

Miles out in the far country
of Quinte the child stands
– senses he is being watched,
glances down at his feet,
which seem supported
by black glass above nothing,
where shadows with eyes,
green shapes whisper
"We'll eat your liver and lights"

Motionless as a waterfall,
he stands in no-time,
where sequence is tangled in creation,
before possible things converge
to be trapped in the inevitable:
the boy's deep sub-self
becomes aware of what looks
like a small hockey player
reflected on the ice watching him –
or else a boy with raw cold nose
– or else a complete stranger,

standing in the high blue barn:
and yet this four-foot two-thirds
man-size carbon of himself is not
himself no matter what it looks like –
An order from somewhere makes one arm
lift up, holding the stick high;
the pinched face smiles grimly;
the body above ice mirror is instructed
to bend down in order that the owner's
eyes may permit a glimpse of the owner
himself, clothed in flesh but aloof
from flesh, remaining hidden:
                              politely
the boy's mouth opens, his lips slowly
carefully form the words:
                         "Thank you –"
After which a whoof
of expelled breath shrieks
a sudden "YEE – OUWW" at the sky,
and black ice with a mile-wide spasm
somewhere beyond the world's edge cracks –

He skates wildly back to town
with long swooping twenty-foot strides,
batting an old tin can ahead of him:
a cold moon hangs above the town clock
tower that strikes hard iron of sky;
the blacksmith in his smoky cave
strokes a chestnut mare with one lame foot;
the elderly pumpmaker in his shop
crowded with pine scent, stops the lathe –
On either side the river lie
dark cubes of houses drowned in snow:
the boy dashes excitedly to one
of them, aching with news of an event
real or imagined, bursts the
door open, "Hey, mom (and forgets
whatever it was) – I'm hungry!"
Weather turns colder, the house

shudders and rocks, frost creeps
on blind white windows: and under
its patchwork quilt time moves
in a drift of birds a dream of horses,
and sticky buds breaking out of snow,
premeditations of flowers and lifting tides,
the sleep of men –

Even the shadow shapes inside their black
prison stay where they are, surviving the night,
and have been known occasionally to sleep –

THE PEACEABLE KINGDOM
*(In Ottawa, after the War Measures Act is invoked
against the FLQ)*

Friday, Oct. 16: Along Elgin Street
traffic crawls at four o'clock
attachés with brief cases
of importance on Wellington
expensive mistresses and wives
of diplomats walking dogs
and babies in Rockcliffe Park
two Carleton students with lettered signs
VIVE le FLQ on Parliament Hill
the Mounties don't lay a finger on them
below the Peace Tower
cabinet ministers interviewed on TV
inside the House
orators drone and wrangle as usual
in a way almost reassuring
In Quebec the Fifth Combat Group
from Valcartier occupies Montreal
paratroopers fly in from Edmonton
infantry from the Maritimes
And the PM's comment
on bleeding hearts who dislike guns

"All I can say is go on and bleed
it's more important to keep law and order . . ."
All this
in the Peaceable Kingdom

Saturday, Oct. 17: No change
the two kidnapped men are still missing
In the House of Commons politicians
turn into statesmen very occasionally
Reilly on CTV news demands Trudeau resign
Eugene Forsey does not agree
Yesterday driving to Ottawa
with my wife
citizens of no Utopia
red autumn leaves on Highway #7
– thinking of the change come over us
and by us I mean the country
our character and conception of ourselves
thinking of beer-drinkers in taverns
with loud ineffectual voices disagreeing
over how to escape their own limitations
men who have lost their way in cities
onetime animals trapped inside tall buildings
farmers stopped still in a plowed furrow
that doesn't match the other straight lines
as a man's life turns right or left from the norm
No change in the news
NDP and PC members condemn the government
Creditiste Réal Caouette does not
Diefenbaker thunders at the PM
a prophet grown old
Police raids continue in Montreal

Sunday, Oct. 18: Pierre Laporte found dead in a green Chev
outside St. Hubert shot in the head*
hands tied behind his back murdered
A note from James Cross found in a church

*This was a false report. Laporte was strangled.

asking police to call off the hunt for him
Crowds gather on Parliament Hill
for the same reason as myself
and stand close to the heart of things
perhaps if some were not before
they have become Canadians
as if it were not beneath them
gathered here to mourn for something
we did not know was valuable
the deathbed of innocence
mocked at by foreign writers
the willingness to pretend
our illusions were real
gone now
Soon we shall have refugees escaping the country
expatriates of the spirit and the body politic
and men in prison raving about justice
defectors beyond the reach
of what we had supposed was freedom
and the easy switchers of loyalty
will change ideas and coats and countries
as they do elsewhere and are no loss
Well
I suppose these things are easy to say
and some think sadness is quite enjoyable
I guess it is too
but this is not an easy sadness
like my own youth full of tears and laughter
in tough middle-age when I'm not
listening anymore sings to me sometimes
Beyond the death of Laporte
and the possible death of James Cross
the deathbed of something else
that is worth being mocked
by cynics and expatriate writers
— the quiet of falling leaves perhaps
autumn rains
long leagues of forest and the towns
tucked between hills for shelter

our own unguarded existence
we ransom day by day of our short lives

Driving west from Ottawa
we stop at a roadside park for lunch
beside a swift narrow black river
looped into calm by the park
thinking in this backwater
how the little eddy that is my life
and all our lives quickens
and bubbles break as we join
the mainstream of history
with detention camps and the smell of blood
and valid reasons for writing great novels
in the future the past closing around
and leaving us where I never wanted to be
in a different country from the one
where I grew up
where love seemed nearly an affectation
but not quite
beyond the Peaceable Kingdom

INTRUDER

Almost sacrilege
for me to wander thru the obstetrics wards
of Johannesburg Hospital with a South African doctor
wearing cloth galoshes against outside germs
me a "tourist doctor" being shown the sights
the terrible commonplace sights
of black women in white
hot shrieking pain but silent
arched black stone flesh carvings
Observing a woman being sewn up
by another doctor who turns away
from his routine hemstitch to chat
with my friend in casual medical gossip

his hands working away without eyes
– a wound more than a foot long
with gaping lips and red interior
a dark flower opening
My face turns a sick yellow
then I guess green and red like a traffic light
I get out fast
and feel like a child discovering the adult world
I'm told later it had been a difficult birth
the woman torn halfway up her navel
myself not having completely realized
it was something more than a wound
the doorway of our last leavetaking
but one into the silent screaming world

South Africa

FOR ROBERT KENNEDY

There are public men
become large as mountains or the endless forests
in the love men bear them
and when they die it is as if a great emptiness became
solid things turn misty and hard to hold onto
and the stunned heart clutches at dear remembrance
retraces its steps back somewhere in the past
when nothing changed and the high sun hangs motionless
friends remain fixed there and dogs bite gently
it is always morning it is always evening
                    it is always noon

And there are men newspapers never heard of
but loved for no reason or every reason
like my ugly grandfather who was
260 pounds of scarred lumberjack
hellraiser and backwoods farmer
of whom I said and say again

"– death takes him
as it takes more beautiful things
populations of whole countries
museums and works of art
and women with such a glow
                  it makes their background vanish
they vanish too –"

But I'm wrong
one drives a beatup Ford to find them
ten towns away across the belted planets
or waiting in the next apartment
one travels light
years across our heavy sorrow
to find the one man one man
and then another yet another
in the alchemy that changes
men but keeps them changeless
and solves the insoluble enigma
of blackjack death and the day's brief tenure
or fails perhaps
and becomes a genetic awareness
an added detail floating outward
inside the collective mind of humanity

POWER FAILURE IN DISNEYLAND

The great Russian poet Dubrovsky stared
out the only window of his state subsidy
deciding that his life's work was worthless
and love possible only to a degree
but apart from that
fame was secure if he kept his mouth shut
and said as much to Ezra Pound
who agreed silently

The long-running stage play
                              life
continues
on a grey day of frequent rain
misty lakes become seemingly
twice as wide as usual
forests mysterious
fields like brown kleenex
trees soft plumes radiating light
– the rabbit chased by a dog dodges
into a mist patch unexpectedly
on the far side his neck snaps
in the dog's mouth like a twig
having zigged instead of zagged
The grey weather flounders into May
June cheer farther away than the liquor store
and it occurs to me
I have not been light-hearted for a long time
nor laughed from the lower gut
apart from obligatory social merriment
in talking with other people
At half-speed the mind runs back
to stand in a field or alone in woods
praising the wisdom that made me possible
an excellent shellfish
parfait gentil tiger
testing my own sincerity
with the sheer humble egotism of demanding
so much from life and getting it
– so much of what other people need
and don't get of praise and love
I am humble damn near almost
the self-drunken moment of awareness in me
multiplied like a thief of time forever
and ever ah men and women
What I mean is
I haven't felt that way in quite a while
things have gotten screwed up somehow
and what future course of action do I

therefore recommend to activate the me correlatives?
Find a handy field and be aesthetic?
Have one drink followed by several?
A good laxative?
Fuck off to Tahiti?
Pretend not to be serious?
Me the first amphibious creature crawling
out of the salt sea wondering
– is it possible to bend a circumstance
bribe the Delphic Oracle so to speak
bugger the Norns with offers of marriage
move the pawns left and right
inside the mind-control-room of course
my own hands or fins reaching inside me
among the dials and instruments
thick knobs of fingers
brush the quivering thought-light
– meat-hooks rupturing reality?

Nothing is different but
swerving in thick mist what might be
another rabbit or the same one
escapes a dog
Rover barks angry and trots off home
lying prone to be tripped over
heavy-hearted in front of a screen door
snapping at flies
Mist lifts slowly into clouds
sunshine predicted by internal weathermen
June is day after tomorrow
the monstrous delicate intuitive stars
change step in their dark prairie of space
allowing me to be reflectively aware
that neural-solar-backyard matter
is phosphorescent and burns protestingly
knowing the lab experiment of life
has several answers but no technicians
with adequate training
as the frantic dials and instruments

flicker wildly
and resume an equilibrium

I pass thru fields and forests
under protocols and directives of light
go home and wait
I am sitting there now
my dear

IN SEARCH OF OWEN ROBLIN

Open the album
it is a cage of ancestors
locked in by metal clasps and stiff cardboard
released by my own careless fingers
And the people literally fling themselves
out of the book into your eyes
the same kind of remote unhumans that scared hell
out of the child who changed into me
years ago when no one else was looking

Seeing those frozen faces again
opaque bulging eyes once more
beards like Mormon elders
bosoms resembling the prows of sailing ships
rumps like overloaded barges
knowing these are your ancestors
but refusing to believe it
hoping for a prompt denial
from snapshot faces of your own parents
– wondering if that frozen blankness
was inherited by them and passed on
to you or was it developed in a genetic vacuum
the trapdoor from past to present?
Stare back at the mirror
seeing yourself a temporal transvestite
wearing black old-fashioned clothes

one hand folded across your breast
about to make a speech or conquer a city
condemn the morals of an entire population
flickering quicksilver image of myself
locked in a cardboard graveyard

The mirror flares blind
in your eyes and the heart beats hard
in the grandfather clock of your body
that leaps with a war-dance of the blood
for which the fiddle-tune comes
direct from those labour-worn faces
and hands seemingly contrived
to swing axes and harness horses
instead of change babies' diapers
but the children also leaped out
from black leather of those awkward bodies
The mirror shows all this
despite a dead photographer's deception
that makes them appear wooden dummies
conceals the grin they never showed here
their laughter muffled by earth
and the long drum-roll of time

Close the book again – but gently
seeing your own unformed face
twisting and leaping at you
from a dozen different directions
reaching back again to them
and ahead
for the book is not closed

First my grandfather
his name was Ridley Neville Purdy
said in full for no part was separable
With only a short plunge back
thru time I can locate him
just before 1930
the year he died age 90

standing in my mother's living room
a giant among the knick-knacks
a monster among the lace doilies
his moustache like the ram on a bulldozer
wearing clothes made of sheet iron
built to last forever in 1930
250 slagheap pounds of ex-lumberjack
barnbuilder and backwoods farmer
all-night boozer and shanty wrestler
prime example of a misspent life
among ladies of the church sewing circle
poker player and teller of tall tales
to a boy – Listen he'd say Listen
and when I listened everything happened
again for the first time
The big lumber camp world came to life
when he came to life a grown man and still a boy
during the early 1850s in Upper Canada
But soon after things began to shrink and contract
slightly when they built the colonization roads

One of them called the Opeongo Wagon Road
beginning at Farrell's Landing on the Ottawa River
traversed the wilderness more or less
west high and low eighty-miles
long connecting with a dozen other roads
– among these the Hastings Road
meandering north from Madoc
connecting with Peterson's Road and Bell's Line
and a green track thru the forest called "The 50¢ Road"
because the roadbuilders were paid fifty cents a day
Everything happens now and then
for the first time Irish immigrant wagons
on the Opeongo Line and settlers on the Hastings Road

And there's my grandfather
a personal family myth as real as hamburger
only 18 years old in 1858 when the roads were built
wearing home-made boots, looking for his first job

in lumber camps at Renfrew and Farrell's Landing
tramping the Opeongo Line
his face the fresh ruddy face of a farm boy
smeared with grease to protect himself
against wild black flies and blazing sun
sweating dust on a road leading into the sky
with a single black cloud near the horizon
a red kerchief wrapped around his head
biscuits and dried deer meat for lunch
six feet tall but only 200 pounds then
axe balanced on his shoulder and stepping it out
the long lifelong journey to anywhere
having decided to live forever
between these blue folded hills
of the hawk's surveillance and sun's dominion
at age 18 there he is
Seventy short years later in a one-room
apartment over the dry goods store in Trenton

Listen he'd say to me Listen
then I could hear in his voice in the room
in his mind the teams jolting past now
and again over corduroy roads thru the wilderness
or jingling sleds in winter
and every teamster with such a pride
before God and Life in himself
that he piled his log load as near the sky
as he dared go and not touch heaven
on earth he called it the "brag load"
– and my grandfather 18 years old
a boy bragging himself into being a man
Listen he'd say to me and the teamsters
and I can hear them

OLD MAN

On the Opeongo Line I drove a span of bays
One summer, once upon a time,
for Hoolihan and Hayes . . .

Now that the bays are dead and gone
and grim old age is mine
A phantom team and teamster
start from Renfrew, rain or shine . . .
Aye, dreaming dreaming
I go teaming on the Opeongo Line . . .

As for my grandfather himself:
well, he died, I guess. They said he did.
Tho I wasn't there to watch him die,
but it had to be like exploring a strange new road
in dusty heat and the drinks far between
unknown taverns with the barkeep fat as God
never inside a black box and the sun gone for good

His wide whalebone hips will make a prehistoric barrow
men of the future may find and perhaps may not:
where this man's relatives ducked their heads
in real and pretended sorrow
for the dearly beloved gone thank Christ to God
after a bad century: a tough big-bellied Pharaoh
with a deck of cards in his pocket and a Presbyterian grin –

Maybe he did die, but the boy didn't understand it,
the man knows now and the scandal never grows old
of a happy lumberjack who lived on rotten whiskey
and died of sin and loving women age 90 or so.
But all he was was too much for any man to be,
a life so full he couldn't include one more thing,
nor tell the same story twice if he'd wanted to,
and didn't and didn't –

Just the same he's dead. A sticky religious voice
folded his century sideways to get it out of sight,
and lowered him into the ground carefully
like someone still alive
who made other people uncomfortable
lowered him into the ground ever so carefully
so he wouldn't wake up and climb out of that pine box

and roar at everyone in his deaf man's voice
"Get the hell away from me you bastards
I ain't ready to turn up my toes by a damn sight
not for another hundred thousand years . . ."
He made other people uncomfortable naturally
a man like a thick-bodied old hemlock
barnraiser and backwoods farmer
soon become an old man
in a one-room apartment over a dry goods store
his head turned listening
to a thousand-mile forest trying to get out
from under the town pavement –

And earth takes him
as it takes more beautiful things
populations of whole countries
museums and works of art
and women with such a glow
it makes their background vanish
      they vanish too
and Lesbos' singer in her sunny islands
stopped when the sun went down –

No, my grandfather was decidedly unbeautiful
carved and gnarled like a weathered tree
blackened by time
that seems dead every winter
an equivalent to three score years and ten
in spring buds sprout like green candles
And I've somehow become his memory
taking on flesh and blood again
the way he imagined me
floating among the pictures in his mind
where his dead body is
laid deep in the earth –
And such a relayed picture perhaps
survives any work of art
survives among its alternatives –

Now I'm talking about myself:
there is a time of defeat in any man's life
any woman's too
If he's a writer that time
is when he's hanging on better writers' coattails
saying or thinking their reputations are inflated
and he's just as good or much better than they are
But comes that horrible time
the realization of knowing
he's not better he just isn't
and finds out suddenly or gradually or crushingly
no one has paid him the least small minuscule
roar of applause or loud whisper of attention
If the guy ain't a writer
but maybe a physicist
architect, ditchdigger or whatever
whatever the rewards of being good are
promotion, money, sex, personal sense of excellence
these come slowly or not at all
and the youth-burning faith in a unique self
dies just damn well dies
and the guy has to buy a woman
or a new car or build a house
have something to show himself for wasted time
surrogate pride and second-hand excellence

Which is by way of being another prelude
for when my wife and I moved to Roblin Lake
Prince Edward County in 1957
after I was a failure at writing plays
a failure at anything in Montreal
poems plays prose and just being a human being
which includes everything I can think of
that was my own situation
So we built a house, my wife and I
our house at a backwater puddle of a lake
near Ameliasburg, Ont. spending
our last hard-earned buck to buy second-hand lumber
to build a second-hand house

and make the down payment on a lot
so far from anywhere
even homing pigeons lost their way
getting back home to nowhere
we built a house so flagrantly noticeable
it seemed an act of despair
like the condemned man's bravado on the gallows
an A-frame house birds mistook for low blue sky
Just outside the cloud of my own black despair
was the small village a mile distant
once named Roblin's Mills

And I got interested in the place
I mean what the hell else could I do
being a little too stupid to ever admit
I was a lousy carpenter and a worse writer?
– Late 19th-century houses in the village
more scattered thru the countryside
many of these old places being
a silent kind of triumph in survival
their owners celebrated with wood and stone
a dozen panes of glass for each window
where glass had been so scarce in the beginning
sign and signal the green waves of forest
surrounding would not wash over them again
Usually they were "second houses"
the first having been log construction
long gone back into earth
And then there were the "third houses"
some with white gingerbread woodwork
complicated as catacombs of the bone brain
a pattern of wood curlicues entangled with time

Blindly staring at the melodious silent gingerbread
I realized that here was the exact spot
where a 19th-century man
worked an hour longer than he had to
because he got interested and forgot everything else
– that lost 19th-century hour

is still visible at one corner of the house
Working on my own A-frame we pounded nails
and sawed boards, cussing and sweating a little
without money for electricity or plumbing
three lamps together and you might read a book
chopping thru winter ice for water
If the result wasn't home it was a place to camp
and whatever gods there were
who permitted pain and defeat
also allowed brief content

When the house was half-built and money ran out
Ameliasburg village became the big city for me
I discovered the old ruined grist mill
built by Owen Roblin in 1842
four storeys high with a wrecked mill wheel
cumbered by stones and time
containing the legend of the Roblin family
and Taylor from Belleville who took over later

Inside the gaunt skull-like stone remnant
dangerous black holes in the floor
as if someone had plunged down screaming years ago
worn-out machinery and great millstones
carved with lovers' initials
some of the boards nearly 30 inches wide
torn from the great pine forests
once blanketing Prince Edward County
19th-century forests seemingly
nearer the last ice age
than the birth date of any man living

Wandering that ruined mill I thought:
Who was Owen Roblin?
what was the man like?
how can I find out about him?
was he human or a creation myth?
did he brush his teeth in the morning?
was he ever despairing and defeated like me?

I questioned every old man in the village:
Did you know Owen Roblin?
and later explored a graveyard near the millpond
beneath the busy black-topped county road
found his red granite stone labeled: Born 1806, Died 1903
and I began to read books about the 19th-century
pioneer forefathers and that kind of thing

In 1958 there were just two people I could find
in Ameliasburg actually old enough
to have had their hand in the hand et cetera
Who was Owen Roblin? Well, maybe they knew
but listening to them I knew very little more
about how the legend had once been a man

In Roblin's Mills old Owen Roblin
came almost fully awake in his lifetime once
owned six houses and built an octagonal one he
slept alone with his woman beside him
beard outside the quilts in zero weather
dreaming not of houris and other men's wives
but his potash works and the sawmill hearing
only the hard tusked music of wheels turning
and hardly ever heard anything soft he
did know one March that June was early
(didst thou then old Owen hear the robins?)
built a gristmill and a village gradually
grew round it and the deep woods vanished and
his wife whelped every nine months eventually
        he died in his sleep age 97
        and everything ended

In the midst of my own despair and failure
I wrote it all down on paper
everything I learned about Roblin's Mills
and the 19th-century village now called Ameliasburg
in a kind of fevered elation at knowing
the privilege of finding a small opening
in the past, shouting questions and hearing echoes

whispering in the tents of the living
In my own desperation also
staying alive on Owen Roblin's coattails
for at least several weeks of intense curiosity
but not realizing what I was doing
not having that much information
about myself then
only that it was important to know:
Who was Owen Roblin?

Two characters in a forgotten melodrama
conceived by an unknown author
first my grandfather then Owen Roblin
both parts minus stage directions

Undoubtedly I made heroes of them
men totally unlike myself
and it never occurred to me
that both were fallible
human beings not entirely perfect
not quite heroic not completely gods
Exploring the old gristmill
that once loomed over its surroundings
like a lord's castle in the forest
and the graveyard like all graveyards
a town peopled by the dead
I wanted to climb over the blank wall
those places represented to me
maybe I thought they'd come to life
again if not in flesh then in spirit
But all my questioning of village people
ended and I drew blank among the old men
their written-on faces fading
After that only books remained
books about the beginning of things in the County
settlement here during the 18th century
in that short silence after the British were defeated
and you could hear birds instead of rifles
after the American Revolution

Citizens of the new United States
who remained loyal to Britain
or those proclaiming themselves neutral
when neutrality was not permitted
were either forced to leave
by the victorious rebels
or decided to go themselves
perhaps because they preferred British rule
or perhaps because they wanted peace
and were tired of having their future decided
by others whether American or British
After the Peace of Versailles in 1783
some 50,000 former citizens
of the American colonies settled in Canada
and became known as the United Empire Loyalists
Among these was a one-time blacksmith
from Kinderhook, New York, Peter Van Alstine
who became a major on the British side
and after the war led a party of refugees
who landed at Adolphustown
some thirty miles from present-day Kingston
just across the Bay of Quinte from Prince Edward in 1784

But there was no town at Adolphustown
a complete wilderness two hundred years ago
forest land had to be surveyed
then cleared by the new settlers
and by a stroke of nomenclature genius
either by Governor-General Haldimand
or Surveyor-General Samuel Holland
the first ten townships were called The Ten Towns
Three of them were in Prince Edward County
Marysburgh was the Fifth Town
Sophiasburgh and Ameliasburgh the Sixth and Seventh
Food and supplies for the new colonists
were provided by the British government
land was allotted and tools supplied
and under the high green ceiling of the forest
they cut down trees and built log houses

I've just been reading about that early log construction
It seems that about 30 years before Christ
a Roman architect and military engineer
named Vitruvius described the method of log building
used by the Colchis people
on the south shore of the Black Sea:
"They lay timbers flat on the ground
one trunk to the left
and one to the right, spaced
one trunk length apart.
The spaces left
because of the thickness
of the material are filled
with wood chips and mud –"

It's springtime now in Ameliasburg
and two thousand years after the Colchis people
seven thousand miles or so from the Black Sea
construction still goes on
dead grass and twigs and mud
also employed by modern carpenters
woven into substantial walls
wood chips only occasionally form part
of the architect's hereditary blue prints
and today one daring house builder actually
filches a piece of white string
direct from my doorstep trailing it
like a long banner in flight
Of course the method of architecture
varies from crib construction to circular
tho in one sense all is crib construction
with marsh builders at the lake edge
and forest builders in chosen trees
Nothing is wasted
no debris littering the floor plan
and the builders go about their work
to the strains of a continual music
rising and falling on the spring air
bright orioles and orange-aproned robins

yellow fluttering goldfinches
brown threshers and red-winged blackbirds
long after the Colchis people
and the Greeks and Romans
long after log houses built here
by people of The Ten Towns

The new settlers sowed their wheat between stumps
inside a great silence called peace
and surely began to understand
the hard politics of wartime defeat
and the civilian exigencies of survival
All this information came from books I read
the well or little-known facts of Canadian history
also the dry record of genealogy
reminiscent of Abraham begat Isaac and Isaac
begat whoever he begat in the Bible
In the midst of genealogical research
with pure joy I spot the Roblin family
feeling like a literary detective
dead broke in Ameliasburg
for nothing could stop me now and then
The Roblins came to Canada with Peter Van Alstine
and records of the first town meeting
at Adolphustown in 1784 name their names
the royal names I almost said
being a bit carried away
Owen, John and Philip Roblin
names twice removed from my boy Owen
John Roblin who wanted only peace
who said in effect to both British and Americans
"A plague on both your houses"

One night the rebels fired 14 shots
into his house then ransacked the place
searching for money and valuables
John Roblin, wounded in the knee
was stripped naked by the soldiers
his brother Stephen hung up by the thumbs

and one soldier shoved his bayonet
at the breast of John Roblin's wife
like a wicked landlord foreclosing life:

SAID THE SOLDIER:

"Your king is George the Third of England!
Go ahead, I dare you to say it!"

AND SHE REPLIED:

"My King is George the Third of England!"
She actually said it
a melodramatic 18th-century heroine
and miraculously didn't get killed
for someone knocked the musket aside
But whether the incident happened or not
the story shows that even then the new-born US
took itself very seriously indeed

Back here at home on page 263
of *Pioneer Life on the Bay of Quinte*
the names of Gilbert Purdy and his eight sons
who were also at Adolphustown with Van Alstine
as well as Philip and Owen Roblin
Barnabus Day and Michael Grass
In fact the two old patriarchs Roblin and Purdy
must have known each other well
maybe drank rum together
sang whiskey songs and dreamt of more children
leaning back against the tree trunks
while the campfire studied their bearded faces
and owls cried "Whoo-who are you?"
and they answered one by one:
MY NAME IS PETER VAN ALSTINE
MY NAME IS MICHAEL GRASS
MY NAME IS OWEN ROBLIN
MY NAME IS GILBERT PURDY

And one far-off descendant Purdy swings
full circle into the needle point of now
and Hey, I say, with silly delight,
Hey, maybe their children intermarried
maybe a boy in my family and a girl in theirs
were illicit lovers bodies strained together
in a haystack or barn loft while the girl's male
parent hunted the boy for a shotgun wedding
Well, okay, it's fantastic, also damn romantic
but who knows, who knows now?

Hard cold fact merges into legend here and legend fact
but the only certain thing is the settlers themselves
restless pioneer nomads fanning out
along wooded shores of the Bay of Quinte
The Roblin family took up land in the Fifth Town
of Marysburgh in Prince Edward
the Purdys stayed put for a while then
scattered out like shotgun pellets
thru all Upper Canada
And in the close-printed genealogy I'm reading
and living I see my own middle name continually
jumping out at me and repeating itself
as if one ancestor had transferred love
for a dead relative to a living one
Also names like McDagg and Hosea
god-fearing Old Testament names
the sons of Gilbert
Biblical fathers and forefathers
forerunners and outriders
patriarchs of the forest biblelands
Owen Roblin begat and Philip begat
they begat and begat and begat
and never missed a tricky stroke
finally with one giant step backward
one dwarf step sideways
in time I find my own Owen Roblin
mill builder and postmaster
son of Philip the son of Philip

In 1829 Owen took up land in Ameliasburg
ten years later traded lots with one John Way
to build his mill and stone house
then an octagonal one for his children's children
But the mill was torn down last year
and stone's internal grey light
gives way to new green
a shading of surface colour
like the greenest apples of several
The spate of Marthas and Tabithas
     incessant Hirams and Josephs
is stemmed in the valley graveyard
where the censored quarrels of loving
and the hatred and by golly gusto
of a good crop of buckwheat and turnips
end naturally as an agreement between friends
       (in the sandy soil
that would grow nothing but weeds
or feed a few gaunt cattle –)
And the spring rain takes their bodies
a little deeper down each year
      and maybe the earliest settlers
some stern Martha or speechless Joseph
perhaps meet and mingle
    1,000 feet down –

And the story about the gristmill
rented in 1914 to a man named Taylor
by the last of the Roblin family
who demanded a share of the profits
that poured golden thru the flume
because the new miller knew his business:
    and the lighting alters
    here and now changes
to then and you can see
    how a bald man stood
sturdily indignant
    and spat on the floor
and stamped away so hard the flour

dust floated out from his clothes
like a white ghostly nimbus
around the red scorn –

      Those old ones
you can hear them on a rural party line
sometimes
      when the copper wires
sing before the number is dialed and
then your own words stall some distance
from the house you said them in
      lost in the 4th concession
      or dimension of wherever
      what happened still happens
      a lump in your throat
      an Adam's apple half
      a mile down the road
      permits their voices
      to join living voices
      and float by
      on the party line sometimes
      and you hang up then
      so long now –

First my grandfather, then Owen Roblin
me hanging on their coattails
gaining strength from them
Then I went still farther back
trying to enter the minds and bodies
of the first settlers and pioneers here
– how did they feel and what were their thoughts?
I tried to feel as they felt and think as they did
thrown out of their homes farther south
the new land bleak and forbidding
promising nothing but work and more work
some of the new settlers middle-aged
others not more than boys
knowing how they were trapped
by the circumstance of loyalty

and trapped by their own stubbornness
even their weakness and pride
But not heroes
in any conventional sense
certainly not the brawny men I once imagined
striding thru the forest that names their names
still impressed on faces of descendants
not heroes but people like all of us
all different and all human

Wandering thru Roblin's gristmill
before they tore it down
and snake fence roads around Ameliasburg
I began to stop feeling sorry for myself
taking strength from them
not their coattails simply hanging on
for a free ride that cost them nothing
because there was no free ride for them
they were born and lived and died
and nothing came easy for them
and dammit nothing is easy for me
Anyhow I feel related to them
by more than blood and just space they occupied
as if I too had hacked at monster trees
sowed between stumps the first grain
and once stood with them in spring
when the quivering air changed direction
from north to warm south wind
the time when seeds leaped under the earth
and green leaves unfurled like sudden flags
stood myself in a log cabin doorway
like some stern Martha or speechless Joseph
and felt what I couldn't say
except somehow they gave me the words

Of course any writer can do this
at least he *ought* to be able to
his mind switching identities
he enters bodies of long-vanished people

the relay race ahead reversed
and I go back down the long stairway
we all came up when we were born
I am myself labouring thru the forest
among the dispossessed, strangers and pilgrims
travelling down the Oswego River to Sackett's Harbour
or sailing rat-infested ships to the Maritimes
in simple desperation
to belong somewhere
no longer alien
and outlawed from the land of their birth:

> "An act for the removal of families and persons who
> have joined the enemy, New York, July 24, 1780.
> Whereas many and great mischiefs do arise by permitting
> the families of persons who have joined the enemy to
> remain at their respective habitations, in as much as such
> persons frequently come out in a private manner to gain
> intelligence and commit robberies, thefts and murder
> upon the good people of this state."

> "A law which shall forbid Loyalists to hold property, to
> be protected by law in any way, or to vote. A special tax
> shall be levied on all Loyalists. Lawyers are to be dis-
> barred. However, since we have need of their services,
> doctors who sided with the enemy shall be allowed to
> practise."

Well, the good people of New York State
and all the other former thirteen colonies
saving one only
made sure their persons and money should be safe
What do you hear in the forest darkness
what are you thinking of
when your head nods a little
and you're neither awake nor asleep?
Something passes across your face
and the fire snaps its red coals

you start awake
and a shadow vanishes?

WOMAN

I am thinking home is the ghost of home
and we are somewhere in between

MAN

And the sounds we hear in the forest?

WOMAN

We have brought iron here
where there was never iron before
iron that is the death of trees
we have brought fire with us
and the forest moans from knowing
"Put the fire out, fire out"

MAN

No trace of deer and even rabbits are scarce
our own food supplies failing

WOMAN

And yet we shall reach the land of Kente
we shall be hungry and we shall have food
I will bear daughters and tall sons
and you shall plow the land
one spring when we are very old
stand between our own fences
among our children
and know that it is finally ours
and the land will take us at last
before we vanish forever
and we shall be born again & again & again
neither waking nor sleeping

After being them I become
myself again rooted in Year One
of all the directions I am travelling
and as much as any place in the world
I claim this snake-fence village
of A-burg as part of myself
its dusty roads and old houses
even the garbage dump sliding
its sleazy treasure chest of litter
and malodorous lastyear valuables
drunkenly down the sudden hill
where winter children toboggan
above two centuries of junk
After the spring run-off in April
at one end of the seasonal time-fuse
before things leap and jump and quiver
and the world explodes with growth
the A-burg kitchen midden is exposed
bright labels faded on tin cans
pop bottles half submerged in dead leaves
broken glass jars from housewives' kitchens
a bulging bosomed dressmaker's dummy
blurred past its fake human shape
a cracked plow motionless in the black unplowed field
that constitutes the shoreless subterranean world
a wornout catcher's mitt and broken bat
baby carriage shattered past repair
farther down milk churns and old harness
under the earth a rusted flintlock rifle
some horseshoes
maybe a lost green corroded coin
minted in one of the lost Thirteen Colonies
or a Queen Victoria shilling flung here
by a disgusted loser in the non-stop
poker game at the A-burg hotel
even a cracked and useless school blackboard
unstuffed teddy bears and fractured dolls
once even the complete skeleton of a dog
and I suppose there must be other dogs here

farm dogs town dogs sheep dogs lap dogs
dogs that say up yours with every snooty bark
all kinds of dogs that ever chased chickens
and dug frantically down groundhog holes
all the evil wall-eyed smelly roustabout
pooches mutts curs bitches hounds and mongrels
frenzied pursuers of sheep and rabbits
from Caesar to Ghenghis Khan and back again
that once were loved by children
here descending the swift/slow elevator of time
reduced to whitening skeletons

All kinds of other bones too
soup bones beef bones pork chop bones
fox bones deer bones wolf bones bear bones
and if I didn't know better
maybe a mammoth's tusk or lizard's forearm
deep down beyond the morning light
that comes bending its way around
this hill a bright flexible shaft of steel
and sees nothing but itself on water
the year's snow or the year's green leaves
or brown land after the spring run-off
the camera eye reversed and turned backwards
showing even myself a man from another time
walking thru the 19th-century village
with a kind of jubilation

And now my mind zig-zags back and forth
like the snake fences around Ameliasburg
from Owen Roblin to my grandfather

Time that tick-tocks always in my body
its deadly rhythm is only a toy of the mind
so that I leap back and forth
from the American Revolution to my grandfather
from Owen Roblin back to the Loyalists
Today at the millpond
below the county road thru the village

sitting on a stone where water foams out
overflowing en route to marshes around Belleville
remembering the slight shock of surprise
I felt to learn that Roblin was not the first man here
not even first building a grist mill

John Way was before him in 1829
a few years after the first settlers
broke land and planted their first dead
a son or small girl or even themselves
buried in one corner of the fields . . .
John Way – about him I know nothing
to that name I add nothing more
except the wooden grist mill
he built near the overflow of the millpond
on land he traded to Owen Roblin eleven years later
That the mill was here is all I know
in fact exactly where I am sitting now
as water flows away into distance
and frogs croak of springtime
that small knowledge of John Way
predecessor, builder and whatever else
for whom no monument
unless this grassy site is included
unless you include what came after
all of us from all of him
as we too have our shadowy children
as close to us as we to him

Clouds cover the sun's face a moment
a moment and I'm not sure where I am
whether the deadly tick-tock in the body
still thunders in 1972
or whether the mind transports me elsewhere
but a related place perhaps
whispering in the minds of my own descendants
who are certainly thinking what I am thinking
because I am there too as they are
saying informally as language allows

"Hello" to John Way
Again searching the records
travelling still farther back
to the beginning where names first appear
attached to land deeds where a village grew
William Giles, Lot 72 in 1835
Daniel Way, Lot 80 in 1810
(and he was John Way's father surely)
Joseph Cronk, Lot 81 in 1803
and that's as far as the records go
with only a few wanderers
trappers and hunters among the Indians here before
but leaving no trace in the record books
Moving forward to 1842
when Owen Roblin built the mill
when everything seemed to happen at once
Elijah Sprague and his carriage factory
who employed and boarded fifty men
under the hill near the millpond
a tailor shop and bakery appeared
bank, hotel, pool room and town hall
with a village lockup in the basement
but the records show one prisoner only
who definitely must have felt himself privileged
an ashery where lye was leached
from hardwood ashes to make soap
a one-room schoolhouse supplied
with half logs on peg legs for desks
(in 1847 the teacher's salary
was two pounds fifteen shillings a month
board, lodging and washing included)
Roblin's own enterprises also mushroomed:
saw mill shingle mill and cider mill
cooperage mill and coffin-making establishment
where your coffin was made while you waited
and the whole village arranged itself around Owen Roblin
By the last half of the century
travelling salesmen in bowler hats
came by wagon and sled to the village

stopping at the new hotel
A village, you might say, like any other
its population in excess of 300
with a wide boardwalk and general store
a village band that practised at night
Also, oddly enough, a company of soldiers
from the 16th Regt. stationed in the village
81 men in all including officers
marched and counter-marched on the dirt roads
orders echoing among the forest trees
perhaps anticipating a sequel to the War of 1812
Owen Roblin himself: councillor and reeve
eventually Justice of the Peace
finally the oldest postmaster in Canada
when he died in 1903
His son Will inherited the postmaster's job
but was fired, and said the only reasons
he knew for his dismissal were political
But names and dates say little
lists of things are only aids to memory
whatever is underneath a village
and one-time pioneer settlement goes deeper
rooted inside human character
contemporary as well as ancient
and the sloppy drunk on a village street
is first cousin to wine tipplers reeling
thru the marketplace of Athens and Rome
the model citizens and much-respected men
all have their counterparts in antiquity
as well as fools and idiots
But no judgement on the past can be made
obviously good and evil are relative
and mean little now when past deeds
are dust as we are children of the dust
not judges and do not bear witness

The long-gone Loyalists stand as forefathers
for one small area of a giant country
only men and that is enough to be

and descendants partake of their own weakness
but also share their strength
it is a human weakness and a human strength
Employing here and now for compass points
space they occupied used again by others
I can visualize many of them
and grappling hooks of the imagination
backed by names and dates and records
produce words and sounds to reproduce them
Here are two people
who never lived but surely existed
fictional people but also prototypes
And certainly in that eternal 19th century
of the mind in which some part of us lives
there was room for these two as well
the village drunk and a lovesick schoolmaster
clichés floating on the surface of complexity
If they never lived dammit they should have
but I believe they did
nameless and unlisted in record books
beyond the constants of birth, death and marriage
I believe they lived

His name was Jib
he drank with the horses sometimes
they staring at him with grave astonished heads
raised dripping from the wooden trough
Sometimes he moved among the cattle
in green fields calling their names
calling Bessie "sweetheart" and Flossie "darling"
they answered with soft wet moos
His fuzziness so completely in character
no one really noticed
his permanent starboard list
or enquired if it was lameness
like a sailor's
at night staring at the stars
not knowing whether they reflected
on water or burst thru the sky in his head

When the miller ran short of help
Jib worked for him
shouldering great bags of flour
weaving in and out
of white clouds obscuring the floury sun
Sweating and stumbling he fell
sometimes grinning his idiot grin
but "Get a move on!"
said the farmer from his high wagon
seat impatient for Rednersville
and foreign ships awaiting cargo

Water crashed at the overshot mill wheel
in his brain falling drifting
toward the far-away millpond
150 feet of bruised spray
After work Jib watched thinking
I could hold onto that rainbow
and ride it down to the millpond
– about to make the attempt
the miller said "Here's your money"

Rye glinted yellow in the dark
tavern spending it all
before the barkeep threw him out
a farmer he knew bought him a drink
and dogs followed him down the road barking
At night in the graveyard
rocking and rocking
he held onto a stone marker
with strangers underneath
not knowing how he got there
but feeling among his own people
And drunk enough for extreme clarity
his thoughts formed without words
as pictures and emotion thinking
I wanted so much to be extraordinary
but always failed until now
now I am extraordinary

and I want to be like everyone else again
but I can't be
He kicked at a grave marker
flour floating out from homespun
world into the strange universe
lost in mist around him
Across the pond he saw a white light
or thought he did
and said "Flossie sweetheart beauty" eagerly
and started to walk on misty water
toward her and sank

SCHOOLMASTER

And I have this other picture
a schoolmaster with a Belleville girl friend
and she is ill with a serious illness
I hear him speaking to her:

Do not die
for if you do
then I shall have no use for women
but that's a lie
they're in my blood and you are too
you most of all of them
and a hunger to say the unsayable
a dream a drink a choice of something
beyond the eyes' closed circuit here
a chance only
a small one
to say something to you
And I repeat the previous instructions
that is – in the positive sense – survive
nor ever rejoice in the idea of death
as escape from anything
there is no escape from anything
not a single damn thing
Blood deals in blood
and love is never less than blood

it deals in truth & treachery & lies
it deals in life & death
but all those big words need transfusions
without blood to colour them red

So I don't understand Tristan and Isolde very well
I don't know much about those others
whoever it was swam the Hellespont
or that lost monk and nun chastely
marooned in the Middle Ages
Abelard and Heloise I think
far from the needle point of Belleville, Ont.
I don't in fact understand myself sometimes
and the schoolmaster in my dreams dreams
of life and death as a choice of things
I wake up cold and sweating
There is no choice except the grave
but a little prior to that
shortly before what happens happens
a prelude so to speak
of something drumming in the blood
of something roaring in the silence
that holds such triumph
it sounds like an overture

There's a line from an old poem that runs:

"And did you once see Shelley plain?"
meaning, I suppose, did you catch a glimpse
of the real man, something essential
that could be no one else but Mr. P. B. Shelley
and even Mrs. Shelley could testify to that
a moment of truth, if you like

Well, I've tried several times
to take that kind of look at my own grandfather
but perhaps all I see is what's around him
his background in pioneer Canada
the way the world looked when he was alive

I see the selective things I remember
nostalgic things that appeal to me
And yet, perhaps it is really so
that I have somehow become his memory
and my survival is the only real trace of his own
which includes the elegy I wrote for him:
"and earth takes him
as it takes more beautiful things
populations of whole countries
museums and works of art
and women with such a glow
it makes their background vanish
        they vanish too"
But that part of the elegy is inaccurate
actually he survives a little longer
and goes with me into the future
flat feet clopping along the street
in my mind like when I was a kid
and he was a very old man
and the questions I asked him

YOUNGER SELF

What was it like? What was it like?

And he replied:

"Not now boy not now
some other time I'll tell ya
what it was like
the way it was
without no streets
or names of places here
nothin but moonlight boy
nothin but woods

Why ain't there woods no more?
I lived in the trees an
how far was anywhere was

as far as the trees went
ceptin cities
                an I never went

They put a road there
where the trees was
an a girl on the road
in a blue dress
an given a place to go
from I went
into the woods with her
it being the best way
to go an never get there

Walk in the woods an not get lost
wherever the woods go
a house in the way
a wall in the way
a stone in the way
that got there quick as hell
an a man shouting Stop
but you don't dast stop
or everything would fall down
You low it's time boy
when you can't tell anyone
when there ain't none to tell
about whatever it was I was sayin
what I was talkin about
what I was thinkin of –?"

And did I once see Owen Roblin plain?
having been on the lookout for fifteen years
reading genealogies and local histories
exploring the graveyard and grist mill
being part of conditions that produced him
talking to old men deaf as tomcats
or nearly – with all their memories mixed together
in one loud single timeless hullaballoo
What do I really know about him

after all that time and speculation?
Item: village people didn't like him a great deal
but I gather they did respect him

Item: he built a water tank for the villagers
so they wouldn't have to haul it from a distance
but the wooden pipes he used burst in winter cold
and the tank was never replaced
Item: Roblin had his financial troubles
selling off his village lands for fifty years
right up to the time of his death
Item: there is a rumour he signed a note
backing a loan by his wife's relatives
then had to pay it off himself
probably mentioning to his wife some small annoyance
the moral being beware of in-laws
but I stress that's a rumour only
Item: I've seen his picture at age 94
he was clean-shaven with a strong face
and looked kinda the way a Roman senator should have
right after throwing some Christians to the lions
or a pirate with religious principles
And that's all I actually know of Roblin
my own wild speculations
and some elusive unverified facts
add it all up and what do you have?
not very damn much –
And yet, as a result of my curiosity
or call it an obsession if you like
certain small rooms in my head are lighted up
the hall bedroom maybe
and definitely the downstairs hallway
I enter them unafraid of darkness or failure

In search of Owen Roblin
I discovered a whole era
that was really a backward extension of myself
built lines of communication across two centuries

recovered my own past my own people
a long misty chain stretched thru time
of which I am the last but not final link
Of course it was an absolutely personal search
including the trivial and inconsequential
and much more important to me
than it ever could be to strangers
They say if you know a thing well enough
it's supposed to evoke either love or hate
but I've never been able to hate very well
because time always seemed too short
and I'm too selfish to waste it that way,
and for all these things I'm talking about
I admit to a strong feeling of affection
which is like being in love with yourself

For it wasn't only Owen Roblin I was looking for
but myself thru him always myself . . .
I am the sum total of all I know
all I have experienced and love
and if that makes me a monster of egotism
bring on your Doctor Freud and Doctor Jung
then go look at the face in your own mirror
I don't mean solipsistic navel-watching either
but John Donne's "I am a piece of the main"
meaning a part of everything larger
and all the things I write about I've done myself
oh not with hands, but with my mind
I am a screen thru which the world passes
a thermometer registering pain and sorrow
and laughter sometimes at being ridiculous
a writer – good, bad or indifferent
embedded in all I've written about
a fly speck in history
dust mote cruising the galaxies

I contain others as they contain me
in the medieval sense I am Everyman

and as Ulysses said of himself in the Cyclops' Cave
                              "I am Nobody"
and a lover

The wheels stopped
and the murmur of voices
behind the flumes' tremble
stopped
              and the wind-high ships
that sailed from Rednersville
to the sunrise ports of Europe
are delayed somewhere
in a toddling breeze
The black millpond
turns an unreflecting eye
to look inward
like an idiot child
locked in the basement
when strangers come
whizzing past on the highway
above the dark green valley
a hundred yards below

The mill space is empty
even stones are gone
where hands were shaken
and walls enclosed laughter
saved up and brought here
from the hot fields
where all stories
are rolled into one
And white dust floating
above the watery mumble
and bright human sounds
to shimmer among the pollen
where bees dance now
Of all these things
no outline remains
no shadow on the soft air

no bent place in the heat glimmer
where the heavy walls pressed

And some of those who vanished
lost children of the time
kept after school
left alone in a graveyard
who may not change
or ever grow six inches
in one hot summer
or turn where the great herons
graze the sky's low silver
– stand between the hours
in a rotting village
near the weed-grown eye
that looks into itself
deep in the black crystal
that holds and contains
the substance of shadows
manner and custom
        of the inarticulate
departures and morning rumours
gestures and almost touchings
announcements and arrivals
gossip of someone's marriage
when a girl or a tired farm woman
whose body suddenly blushes
beneath a faded house dress
with white expressionless face
turns to her awkward husband
to remind him of something else

The black millpond
                holds them
movings and reachings and fragments
the gear and tackle of living
under the water eye
all things laid aside

        discarded
                forgotten
but they had their being once
and left a place to stand on

LAMENT

They are gone the mighty men
they have vanished utterly gone the record-setters
once as a child I remember
the achievers of forty feet at a brass spittoon
– and it sang like the birds

Uncle Wilfred was my non-uncle uncle
I called him that because I loved him
sitting in semi-darkness he could knock a fly
off the dinner dishes with one bronze splash
– my Uncle Wilfred will never die

Teamsters were lords of that kingdom
they raced their wagons and fought duels
they let go at open windows they had jumpy wives
nervous with close calls from straw-coloured fluid
an evil the preacher mentioned on Sundays

The Gilbert House had leather chairs in the lobby
and maybe half a dozen very old men
dozed there taking pot shots at the rubber tree
which died slowly and dust settled on them slowly
until Spang went the spittoon singing you're dead

When I lay in the grass staring at clouds
I imagined them up there sighting at planets
now the shoe-spattered targets and dead shot dowsers
blacksmiths horses teamsters all are gone – even at length
mouth pursed and ready my Uncle Wilfred

KERAMEIKOS CEMETERY

So old that only traces of death remain
for death is broken with the broken stones
as if convivial party-goers came
and talked so long to friends they stayed
to hear the night birds call their children home

All over Athens rooster voices wake
the past converses with itself and time
is like a plow that turns up yesterday
I move and all around – the marketplace
where something tugs my sleeve as I go by

THE HUNTING CAMP

Lost and wandering in circles
the camp seen for a third time
was like stubbing your toe
on a corpse
mouldy rotten logs an open grave
but the woods myth of continual circling
comfortingly verified as accurate
seemed a remote contact with warm human wisdom
It also seemed natural to address the trees
as a people substitute
but they would not speak
made no reply to his whispering yells
altho some were fat or thin
a few even looked a little friendly
but he told himself they were only trees
and said to them "You're only trees"
unsettled to hear himself
talking to a forest
That last time he saw the hunting camp
spectral with decay among the green life
something seemed to delay his own continuance

assuming continuance to be the sequence of thought
at least there was a gap in his life
he couldn't explain until afterwards
his last memory standing at an open tomb
which must have been the camp – then nothing
Afterwards
new-arriving bruises were evidence
of a few seconds when his brain had stopped
but feet had carried his mindless body forward
the forgotten feet slammed against trees
forest undergrowth whipped against his face
the feet bounced a body from tree to tree
and someone who was not his someone
had lived in his body during his death
then he re-occupied but without memory
only pain-evidence and a feeling of violation
his own thoughts beginning again and searching
for the stranger in his sixteen-year-old skull
In Hawk Junction distant as the moon
but only five miles away
he heard the trains' bodies shunting together
puzzled that sound came in waves and eddies
zig-zag voices that weren't there surrounding him
quite different from leaves touching other leaves
among which if you listened long enough
you might distinguish vegetable words
and he said to the leaves "What are you saying?"
In a clearing unaware of the sun
he might have seen a hairy man with humped shoulders
passing by intent on his own purposes
and wondered whether to ask directions
and wondered if he was capable of knowing
whether the thing was man or a bear
and felt pleasure at this intuition of instability
comforting as a pledge of fear of fear
Whatever time was went by
contracted or expanded somewhere in his skull
one thought went out to explore the brain's territory
among locked doors and doors slightly ajar

he kept arriving at blind alleys and places of no intention
– a second thought said trees had stopped speaking
a sub-thought said the trees had never spoken
but his thought consensus said they would someday
even tho trees were fat or thin but not human
trains actually were the hoarse voice of reality
Cooling sweat streaked his face and it pleased him
and the word for it pleased him: anodyne
which means release and solace from terror
he thought to make a song of it singing
and managing two syllables for every step
"O my darling O my darling Anodyne
You are lost and gone forever
dreadful sorry Anodyne"
and chuckled about the ridiculous sound
so exactly right for his regained calmness
then turning a street corner
in the forest found again
the hunting camp

INSIDE THE MILL

It's a building where men are still working
thru sunlight and starlight and moonlight
despite the black holes plunging down
on their way to the roots of the earth
no danger exists for them
transparent as shadows they labour
in their manufacture of light

I've gone there lonely sometimes
the way I felt as a boy
and something lightened inside me
– old hands sift the dust that was flour
and the lumbering wagons returning
afloat in their pillar of shadows
as the great wheel turns the world

When you cross the doorway you feel them
when you cross the places they've been
there's a flutter of time in your heartbeat
of time going backward and forward
if you feel it and perhaps you don't
but it's voyaging backward and forward
on a gate in the sea of your mind

When the mill was torn down I went back there
birds fumed into fire at the place
a red sun beat hot in the stillness
they moved there transparent as morning
one illusion balanced another
as the dream holds the real in proportion
and the howl in our hearts to a sigh

PRE-SCHOOL

Black was first of all
the place I came from
frightened because I couldn't remember
where I'd been or was going to
But when did I find yellow
in buttercup and dandelion
in the meadowlands and hill country
discover them in my mind
as if they had always been there
yellow eyes yellow eyes?
Red was about then too
and the river discovered me
lying upsidedown by the water
waiting for myself to happen
all the unfolding summer
while red willow roots waved
thru the water like a drowned girl's hair
I said as slowly as I could "You're red"
and it was so and I knew
I knew for the first time

that I could invent the world
Dark colours came later
of course after the blue sky
brown takes study to like much
tho some of the brown kind of people
have silver lights in their eyes
from the time the moon left here
because of a solemn promise
it gave the sun earlier on
and the brown people wanted to stay
in that gleaming landscape
and waited too long to leave:
in their minds are not quite clear
they haven't dreamed their sleeping
why it was there were no shadows
in that country without colour
but silver silver silver

Later on
the house went smaller and smaller
and green moss grew on the shingles
and all vegetable things in red and yellow
flowed orange and gold into women
and the grey child
went searching for one more colour
beyond blue eyes and brown hair
past the red tremble of leaves in October
and the silver women
beyond the death-black forest
to where all colours begin

THE CHILDREN

By day
Chipewyan children scavenging
the garbage dump for food
Churchill housewives throw away
stuffing it into their mouths

as if they didn't remember how
and their rival scavengers
half-ton polar bears
slumbering down from the high Arctic
At the HBC store their parents
carting off boxes of garbage
by taxi and paying the driver
with social assistance money
At night children
in misery and boredom and hunger
wander the town
smashing shop windows
breaking into empty houses
the plague of Egypt in Churchill
platoons of children
ten-year-old privates
and twelve-year-old captains
creep thru shadowy backyards
raiding the white settlement
Joe says: no one watching
Elijah answers: now then
John says: burn it down
and their breath stops
a match flares bright blue
over Henry Hudson's sea glimmering
into a flame house
reflecting roof rafters of a sky
the white whale dreams under
the white whale dreams winter
sometimes John whispers to Elijah
but Elijah is dead
as droning taxis murmur
on the main drag of the town
Joe whispers to John
but John is dead too by then
Ghost children
skip stones over the ice
and whisper to each other:
suppose the whole world

is a garbage dump
well just supposing it's so
and old tin cans are lovely
as pearls for a lovely princess
on the front of her lovely evening gown
and rotten spaghetti isn't
crawling white worms crawling
under the falling snow
that makes all things beautiful
Well just imagine just supposing
Mother Goose lived here
whispering stories to the dead children
about home sweet home on the garbage dump
for another million years
while Hickory Dickory Dock solemnly
concurs and Humpty Dumpty never
fell before Peter Rabbit became rabbit stew
and it isn't true
that Indian kids live like that
and die like that it isn't true
somebody's bound to say
besides it doesn't make a very good poem
and isn't pleasant either I guess
but to hell with poems
to hell with poems

Churchill

DEPRIVATIONS

Stand quietly here
on the lake shore and fish
swim up in their lighted ballroom
at your feet doing a sundance
small bass so near transparency
they're nearly not here at all
but peering back from the other

side of becoming coming
closer closer very close
and I'm a thousand-foot
giant to them certainly not
supremely unnoticed not
less than nothing no
tear or blank spot
would suddenly appear
in the landscape
if I weren't there
but dozens of my selves
in their eyes would wink out
Among the fingerlings two
bullet-bodied cruising adults
drift dark with adult problems
– if there was a post office down there
they'd be leaning against it
if there's employment
they don't want to find it
they are incurably
fish and for that reason
a faint disturbing reproach
to whatever I am
I stand a few moments
in my aquarium of air
and they examine me
from their water incubator
a key turns somewhere
in a lock
now stops and stays here
and clouds are motionless
– to think that these
are prototypes of that first one
definitely weirdo and oddball
who dragged himself painfully
away from the salt waves
away from his quicksilver buddies
crawling up a gritty sand beach
for stubborn personal reasons

to set up dry housekeeping
and raise a family
I can't return there of course
have only this moment
of childlike rare communion
and sudden overwhelming envy
of things without the heritage
and handicap of good and evil
which they escape easily
with one flick of the tail
And something they do not know:
when I move my slowly stiffening
body and they scatter into diamonds
it is like a small meanness
of the spirit they are not capable of
and that is one difference

IN THE DARKNESS OF CITIES

How does one come to terms with the terrible beggars
staring straight at tourists near Minos' ruins say
or looking sideways at you in Oaxaca market as
if you held the only key to their survival in your pocket
and used it to unlock the door of a new Chevrolet?
I mean the very poor poor plentiful as money
things with withered breasts hands like claws
in Singapore and Karachi and mud huts in Yucatan
Indians scavenging garbage dumps behind factories
and how could you imagine their name is Mohawk say
Aztec Inca or anything proud enough to forget
their name ever meant anything but death?
I have a feeling about them sometimes
that they know all the books are nothing
and tall glass towers of cities and river bridges
and brains to harness the sun and moon tides
and send ships whooshing beyond the flowering earth
I have the feeling they know and know I know

that nothing in the world no feat or accomplishment
no riches from the ground or thought of men's minds
they know that nothing is ever done for them
no matter what extravagant words proclaim that it is
The fish is a thing only and we do not care
if it starves unless we need its body
the beast is slightly less of a thing for we know
we do need beasts' bodies to feed our own
and all other creatures merely supplement our own
existence each in its manner and for our benefit
But the poor are a needless luxury and they know it
they know the world would lose nothing if they left us
if they were squirted with liquid fire or disease and left us
alone on a solar tertiary adrift on our swaying raft
somewhere between nowhere and what might be someplace perhaps
and terribly they know this for I see it in their eyes
as I hold onto the lovely difficult money
the needful minimum sample of all good things
that seemed so necessary and worthwhile
and as I guard my little knowledge my precious thought
as I applaud the rocket cars motoring into absence
to explode in a dream on a picture-tube somewhere else
they know our bright lights in the sky are not their lights
they know the beast is not fattened or the seed planted
for their harvest they know sun and moon are heat and cold
and mountain streams with deep amber coins in autumn
are not for them to spend on idle thoughts of beauty
they know
And in the face of their knowledge
all these mere words on paper
ring soundlessly in the vacuum of inattention
I know they mean nothing
as the terrible unaccusing poor know also
while brightly coloured birds
fly in and out from lonely caves of my imagination

ALIVE OR NOT

It's like a story
because it takes so long to happen:

a block away on an Ottawa street
I see this woman about to fall
and she collapses slowly
in sections the way you read about
and there just might be time
for me to reach her
running as fast as I can
before her head hits the sidewalk
Of course it's my wife
I am running toward her now
and there is a certain amount of horror
a time lag in which other things happen
I can almost see flowers break into blossom
while I am running toward the woman
my wife it seems
orchids in the Brazilian jungle
exist like unprovable ideas
until a man in a pith helmet
steps on one and yells Eureka or something
– and while I am thinking about this
her body splashes on the street
her glasses fall broken beside her
with a musical sound under the traffic
and she is probably dead too
Of course I cradle her in my arms
a doll perhaps without life
while someone I do not know
signals a taxi
as the bystanders stare
What this means years later
as I grow older and older
is that I am still running toward her:
the woman falls very slowly
she is giving me more and more time

to reach her and make the grab
and each time each fall she may die
or not die and this will go on forever
this will go on forever and ever
As I grow older and older
my speed afoot increases
each time I am running and reach
the place before she falls every time
I am running too fast to stop
I run past her farther and farther
it's almost like a story
as an orchid dies in the Brazilian jungle
and there is a certain amount of horror

ANTENNA

Waiting:
everything in the city park super
real – trees – anonymous buildings nearby
are symbolic any-buildings at ten
below zero then the entire
background world just goes Phuutt
long pause then Phut more briefly
and can't be translated back – it
(the world) practically doesn't
exist except as something
to be stepped on crossing
Yonge Street in heavy traffic
to discover someone's nose is
a cold rosebud and jumping
off a plane or taxi or rocket
at Marsport drugstore the
unlucky martians almost human but
lack something fundamental for
instance not knowing
your thick pubic hair is
composed of a million tiny watch

springs inside an immortal hour
glass and one particular kind of
look is not yours alone but given to
a switchboard where little lights
flash or a bell tinkles
in the forehead answering
service announcing
an absence of before and after
but refuting that conjecture:
in some prehistoric forest
where happiness was not
thinking of anything but eating
someone before killing
his noonday meal and hurrying
thru the rustling silence
of himself must have
stumbled on this sadness
slightly similar to hunger
something he was the first
man capable of feeling
– and the woman knowing it
must have looked at him
a million years ago
questioningly

PAPER MATE

They meet in heavy snowstorms on streetcorners
muffled in thick overcoats and thermal underwear
– other storms storm thru their bodies
every snowflake is a cry
from not-meeting and never being
prompt for appointments of this nature
which are cancelled if not dealt with by proper authority

The proper authority for lovers is pain
they know each other's telephone voices

and joy-pain whispers over wires
not knowing they're fools is not enough
they must be aware of losing the whole blue world
which obviously amounts to nothing compared to each other
and break every phony vow for their sacred selves
of course moaning in near-agony and disbelieving
sensible advisers if any

Meeting in bare rooms and parks on aforementioned
wires everybody knows everybody guesses but trees
conspire like loyal slaves porch lights wink
out to hide them from themselves
day is reversed night dreams in all of us
but morning is a grey prophet when the angry god
of everyone arrives at noon to cast the first stone
– they are forced finally to ration the quantities
of self each gives and takes from the other
like medicine in teaspoons to cure themselves
from themselves but the malady is not susceptible
to standard treatment – only boredom is curative
they fear it and fear their own repeated necessities

Is magic then an everyday thing they say finally
is it sordid as tenements underhanded as rich men
can it be measured codified and shoved into time slots?
does it survive as itself or memory of itself
in absence or rare presence?
                                – it does survive however
all high points are loftier and depths much farther down
they find themselves alternately in clouds or dark caverns
(Jews and Arabs and the Irish Republican Army
indulge their different insanity somewhere in between)
and preoccupied with mapping the territory
they are in love with maps and charts of themselves
where a paper woman whispers to a paper man
"I love you" and he obedient "I love *you*"
and the phrase floats backward and forward
along the time lines among historic longitudes
where Troilus says to Cressida "He's a liar"

Beatrice to Dante "Let's hope so"
Nelson to Emma "Give them more rope"
and whatshisname that castrated monk
– Abelard plaintively "That sonuvabitch Plato
has much to answer for" (to Heloise)
In the opposite direction they hear us
but we don't hear them: our bedsprings musical
and ballpoints vociferous while some possible someone
might say wistfully "We are hostages to fortune"
– and science Great Science takes precedence over all
the High God of Genetics says "We're mortgaged to the future"
the living and the dying are a means before the end
but to paraphrase another whose name I've quite forgotten
"My dear oh my dear"

SUBJECT/OBJECT

What shall we say of these lovers
that has not been said of others?
Except – all doubt and self-derision
swept away even if temporarily
Except – mad wrestlers in the blood appeased
vampires refreshed from eating the god-selves
Except – reiterated personal signals
whose monotony and frequency are clichés
yes pure cliché remembering later
                    but yet also this
hard pride in defeat yes defeat by choice
submitting to apocalypse in a simple fuck
– a simple fuck?

Give me
the great ambitions
to scribble your name on a planet
to be a minus sign on the universe
yet be everything feel everything
obsessed with one single excellence

knowing
all these things sound trivial
when frozen to death on paper
to be what you are so fully
all questions become answers

Give me
chemical constituents of this dirty pair
of dogs grappling in some backyard
to reproduce more dogs   dogs stuck together
as panicky twin witnesses of themselves
morally responsible for their own predicament

Give me
the dictionary word and grunts and mutters
unthought sounds of fucking in bevel-aching ear
synchronized with blood and breath and bone
as fucking is the lost-and-found of love?

Give me
my guts return them immediately
subtract yourself from my self wholly
retract also your believable lies
                your crooked straightfulness
by mail or runner native to the country
and know that isn't possible
in lands beyond our lifetime
                the runners pull up lame

Give me
what you have already given
your own silence
balanced on the moment
in the waiting early morning
and the still air between us
the fullness and the emptying
this little place

THE COLOUR OF REALITY

You were lying in my arms
one hand running over all your soft smooth places
and this little girl kept looking in the window
I said "Scat, beat it, go find yourself
a nasty little boy to play with!"
– the kid disappeared in a big hurry
My hand walked into the anteroom
of where we had often come together
a place of warm gardens and bright blue thistles
disguised as forget-me-nots
"I won't see you again" you said suddenly
"For God's sake doesn't all this mean anything?"
I said angrily and opened my eyes
noticing your hair was a dull red colour
like a rusted piece of tin
and with an uncanny feeling
I thought – what the hell's going on here?

Awake
the correct video tape clicked into place
your hair once more a bright yellow
– but the desolation remains
I can hardly bear it being even a dream
and think – what if all those other times . . .

BORDERLANDS

No way of knowing where we went
on those long journeys
Sometimes there was a whiteness
as of snow that obscured everything
but it wasn't snow
Sometimes it seemed we left a campfire
and looking for it again
couldn't even find the burned place

blundering into trees and buildings
– but then nothing
has ever confused me as much as light
Sometimes we arrived back separately
but still seemed inside the borders
we crossed by accident
and want to be there if we think it real
but we do not think it real
There is one memory
of you smiling in the darkness
and the smile has shaped the air
                          around your face
someone you met in a dream
has dreamed you waking.

SEPARATION

Then neither of us will see the other die
no oozing tears and pity
the close watching
wondering who's first

It will happen some place else
one of us will know later
among the crises of blurred eyesight
constipation and insomnia

A sick old woman a sick old man
spared something
spared pain and unnecessary grief
spared love

PLACE OF FIRE

There are smokestacks hundreds
of feet high, disciplined phallic
chimneys penetrating the helpless sky
in ritual rape, towering above dead bodies
of factories. But technology built them –
I mean, they're too cosmic to be personal.
Ours is twenty feet. And still climbing.
Ingredients: limestone from an 1840 Regency cottage
(I told Bill Knox he was nuts to tear it down);
historic stone from the Roblin gristmill site;
anonymous stone from Norris Whitney's barnyard;
and some pickup loads from Point Anne quarry.
– All this to toast marshmallows?

But you'll have to admit the ritual significance
of not being above working with your hands?
You don't admit? Okay, I guess you're right.
But you must agree it's the hard way
to gather ingredients for a poem?
– lugging tons of CaCO2, stone plus fossils?
Symbolic as hell too: you can't beat limestone,
which Auden said was very important stuff;
W. Yeats and R. Jeffers kept building towers as well,
so they could write great poems about it.
I'm just the latest heir of the hearth-warming
tradition, eh?

You know, I've talked myself into a corner:
it would be silly now to mention that at my shoulder
the dark tribes are hovering and worshipping,
stone people who preceded the jukebox people;
and before them the first fossil critters,
having such a nice trip in their stone coffins.
I won't mention them. That would be too much.

I did forget to include the inheritors bit,
mystic stuff about hearing whispers from the far

past, me a listening lowly high priest,
unacknowledged legislator or something –
Of course what I'm actually doing, or seeming to,
is telling anyone reading this how to write a poem:
so build your fireplace, raise your stone tower,
fall in love, live a life, smell a flower,
throw a football, date a blonde, dig a grave
– in fact, do any damn thing, but act quickly!
Go ahead. You've got the kit.

TEN THOUSAND PIANOS

The Arctic is mostly silent in summer
seals bark only at a distance
from the rifle's mean crack
or a motor's stutter
breaking the blue glass of water
In evening ducks mourn
eerily their fate as ducks
the killer whale ghosting along
hiding beneath a dorsal fin
soundless as words on paper
Idling past a mile-wide iceberg
in the canoe listening
to meltwater dripping in the sea
ice marries itself to water
as red leaves float down in fall
as snow or rain or lost words
wandering beyond hearing
Listen to your blood negotiate
interior roads in the brain's back country
or lying on your back in grass
clouds buffet clouds in leaning silence
under the upsidedown mountains
I am an elderly boy come here
to take piano lessons
realizing one should be born

in silence like a prolonged waiting
after the first death-cry
knowing this music
is what silence is for
in a canoe in Cumberland Sound
waiting among the white islands
for summer's slow departure

Baffin Island

SHALL WE GATHER AT THE RIVER
for Dave Williams

Riding a freight train for the first time
I was seventeen
and it rained
it rained like God was weeping
so hard he never noticed me
cowering in the shadow of his throne
When the steam rattletrap stopped
for water at Hawk Junction in NorOnt
I ripped the seal off a boxcar
trying to get inside out
of the rain and couldn't
budge the sliding door
Back on the flat car shivering
the CPR cop found me
and said I could get two years for my crime
and locked me in a barred caboose
to begin and end this sentence
I escaped (hardened criminal me)
and started to walk back to Sault Ste
Marie beside the tracks and figuring
that cop would be looking
stayed outa sight maybe thirty feet
inside the woods being fairly
cunning even at seventeen

Upshot was I outsmarted myself
got into the bush too far
lost in trees for two days
while it rained then it rained some more
For the last time in my life
I prayed and prayed some more
agnostically declining to take chances
Then very rationally I remembered the river
crossing under the tracks at Hawk Junction
river and tracks forming two sides of an isosceles
triangle so chances were two-to-one in my favour
that I could locate one of them
and did – I found the river
The question is: did God help?
I wondered afterwards
and answered my own question: NO
I worked out the problem alone
except for my friend Euclid
Years later another friend
(hearing this story)
has made me somewhat uneasy
and says "If there's a God
then the river was made by Him
rivers being part of nature
whereas the railway was man-made
and it would have been more in keeping
with your self-help theory
if you'd found the railway tracks instead
thus having no truck or trade with a possible God
Yes (my friend went on judicially)
it's too bad in a manner of speaking
that you ever found that holy river"
All these long years later
my mind was quite at ease
now it chills my backbone
to think of that unprovable God
meeting me at the river
and saying nothing not a word
just sitting comfortably on his golden throne

the second-best one in muddy shallows
where little green gun-slingers
of frogs were shooting down bugs
and birds chasing desperate minnows
dive-bombed in the sudden sunlight
while God the scientist watched
observing a terrified boy
wandering thru hell
to rejoin the improbable world

"I AM SEARCHING FOR YOU"

There are twenty Eskimo words for snow
and many more for different kinds of ice
but two Labrador hunters
in a blue snowmobile failed to recognize
the word for treacherous ice they encountered
when their machine and themselves
drifted away on a floating island
broken from the sea ice
Jacko Onalik and Martin Senigak
you do not know me
have never seen my face
I mean nothing to you
and yet at this moment I am searching
for you 500 feet high
above the fifty or maybe
a hundred kinds of ice below me
and if you are alive down there
might see my eagle shadow
mirrored on the pack ice
might hear dark thunder and look up
Myself clothed in a giant aeroplane
circling in the high clear blue
therefore Martin and Jacko make a sign
I don't know how but make a sign
— and while I'm waiting let me tell you

the odd circumstances of my being here
unmistakable civilian among the uniforms:
six weeks ago I had this bright idea
for writing an article about Search & Rescue
sovereignty overflights and northern patrols
wanted to stare eyeball to eyeball
with Russian trawlers fishing inside
or outside the Canadian twelve-mile limit
carpet-sweeping the ocean of everything alive
So I arranged for that to happen
(made some phone calls to Ottawa)
and here I am with sixteen crewmen
cooking steaks 500 feet above you
in the galley of an Argus aircraft
Anyway at least eight observers up here
are trying to catch sight of the two lost hunters
small black bugs on the white desert
and I am briefly inside the plexiglass bubble
of the aircraft nose feeling like a tear
about to fall back in Nain where village elders
requested the big bird to try one more time
because they are also thinking of you
We have covered 2,000 square miles
of North Atlantic off the Labrador coast today
examining anything the least bit unusual
instruments supplementing the hundred eyes
of Argus in Greek mythology
crossing and re-crossing Dog Island
where you intended to hunt foxes
until the blue snowmobile
misunderstood the word for treacherous ice
as machines sometimes do
leaving a track ending at open water
Jacko Onalik and Martin Senigak
it seems unlikely we shall ever meet
but I wanted you to know something about me
altho I have told you almost nothing
except the fact of searching for you
And now all of us think the search hopeless

the captain and co-pilots and navigators
engineers radio men and observers
and me the civilian
it is hopeless
because six days have come and gone
since you and the blue snowmobile
disappeared in the direction of Dog Island
But I have a reason for writing this
even tho it's absurd to think you could hear
anything said above the high sea barricades
over you and under the aeroplane
– the reason is an illusion
an illusion so strong I feel
I am speaking directly to Jacko and Martin
their souls maybe tho I don't believe in souls
and saying to you we tried all of us tried
because on some night not long delayed
when I have necessity for hope
I hope beforehand someone will be searching
for me however impossible

RODEO

Inside the Stockmen's Hall drinking
beer with Marvin Paul who looks
like a tragic poet and carves totem-poles
taking three weeks to earn four dollars
Outside in the dusty arena horses explode
with arched backs and William Billy Boy
sails upward in air and downward to dust
Another bronco refuses to do anything at all
just stands there somewhat reminding me
of a friend saying "It's better not to be born"
There is free will it seems here in the Chilcotin
a semicircle of mountains stares at the sun
an old Indian with his face a dark forest
outside the Stockmen's Hall sleeps tenderly

I am waiting with Marvin Paul for one of those
moments when all will be made plain
to me when the calf-ropers build their loops
and lasso the stars as William Billy Boy rides
to his inheritance on earth in eighteen seconds flat
his own people quiet and the whites noisy
while our round earth resumes colloquy with the gods
As things stand now Marvin Paul incoherent
with beer sells me his pencil portrait
which translates him to a tragic dimension
the wild cow-milkers clutching beer bottles
strain for a few drops but the beasts refuse
William Billy Boy is slammed to the dust
his bent back aches and he won't ride for a while
Nothing is finally made plain to me
but I have stated my intention set the scene
the same one in which a bored housewife
prays for a romantic lover and the bankrupt rancher
stares at his parched range and starving cattle and spits
Both settle for less than their dreams: the woman for a man
the rancher for one more year in the high Chilcotin
myself for something less tangible
hovering in my mind close to this poem

HOMAGE TO REE-SHARD

Frog music in the night
and all the dogs and cats and cows
on farms for miles in all directions
screech and howl and moo from shore to shore
the beasts of God bust their guts with song
and the sun a great bonfire burning away
darkness on the lake's little republic
but so delicate a rose tint on water
no girl has steps as light
Hockey – we have been talking hockey
Dave Williams and me at Roblin Lake

then slept and I wake him up later
to witness this birth this death of darkness
but how it relates to hockey – don't ask
tho maybe frog-music frog-music
of Montreal and Ree-shard the Rocket
"First madman in hockey" Dave says
not sensible and disciplined
but mad mad mad I see him
with balls shining out of his eyes
bursting a straitjacket of six Anglos
riding his back a thousand miles
of ice to beat the Anglo goalie
while all the dogs and cats and cows
from Toronto to Montreal and Roblin Lake
and Plains of Abraham forever
moo and screech and howl from shore
to morning shore in wild applause

The first madman
first out-and-out mad shit disturber
after cosmic duels with Bill Ezinicki
now sullen castrated paranoid Achilles
with sore heel in a Montreal pub retired
to muse on wrongs and plot revenge
with long memories of broken storefronts
along St. Catherine Street
when Maisonneuve's city made him emperor
for a day and hour and a moment
But Dave if I may interject a comment
difficult tho that may be
I think compared to the Rocket
all Iron Horses Catfish Shoeless Joes
and the Bambino's picayune meal of a mere
planetary dozen steaks and hotdogs and mammoth
bellyache sink to a minor tribal folk tale
in a trivial game of rounders somewhere south
"Hockey" says Dave pontifically
"is the game we've made of all our myth
of origins a million snot-nosed kids

on borrowed bob-skates batting lumps
of coal in Sask and Ont and Que
between two Eaton's catalogues in 1910
these are the heroes these the Alexanders
of our foetal pantheon and you know
you eastern bastards froze in darkness
you don't know Bill Cook and brother Bun
they came from my town Lac Vert Sask
they came each spring showering ice cream
and chocolate bars on all the kids
in my home town they were the new gods
almost replacing money
and you could see they knew
they were the gods. . ."

The sun now shines upon our right
out of the sea came he
for god's sake get ye hence to bed
no early risers we

And then I dreamed I dreamed Ree-shard
ancestor Maurice incestuous mythawful Rocket
standing at my bedside
I fled Him down the nights and down the days
I fled Him down the arches of the years
I fled Him down the labyrinthine ways
of my own mind – but he was too fast for me
his eyes blazing blowlamps
on Décarie and its cloacal hellway
and Montreal East kids with ragged Canadien
sweaters on St. Germain outside the factory
I worked in all the little Ree-shards
failing to negotiate contact
with their dream among the greasy-spoon
cafés and their out-of-work pères
and mères among the non-Anglos
among failed gangsters and busted drug peddlers
and '48 Pontiacs with bad lungs
coughing their own smoke in Montreal East

I dreamed Ree-shard and the kids
Me the failed athlete and failed lover
absurd idealist and successful cynic
I dreamed the bitter glory-fled old man
nursing his hate and grudges and memories
his balls making only sewer water
with Jung and Freud as solemn witnesses
But that man disappeared suddenly
and what took his place was the real thing
honest-injun Rocket indubitable Maurice
mad mad Ree-shard in fact the first and only
berserker astronaut among the lesser
groundlings their necessary flyboy
who slapped a star along Décarie hellway
and rang a bell in Bonaparte's tomb
and knocked a crumb from Antoinette's pastry
waved his wand at Anglos Howe and Ezinicki
and made Quebec Canadian

Rocket you'll never read this
but I wish for you all the best things
whatever those may be
grow fat drink beer live high off the hog
and may all your women be beautiful
as a black spot of light sailing among the planets
I wish it for just one reason
that watching you I know
all the things I knew I couldn't do
are unimportant

POUR

My love is a winter woman
floating down mountains on skis
I have seen no mountains without thinking of her
no high Sierras or Purcells not even a small goose bump
on the horizon without dreaming of her before breakfast

racing under an arched blue sky
trailing her breath behind
like white roses

My love wears a yellow dress and has long gold legs
they walk her to groceries and libraries and pharmacists
they carry her to taverns and toilets and town houses
I think I'll never again ride aeroplanes or motor cars
but walk always just on the chance of seeing her
doing what everyone else does but so differently
And perhaps I'll walk to California or Montreal
like an out-of-date highwayman with blisters
on both feet and the street empty of her
but walking the city I'll never see forests again never again
unless water remembers unless clouds remember

My love and I were in bed together
and she told me the story of her first lover
she was ten and he was twelve
and he told everyone all the kids in school
the kind she was and what she let him do
and everyone laughed they all laughed and pointed
and crossed their fingers and cried shame
shame on you and I am laughing too it was so serious
the shame and the way her blue eyes must have looked
and the way they are looking now
when we were young together

I tell her the story of my own first love
how my nerve failed and I failed and kept on doing it
the way some of us fail when anything is very important
fail to dodge the snowflakes dodge the rain
fail to escape the town houses and grocery stores
if hell bars the way we fail to keep on coming
fail to realize how valuable we are
to each other alive in bed but only slightly moving
for we are tired too tired to love each other
and failing to find our way home one evening
fail to know how the story ends

My love stands naked by the telephone
talking to someone who doesn't know
how much he's missing
but I know and knowing burns my throat
for all the moods and times and moons of night and morning
belong to each of her for each of her is a different woman
and I have loved all of them
they are running water under ice and snow like white linen
they are suns rising and setting on the innocence of children
they are little girl manikins dancing on my balls
When one of her has dressed and fixed her hair
checked purse to make sure she has the car keys
then I go down with her to the street
a privileged old retainer anyway not a lover
only a name she thinks of sometimes
sometimes in the snowflakes or the rain
a man walking back to an apartment
tearing off a leaf from the calendar
watering some houseplants.

THE DEATH MASK
(dated before 1200 BC,
therefore too early to be Agamemnon's)

Thin gold pressed against a dead man's face
the tangible
            shaped by shadows
of the intangible and an error
on the draughting board of God
(some god or other)
transferred to a mask
The look of death that is a metal look
where the lines of a smile
of fear that began in life continue
changed into death's unindifference
for the double axe again poised
over scented bathwater and the Furies

gurgling down the drain
If death is like to death it is the bored face
that thrilled to other deaths
the going forth the not returning
and tall grass growing high on other streets
where others walk and meet and gossip
that now are goat-paths on a day
in Athens when the rain-dark hurrying clouds
that drown Apollo in their ragged hearts
and skirt museum walls but can't
douse the red flames of Troy
alight across the face of gold

Athens

ALONG THE IONIAN COAST

White gulls and sponge divers with bloody ears
float still in water along this coast
where old ships went down their captains yelling
"Beach her! Beach the bastard quick!"
or "Great is Diana of the Ephesians!
                    Save us you bitch!"
They drown the green urine takes them
all those ships and dark round-shouldered oarsmen
chained to the bench screaming
hawk-faced captains sinking like the others
hairy bullies and cringing cowards
outnumbered by the good men in between
bodies predestined for death their minds
groping for reasons
with cargoes
            "beads of tawny Baltic
                red Sicilian amber
                    girl slaves
                        for fish to nibble
                            their soft pink toes"

The world itself disappearing in water
crews staring at the tilted stars
their names lost home ports unknown
– in dockyards grey old master shipwrights
mourn the children of their hands and not sailors

Cave dwellers in the night who found or made fire
actually created the tiny flicker of red something
conceived a wheel in their minds that rolled into daylight
and the first moving day from rock cave to mud house
the first beast tied to a tree and milked accidentally

Beyond a hill or forest water that must be
walked around or travelled over by magic
tamed with a word so that a man's mouth
might hold the morning noon and midnight sea
in one gulp of sound
or walked away with to the parched inland
where an image of the bald sea roared in skulls
borne into time by generations of children
who knew nothing of the sea

Below dark headlands of racial memory
the first ships turning fearfully out
from land and single double triple rows of oars eventually
a drum-heart beating time for the oarsmen
a ram pointing its bronze boxing glove at the sea

Was it like that? Not just like that not only
the men and sea and ships and a memory of Icarus
or white legs of the drowned dancing in kelp
also electron and molecule the dance of things
For instance here and now between night and night
in this hotel room I watch how a glass of water climbs
against the momentary horizon and achieves a silhouette
books fall open and dust motes drift almost alive
a wash of sunlight touches and touches not
me held in a frame of the mind's lapsing inattention
and what I think of as myself slows down

I wander the blind beach
to watch sponge divers far out from shore
and how light dances on the yellow sand
the sea we came from dancing
inside me the heart's tides lift

Turkey

FUNERAL

The preacher called beforehand
to make sure God
occupied a place in my heart
or somewhere nearby
I made a mistake
told him the truth
said I wasn't religious
During the funeral chapel sermon
called a eulogy by some
among my mother's friends and relatives
dressed in their black Sunday best
and the smell of sweat and formaldehyde
he preached the evil of unbelievers
clubbed me with clichés
stunned me with Job and Jeremiah
and the sheer surprise of it
pinned me to the chair
The United Church minister
kept hammering away
knowing I was a prisoner
and couldn't escape
because a son must be there
because a son must bear witness
when half his reason for being
vanishes into the earth
and there is no longer
a warm presence behind him

he stands naked
on the needle point of now
before the rushing winds of time

At first it was exhilarating
being so damn furious
drunk and sober simultaneously
atheism seemed glorious
then changed my mind
wanted to be a believer
in order to render aid
and comfort to Satan
Finally some relief
that it took a phony god
to make this bastard possible
then amusement that my immortal soul
was worth only twenty minutes
as the red-faced prick thundered on
for his audience of one
and the dead woman listening

IN THE DREAM OF MYSELF

Father and grandfathers are here
grandmothers and mother
farmers and horsebreakers
tangled in my flesh
who built my strength for a journey
Their old habits with rifle and cradle
their ways of listening
these made me lefthanded
inclined me to baldness at fifty
and gave me their silence

These too await you
spread their fine linen
laid out their best plates for you

expecting your coming
opened the warm rooms and waited
and my being is theirs
Old hunters and farmers and woodsmen
who lived in the bright day
and sowed earth with their bones
alive in me
theirs too is your welcome
brown-haired woman

STARLINGS

The starlings strut jaunty and raucous
with just that little swagger which says to hell with you bud
orioles glow like orange napkins at the world's dinner table
by twos always by twos being lovers
things shine internally and it's spring
everything is all that it is and complete as it is and the sun
just coming up

By contrast:
before I returned to the house this spring
three starlings were trapped
in the shed between wire mesh and door glass
and died there shitting and squawking
their heads projecting inward thru the wire their bodies rotting
and I left them there for I'd have been sick
if I tore them out with pliers
This morning the shed floor was covered with cream-coloured
            maggots
wriggling worms helpless as human babies
having abandoned host bodies of the three starlings
desiccated and part mummified in the shed window
while other sub-microscopic organisms hold high revel
in the corpses and fester onward in the condition which is life

At times it is brought home to one
as viewpoints change according to age and exuberance
this continual process
– as human bodies are shovelled quickly into the ground
decaying soldiers on battlefields glimpsed only briefly
by burial details and cameras   a single maggot crawling from nostrils
evoking casual grunts of horror on television
rioting students die outside chemistry classrooms
guns bark muted and witnesses give brief testimony
then move on elsewhere into a morning more or less like this one

No reason to write a poem
except to say that the morning is bright
your breasts my dear are lovely
and suspended somewhere between birth and decay in
        a single moment
melancholy fuses with wonder   the body stiffens alertly
as if something had been hinted at
– vouchsafed perhaps the word is? – or the realization is
        achievement?
– pinned down by particular words – arrived at like a streetcorner
while the grass grows an eighth of an inch as the maggots converge
like arrows   labels on medicine bottles read backwards   the colour
of thoughts turns grey   bacteria glimmer in the stars' experimental
stations   your breasts are lovely
three dead starlings strut onto the lawn stage jaunty and raucous
and impossible to do without
it is a bright day

A HANDFUL OF EARTH
   to René Lévesque

Proposal:
let us join Quebec
if Quebec won't join us
I don't mind in the least
being governed from Quebec City

by Canadiens instead of Canadians
in fact the fleur-de-lis
              and maple leaf
are only symbols
and our true language
speaks from inside
the land itself

Listen:
you can hear soft wind blowing
among tall fir trees on Vancouver Island
it is the same wind we knew
whispering along Côte des Neiges
on the island of Montreal
when we were lovers and had no money
Once flying in a little Cessna 180
above that great spine of mountains
where a continent attempts the sky
I wondered who owns this land
and knew that no one does
for we are tenants only

Go back a little:
to hip-roofed houses on the Isle d'Orléans
and scattered along the road to Chicoutimi
the remaining few log houses in Ontario
sod huts of sunlit prairie places
dissolved in rain long since
the stones we laid atop of one another
a few of which still stand
those origins
in which children were born
in which we loved and hated
in which we built a place to stand on
and now must tear it down?
– and here I ask all the oldest questions
of myself
the reasons for being alive

the way to spend this gift and thank the giver
but there is no way

I think of the small dapper man
chain-smoking at PQ headquarters
Lévesque
on Avenue Christophe Colomb in Montreal
where we drank coffee together six years past
I say to him now: my place is here
whether Côte des Neiges Avenue Christophe Colomb
Yonge Street Toronto Halifax or Vancouver
this place is where I stand
where all my mistakes were made
when I grew awkwardly and knew what I was
and that is Canadian or Canadien
it doesn't matter which to me

Sod huts break the prairie skyline
then melt in rain
the hip-roofed houses of New France as well
but French no longer
nor are we any longer English
– limestone houses
lean-tos and sheds our fathers built
in which our mothers died
before the forests tumbled down
ghost habitations
only this handful of earth
for a time at least
I have no other place to go

PRINCE EDWARD COUNTY

Words do have smell and taste
these have the taste of apples
brown earth and red tomatoes
as if a juggler had juggled

too many balls of fire
and dropped some of them
a smell and taste and bell sound
in the ear of waves
– not princes

Conservative since the Romans
– altho it's only animals
that are true conservatives
using the same land and water
and air for countless generations
themselves their own ancestors
each their own child
rabbits and groundhog tenants
porcupine leaseholders
and the wide estates of foxes

This is an island and you know
it's like being dressed in lace
as only a woman may be
and not be laughed at
around her neck and throat
the silver dance of coastlines
and bells rung deep in limestone

Animals having no human speech
have not provided names
but named it with their bodies
and the long-ago pine forests
named it with their bodies
and the masts of sailing ships
around the century's turn
named it to the sea
and a bird one springtime
named it bobolink bobolink
even a small unremarkable flower
I saw last April blossoming
that died shortly after

named it for herself
trillium

And we – the latecomers
white skins and brown men
no voice told us to stay
but we did for a lifetime
of now and then forever
the fox and flower and rabbit
and bells rung deep in limestone
– for any who come after
you have heard our names
and the word we made of silence
bobolink and –

MONASTERY OF THE CAVES

Which should I remember?
– 11th century monks in deep caves
mummified to non-edible brown
blobs in glass cases –
or the dog with a crushed paw
outside on the sunlit courtyard?
Not a choice between men and animals –
the darkness seekers the non-Icarians
or one poor beast waiting to be kicked
because he can't run away fast enough
– nothing is quite that simple

Great men unburied here
from shadowy kingdoms
of long-ago Muscovy:
                O Redeemer of Berestovo
                & Yuri Dolgoruky
                founder of ancient Moscow
                you Anthony & you Theodosius
                co-founders of this underground rat-trap

& you Nestor the Chronicler
                entombed in the 11th & 12th centuries
– wouldn't you trade all your greatness
your hope and heavenly ambitions
for a crushed foot in bright sunlight
among the tourists
and another moment of life
before you escape back into darkness?

Kiev

ON REALIZING HE HAS WRITTEN SOME BAD POEMS

I am ashamed of you
my poems
you owe me something more
than you've given recently
my poems
you have forgotten your duty
which is to make me important
your function in this life
to march ahead of me
with fife and drum and skirling pipes
to encourage my own halting steps
my poems
your obligation is to cause people
to look at you and glimpse between your lines
indistinct and ambiguous my own face
enigmatic almost majestic certainly wise
my poems
your responsibility is to lie about me and exaggerate me
allow me to bask in the esteem of a million readers
or a million in one
and so to shine under their focused intense regard
that my fossilized flesh will precede my dying
preclude my loving replace my actual living

(and that other
the jewelled hunchback in my head
seated brooding in a dark bone corner
who will not be placated
by such rewards
he too has ambitions
– different ones –)
my poems
you have betrayed your creator
I would discard you deny you condemn you
and since the life I have given you is not requited
the love I poured forth on you has not brought children
I will abandon you in some gutter blown by the wind
until the long rains beat on you and snow shall blur your meaning
with noon heat night cold on the swaying space ship earth while the
         morning star
shines over your graves
my poems you have failed
but when I have recovered from
this treachery to myself
I shall walk among the hills chanting
and celebrate my own failure
transformed to something else

AFTER RAIN

The world pulses and throbs
bathed in a thick gold glow
the world is a heavy
gold bangle on the universe
burnt brown grass turns live yellow
the shithouse is a green dollhouse
even grey muffin-shaped stones
are throbbing small hearts
across the dark south
lightning semaphores north
Suddenly – say ten seconds

– everything thickens
as if someone had stirred
and mixed in another colour
I am almost what I was
a bored child again
experiencing magic
but that's a lie
I never did experience magic

Now I'm old as Houdini
without any sleight of hand
and know there is nothing
nothing I could possibly need
or want more than is here
only this thick brown-gold glow
turning the tall cedars
into one-dimensional cutouts
the shithouse a gingham highrise
Oh yes one thing more
come to think of it I saw
a blue heron this morning
on the lawn like a fake ornament
but he was blood real
I held my breath and didn't move
and the world stopped shoving
then he stopped being
a work of art and changed
his shape becoming
a bird flying in my mind
Of course there's death
cruelty and corruption
likewise shit in the world
to hell with that
one day at least stands
indomitable as a potato
its light curving
over the roof of the world
a samovar of the sun
enclosing my guest

the great blue heron
including a hunched figure
myself
on some porch steps
between lightning flashes
writing

THE EIGHTIES

THE DEAD POET

I was altered in the placenta
by the dead brother before me
who built a place in the womb
knowing I was coming:
he wrote words on the walls of flesh
painting a woman inside a woman
whispering a faint lullaby
that sings in my blind heart still

The others were lumberjacks
backwoods wrestlers and farmers
their women were meek and mild
nothing of them survives
but an image inside an image
of a cookstove and the kettle boiling
– how else explain myself to myself
where does the song come from?

Now on my wanderings:
at the Alhambra's lyric dazzle
where the Moors built stone poems
a wan white face peering out
– and the shadow in Plato's cave
remembers the small dead one
– at Samarkand in pale blue light
the words came slowly from him
– I recall the music of blood
on the Street of the Silversmiths

Sleep softly spirit of earth
as the days and nights join hands
when everything becomes one thing
wait softly brother
but do not expect it to happen
that great whoop announcing resurrection
expect only a small whisper
of birds nesting and green things growing

and a brief saying of them
and know where the words came from

JOURNEY TO THE SEA

Zig-zag on the switchback road
over mountain country
in alpine clarity
trees have eaten their shadows
and many-fingered cactus
stand like prophets
pointing in all directions
to the Promised Land
Then down to the tropics
in sweatbox heat
and comet-blossoms of flowers
the yellow torch of primavera
a blue one for jacaranda
tents of blue-yellow
as the man-beetle floats down
– floats heavily down
with a pig-squeal of tires
Then a road not on maps
still being built
by prehistoric engineers
I daydream in the heat
of seeing a man waving
a red flag on the road
shouting Turn Back Turn Back
We slosh and dribble
thru thin brown rivers
near half-built bridges
and overturned wheelbarrows
– a crashed airplane at roadside
mashed aluminum bug
the pilot certainly dead
and thinking: how awful to die

reeling down from up there
allotting yourself just seconds
to remember the best things
counting from one to twenty
– eight my love and six my love
and three for yellow primavera
and then forgetting
Washouts and stone slides
where the mountain spared us
by acting a moment before
we came or a moment after
At the world's last corner
a mountain shelf
maybe a thousand feet high
and nothing but space
an empty blue room
– and if there was anywhere
a First Cause
it had hidden itself perfectly
by remaining in plain sight
without intention or design
blue robes and blue sandals
spread out before us
like the altar cloths of heaven
an aching majesty of nothing
while we drink beer

Mexico

ON THE HELLAS EXPRESS

We were two and claimed it
but the compartment could hold six
            – sometimes we saw the other four
            looking in our window
            from the outside corridor
            with tired faces

and pulled the curtain
        hurriedly
All the way from Luxembourg
thru Germany Austria and Yugoslavia
to Greece we guarded that compartment
slept in shifts
left singly to bring back food
crept out at night for air
thru snowy mountain villages
and dark night streets of towns
in Alexander's Macedonia we galumphed
triumphant North Americans
street lights lamp lights starlight
shining on our grey blankets sideways
Of course an officious little official
helped us at the barricades
thinking we might be important
and wanted a good word placed
in a superior ear in Athens
And we chuckled
pleased to be so clever
        – drank tea in Austria
        beer in Germany
        ate our sandwiches
        in Yugoslavia
where Tito's brand of socialism flourished
while those four other people
waited outside
And years later
we are still defending that compartment

BESTIARY

Burro sounds
in early morning
six eight ten syllables of a rusty iron gate
squeaking open and closed

the long guttural word of speaking
that hears itself from outside the burro's body
earth-wail of the burro-soul
and hairy old man's ears lift listening
unheavenly jewsharpgutstretchingmouthfartingmusic
stymies sleep
touching the far rim of being
the solemn lost edge of things
when the first cry was a new thing
that said this is who I am
and to hell with mountains

Mourning doves
roosting in eucalyptus trees
above flaming poinsettia
a throaty non-bird sound
gurgling insomniac sound
that goes whispering back and twists
itself into serpent hiss
old father of lies on his crawling belly
reptilian ancestor without song
goes slumbering back to the great lizards
kin to the lizard
chickadee chirp
in a snake's mouth

Rooster boast
two short and one long syllable
sends blood plummeting skyward
where he can no longer go
and declares in rooster
earth is best earth is best
and heart knows that isn't true
the brag-song is a grief-cry
earth at best is second-best
he mourns the sky the lost sky
with a metal windvane rooster
dodging lightning atop a northern barn
he is sky-lost

the white stovelid a lost glory
poor flightless bird

Dogs
barking and threatening
harassing each other
then into the mob-gabble and out
again emerges one long wavering howl
so close to the man-howl in extremis
self-pitying man-cry
all is lost all is lost
then moving along the scale down down
the dog-soul plaintive and wavering
saying piteously
I am so lonely so one-single
I have so much personality
such tragic grandeur
then frightening himself into seriousness
a disembodied ghost-voice trembling
among red pomegranate and mango trees
calling Father Dog and Grandfather Wolf
all the way back to the Cambrian
and Precambrian when there were no wolves
no housepets
only the still cooling world
earth steaming and boiling
in the ovens of creation

Mexico

D.H. LAWRENCE AT LAKE CHAPALA

Try to simplify your life
you cannot
try to live a new life
and the old one complicates the new

– today's details like sand grains like commas
mind-lost in an immense
garbage heap of yesterday's details
yet I am preoccupied by this phoenix
with moulting tail-feathers:
Lawrence grows small in the midst of all this
– this lost importance this scribble of things
How could you pick him out now
see him from one corner of your eye
scrubbing the tile floor at Zaragoza 4
throbbing with tubercular life
bossing Frieda around on Chapala beaches
and why for gawd's sake do you want to?
answer: for your own sake only

A fly speck seen from fifty miles up
memory dismisses him
he's dead long after his death
fading despite all those once-shining thoughts
disagreeable little prick
a bit anti-Semitic and self-important
– get the hell outa my head
begone take off split get lost et cetera
and finally incredibly I find myself
arguing with him saying:
"Listen you one-fifth Cockney bastard
(I'm anti-Cockney) you're a liar
life is marvellous only
when you're in love
with a woman-echo or your own genius
Murry had you pegged but good
too bad it was him tho he being
only 'one-fifth of a mud-coloured man'
Whaddaya say to that Lawrence whaddaya say?"
Apotheosis takes over
and he says he's like "some horrid hairy God
the Father in a William Blake imagination"
That kinda stops me that really stops me and

he all the time coughing his guts out
where Nobodaddy listens to plasma-gargle
soaking the drainpipes of God

His vehemence fades not at all
among the details random details
that litter the brain's red dung-heap
cover the real earth and mind-place
we hold that is private ourselves
resist knowing we're only details
demand glory require importance
somebody cut the sky's throat when we die
strike up the band rouse the horsemen of God
And Lawrence
no doubt he wanted that too
illusion the endless infusion he lived by
so real when Frieda remembered long after
and tried to repeat them the song
of the senses hymns of the dark gods
she could only stutter the details
to some young interviewer some boy
with steno pad and the best of intentions
stutter the details of Lawrence
and they sounded so mundane and meaningless
sounded so flat and commonplace
the kid gave up Great Literature
and opted for forensic medicine instead
Of course they are flat and commonplace
but not meaningless
– not when you remember the details of Lawrence
and include the glowing question mark he wrote
after every single one
of the million names of God?

Mexico

IN THE GARDEN

Poinsettias blaze red bougainvillaeas burn
the lake is a smooth blue plate
for sun-tongues to lick clean
Once maybe at the very beginning of things
everything was mud-coloured
you could look out and see only grey sand
you could see nothing to send messages
back from it to you
just dirty-coloured seawater
where rain had lashed things in fury
and wind mixed everything up like soft porridge
and only the pole-star shone like a white lever
for gods of the sky to shinny down
on long slender columns of light
and arrive on earth with a cry
Then we had blue and scarlet and silver
then we had vegetable love
whoever was looking for something
dreamed it first of all
then we made a wanting song of sadness
then we made a finding song of joy
when the Moon said "Here I am Sun"
so he was
and went on sailing up there
all night for the first time

It must have been if you were watching
if you could have watched in the morning
a time to stand naked in rain
a time to feel the fingers of warm rain
touching your new human body
and stammer some praise for it
        your thanks – and you had to thank someone
why not the earth?
Thank you earth thank you sea thank you sky
the beginnings of human love
when we said:

these things are dear
they are bought with your life
they are yours for only an instant
they are yours unconditionally
then you must give them away

Mexico

BIRDWATCHING AT THE EQUATOR

The blue-footed booby
stands on her tropic island
in the Galapagos group
stands all day long
shading her eggs from the sun
also protecting her blue feet
from too much ultraviolet
Sometimes the male booby
flaps his wings and dances
to entertain his mate
pointing his toes upward
so they can discuss blueness
which seems to them very beautiful
Their only real enemy
is the piratical frigate bird
floating on great black wings
above the mile-long island
Sometimes the frigate bird
robs them of their fish
whereupon the booby
is wont to say "Friggit"
and catches some more
When night comes all the boobies
sit down at once as if
God had given them a signal
or else one booby says

to the rest "Let's flop boys"
and they do

The blue booby's own capsule
comment about evolution:
if God won't do it for you
do it yourself:
stand up
sit down
make love
have some babies
catch fish
dance sometimes
admire your feet
friggit:
what else is there?

Galapagos Islands

MOSES AT DARWIN STATION

Tortoises
like small boxcars
a baker's dozen of them
one seven hundred pounds
and 160 years old
(call him Moses
predating Darwin's
Voyage of the Beagle)
body a huge strongbox
plundered by 18th-
century seamen for food
but nearly impregnable
for non-human burglars
We're shadows to him
two-legged shadows
ungainly whirlpools

of bifurcated motion
black and white only
in his optic register
the scrawny old-man's neck
motionless buckboard of shell
galumphing *galapago*
exploring silence
investigating the either/
or of persistent rumours
that God exists
or does not
Scratch his long neck
and he suffers me
after 160 years
one can afford
indulgence of shadows
tolerance of transience
Tortoise-*chelonia*
science nomenclature
animal identity
and yet I think
who are they?
despite trite labels
perishable description
vanishing sound-glyphs
who are they?
– would I recognize Moses
in a downtown galaxy
or asteroid hotel room
of neon and strippers
in New York and Vegas
his buckboard shell
traversing 160 years
his ponderous ancestors
hop-stepping ages
reptilian acrobat
one hundred million years
of fence posts of time
a phantom charioteer

called soul or spirit
or even instinct
urging him on forever
We of course are human
but not recognizably so
as long as he was tortoise
in fact confess it:
remembering far ages
when birds and mammals
branched off from reptiles
and therefore those distant
ancestors of old Moses
are unrecognizably
but yet indubitably
my own
It is chastening
it is downright chastening
to have your forefather
barely acknowledge you
when you scratch his neck
but snuff at greenstuff
you proffer cautiously
his pleasantly ugly
face a road map
to your own past

Therefore go back there
following your footprints
a lost time-traveller
when things were beginning:
while comets crash
and ricochet on earth
the *phyla*-families
take evasive action:
one-celled *protozoa*
dodge fire-balls
way back in the Cambrian
worm-*annelid* slips the punch
fish-*chordata* becomes

a clumsy amphibian
and seven-come-eleven
the dice turn snake eyes
tortoise-*chelonia*
does a tricky dance step
and we're on our way
Ol Granpappy Moses
brushes off this nonsense
of uranium clocks
and scientific theories
of continental drifting
glaciation and star-birth
remembering only
the linchpin now
this permanent moment
the same as always
its name is Moses

Galapagos Islands

(Note: *Galapa*go is a Spanish word for tortoise.)

DARWIN'S THEOLOGY?

– stand under the great sky round
      circling these islands
where the absence of a god
leaves a larger vacuum
than a presence could fill
with a presence
sea and sky completely occupied
by the non-existent monster

Galapagos Islands

MOONSPELL

I have forgotten English
in order to talk to pelicans
plunging into tomorrow
disturb the deep reverie
of herons standing
on yesterday's shoreline
find the iguana's secret
name embroidered
on his ruby brain
it is milk
it is moonlight
milk pouring
over the islands
stand in a doorway
listen
I am drowning
in sky milk
and those soft murmurings
of moonlit vertebrae
these deciphered codewords
are spoken names
of island dwellers
they will not be repeated
pour on my bare shoulders
are small extensions
of themselves
as the manta ray bubbles
rising in water
gleams in moonlight
small fish tremble
I know I know
my speech is grunts
squeaks clicks stammers
let go let go
follow the sunken ships
and deep sea creatures
follow the *protozoa*

into that far darkness
another kind of light
leave off this flesh
this voice
these bones
sink down

Galapagos Islands

NEAR TOFINO, VANCOUVER ISLAND

The great auk and passenger pigeon
extinct a hundred years
close relatives of mine
at least compared to Tyrannosaurus
the lizard king whose tyrant head
was fringed with clown's tassels
his dinner-plate eyes
from an old horror movie
postmarked a hundred million years

Now the blue whale lollops
like a neighbouring planet
and orbiting the earth passes
my dirty Ford doubleparked
on the beach illegally
– the great blue whale
soon no doubt to die
five miles out at sea
spouts like a car wash

I stand for hours
to watch the great auks pass
Tyrannosaurus in his swamp
challenging eternal mud
glaciers receding at last
meltwater surging on the Ford

(Save me Save me maiden cries
in colour movies of the brain
I seize her by the hair and climb
high up some Quasimodo stairs
rest safe at last in Notre Dame)

My poor blood relatives
whose fossil bones are found
in limestone strata lying prone
or upright in earth catafalques
as if beseeching time more time
for reaching mammal status
or else descending back to slime
and praying to a lizard god

The man Neanderthal departs
and drives his car along the sand
(with seat belt buckled)
upright a little longer maybe
who loved a little
            thought a little
                    and drank a lot
bequeathed the stars some Latin names
                    which they forgot –

SHOT GLASS MADE FROM A BULL'S HORN
(once owned by Ralph Purdy)

A young ensign set lips to this cup.
I drink from it now. In 1815,
one Francis Gore, Lieutenant-gov.
of Upper Can., gave him his commish.
The cup is dark brown with gold lights.
It's attractive to me for such reasons,
with initials R.P. deeply incised,
and a crude Brit. flag cut in bone.

I presume R.P. was my ancestor,
when George something-or-other was king,
at a time when the French Rev. was
alarming grocers: Ralph went swaggering
into a pub full of joy in himself,
and talked nonsense in some girl's ear:
after the fiasco of 1812,
love was the thing and war a bore.
Here's to you Ralph with good rye,
when kings are quaint and Canada is
a country ending at the beginning,
but love and sex continue thru history:
somewhere a phantom ensign is waving his sword,
and somewhere his backwoods Jerusalem survives:
wholly ridiculous and quite unreal,
where the great trees stand and a stone sun
glares down on settlers in the remote forest:
a mythic country that disbelieves in itself,
but whose citizens yet declare allegiance,
and still feel mortal love and hurtful pain,
and drink to both from a bull's horn . . .

RED FOX ON HIGHWAY 500
(near midnight)

All I saw was the tail of him
the dream fox ahead of me
his rump a red light flashing
in a thousand movie still shots
(callipygous screenland special)
forty feet ahead of me
feet red hammers hammering
light as air on the highway
running from death on the highway
he died or dreamed he did
– his tail a flat red poker
flung straight back toward me

his eyes overtaking his shadow
his tail bisecting the moonlight
he was fox fox fox

It was like a stage play
it was like my childhood nightmares
the guilt-ridden dreams of running
when all the adults chased me
but nobody ever caught me
it was like time had stopped for us
and never begins again
His shadow black as a monster
his shadow a soundless monster
stomping the dark ahead of us
suffering when we suffer
dying when we die

And I saw us running
I watched us doing it
the car the fox the shadow
those other selves for witness
– and I wondered about things
I wondered about all sorts of things
his face and what he looked like
apart from a million foxes
the rest of his breed and kin
and whether his foxy character
glowed in his brain and eye
and about this damn predicament
of having a dozen bodies
like fascinated observers
all of them watching us watching
deep in the moonlight forest
or under the bedclothes loving
or killing another animal
I was really philosophical
it was almost like a poem
and it had to end precisely
at ten minutes after midnight

so that I could drive to Belleville
keep an appointment in Belleville
and never forget a word

So here we are
and here we have been forever
running and running and running
your mate in the nearby forest
wondering where you got to
and failed to keep your appointment
an hour ago in the cedars
the mystery of why things happen
this way and never that way
the reason you kept her waiting
an hour or was it your lifetime
in case you go under the wheels

Of course I stopped
and gates of the moonlight opened
and lightly he stepped inside
– it was silent that kind of silence
when live events are waiting
jammed at the doors of time
frozen in silver moonlight
then leaped into flux again
– he had to keep his appointment
no matter how late it was
and I had to drive to Belleville
both of us had our plans
plans of the utmost importance
for going on living longer
for eating and drinking and sleeping
and maybe loving someone
for killing other animals
for being noble and human
or fox fox fox

THE NURSELOG*

These are my children
these are my grandchildren
they have green hair
their bones grow from my bones
when rain comes they drink the sky
I am their mother and grandmother
I am their past
their memory is my thousand years
of growing and waiting for them

Four hundred rings past
in my body count
there was fire
it touched me and I glowed
with blue fire from the sky
the sky was so close
it hissed and shimmered in me
then rain fell
Three hundred and fifty rings
past there was no rain
for many growing times
but when it came I heard
the forest talking together
How great a time ago
is lost but I remember
long-necked animals eating me
one great-jawed creature eating them
everything consumed everything else
and wondered if living was eating
Then the birds came
but strange birds like reptiles
with broad leathery wings
flapping and crashing through me
they changed to specks of blue
and orange and green and yellow

*When a fallen log in the BC rain forest begins to decay, its trunk becomes a nursery
for hundreds of tiny tree seedlings.

little suns sleeping in me
I remember this in a dream
when we all dreamed
as if I were an old repeated story
once told to me that I retell
And now the little green ones
nesting cleverly in a row
some love the shade and some the sun
another is growing crookedly
but she will straighten given time
one grows more slowly than the others
and has my own special affection
They are so different these small ones
their green hair shines
they lift their bodies high in light
they droop in rain and move in unison
toward some lost remembered place
we came from like a question
like a question and the answer
nobody remembers now
no one can remember . . .

SPINNING
for Colleen Thibaudeau

"Can't see out of my left eye
nothing much happens on the left anyway"
– you have to spin around right quickly
then just catch a glimpse
of coattails leaving the room
(lace doilies on the settee)
light foot rising and disappearing
the last shot fired at Batoche
or maybe it was Duck Lake
– thought I saw someone I knew
and turned faster and faster
said wait for me

it was my grandmother I never knew
before I was born she died
– sometimes I turned fast enough
and nearly caught up with the sun
it bounded like a big red ball
forward and then went backwards
over the mountains somewhere
– thought I saw someone I knew
she was young in an old summer
I tried to remember very carefully
balanced on one foot
and concentrated and concentrated
lightfoot white feet in the long grass
running to meet her lover
I couldn't stop turning then
wait for me wait for me

MAY 23, 1980

        I'd been driving all day
arrived home around 6 p.m.
got something to eat and slept an hour
then I went outside
and you know
– the whole world smells of lilacs
the whole damn world

I have grown old
making lists of things I wanted
to do and other lists
of words I wanted to say
and laughed because of the lists
and forgot most of them
– but there was a time
and there was this girl
this girl with violet eyes
and a lot of other people too

because it was some kind of a party
– but I couldn't think of a way
some immediate plan or method
to bathe in that violet glow
with a feeling of being there too
at the first morning of the world
So I jostled her elbow a little
spilled her drink all over
did it again a couple of times
and you know it worked
it got so she winced
every time she saw me coming
but I did get to talk to her
and she smiled reluctantly
a little cautious because
on the basis of observed behaviour
I might be mad
and then she smiled
– altho I've forgotten her name
it's on one of those lists

I have grown old
but these words remain
tell her for me
because it's very important
tell her for me
there will come one May night
of every year that she's alive
when the whole world smells of lilacs

THE DARKNESS

– particularly in Renfrew County
when I chased that porcupine
from cellar to woodshed
from lawn to road with flashlight
and felt affection for it

that I couldn't explain to myself
but do explain
as if it embodied all the lost
doomed animals crushed to death
on highways or swallowed and eaten
by fiercer animals – by man
Why should one comic beast
like a briar patch on four legs
be anything but that?
Anyway I'd stand there
beside the porch when bugs were gone
with everyone else asleep
looking up at that great ocean
that place where you're able to think
farther than you're able to see
billions of miles – or think you do
for surely observing light from that distance
is having your mind touch its source
having it brush against stars?
– my smallness therefore conversely important
my heart beating across that void
a tiny pump supremely unimportant?
Then I laugh
how ridiculous to invent methods
of deceiving yourself or pretending
you touched the far edge of the cosmos
Only settle yourself on the shore
of this bright sea this glittering enormity
and close your hand on a scrap of it
the darkness the massed nothingness
say I have grabbed some and held on
Surely if that frightened porcupine
could represent all dead animals
then I may allow myself this conceit:
to feel with hands and heart
the black reaches of light-absence
and the whip of comets
pulsing like swift little fish
when lights leap like car headlights

gleaming on wet pavement in the sky
What this comes to is religion
not the conventional stuff
but some lost kind of coherence
I've never found in people
or in myself for that matter
only in the unhurried natural world
where things are uncrowded by things
with distance between animals
star distance between neighbours
when the grouchy irritable universe
fumbles with understanding
and a god's coherence
               Look down on me
spirit of everyplace
guardian beyond the edge of chaos
I may be a slight reminder
of a small tribe that occurred to you
when you were thinking of something else
even tho I am of little importance
and conversely of great importance
I am waiting here
until the dark velvet curtains
are drawn and the scrap of darkness
I clutched in my hand
has changed to light

ARCTIC PLACES

– they are mileposts of old passage
echoes of our hinterlands
plunging name-sounds
of things we felt or dreamed or imagined
this farthest earth
the shuffling roof of clouds
summers beyond our lives
with nothing of ourselves wasted

we used what there was
our bones flow onward
blood breaks and stops –

FATHERS
for Ron Everson

This year I realized my dead father
was sixty when he died and I am sixty
but it's a year like any other year

(The annuals in our garden
are only two months old
just babies in the arms of earth
our perennial peonies are fifteen years
and fifteen years I've watched them rise
in scarlet jets from earth
– their time is earth-time and the sun's)

He was fifty-eight and suddenly
became an unexpected father
with a look on his face in old snapshots
as if he'd never enjoyed himself much
and two years later he was dead

In 1919 the year after the first war
there must have been several times
when the baby face and old serious one
looked at each other like blank coins
a thought registered a look stamped itself
something now forgotten was interchanged

It seems there should be more
something I can put my finger on
when a spark jumps between connections
a flame wavers from bone to bone
– reach out beyond the tangible

to those dark castaways
flesh of my flesh that dies
that touched and held

NEAR PÁTZCUARO

Sun dominates
a glass ball dashing back and forth
in the space between your eyes
It's like a disease you catch
but after exposure to fire-germs
a cure is effected
when the bugs begin to love you
Arriving from the 16th century
dugout canoes with fishermen
and the death-mask of Father Morelos
inside his 132-foot statue
gleams across Lake Pátzcuaro
blessing damn near everything
which includes Indians market women
and near the *farmacia* a dog
with arched back shitting
I have to learn how it is
to be alive here all over again
do as the brown people do
and their don'ts a dance step
I look out from a blind beggar's eyes
and see myself a northern myth
a tall grey gringo illness
and shudder away from me
Driving to Tzintzuntzan
Place of the Hummingbirds
ancient Tarascan capital
I learn how they defeated the Aztecs
in battle by shouting
Tzin-tzun-tzan at them

reducing Tenochtitlán to a whisper
of many hummingbirds' wings

How to be alive again?
Did Father Morelos know
or Bishop Don Vasco de Quiroga
with their transplanted God?
– the flowers with their brilliant
rainbow faces turn
toward the mountain morning
– among the innocent mountains
unnoticed are the guilty ones
where 500 dormant volcanoes shudder
whatever uncertainties there are
expressed in that shudder
– and love which is the inexpressible
turn to me in this place
and from my continual turmoil
grant me some knowledge of myself
and of my residence on earth

MANTIS

As for me: natural things would prevail
shadows would always move like sundials
their black rafters menacing and permanent
after a few centuries you could return
here and still notice ghostly 2 by 4
landmarks of perpetual nothingness

As for her: in her wake permanence is flux
trees fall down shadows rearrange themselves
one thing joins itself to another
flowers whirling in mist are her compass points
and the bees have selected particular blossoms
which become vegetables at her direction

Unresistant I am manipulated
as an object placed or displaced
I cannot say no or yes only stand
thinking I have stood here a few moments
only where she has moved the shadows
into more symmetrical arrangements
and shortly no doubt will be dissatisfied
I shall be asked to stand thus and so
to enable the fulfilment of her purposes

I am sideways-on to the big events
mushroom clouds rise and are swept away
by high upper winds circling the world
and lying in bed enclosed by no light
I hear the plop and again plop of apples
falling outside from the over-ripe tree
and think to ask when she awakes
how she will dispose of those sounds
and hear my own small whisper not
of protest but some latent curiosity
in the disposable darkness
where I await my discoverer

ORPHEUS IN LIMBO

If you arrive late, don't worry,
I'll still be there. If you don't come at all,
I won't gnash my teeth in blind fury,
no blood or formaldehyde rush to my head.
But it'd be nice to think of you now, hovering
then over raw earth and dirtying your shoes.
Understand, you needn't mourn, howl or sing
a sentimental dirge about true love lost.
I don't require it. Only that direct evidence
of feeling for other than lame dogs or wet kittens
be submitted in the interests of authenticity.
I'm told some guarantees are reliable:

GMC and Ford rarely; pet foods sometimes;
Chase & Sanborn coupons are legal tender;
Bell and ITT seldom observe the small print
in contracts: nevertheless send me your soul
(prepaid), if you can get it out of the carton.
Lady, sensitive, intelligent lady,
worried about just about everything,
please be advised of your rights, which are
one only, namely: the right to be afraid,
the only inalienable right we animals have:
to arrive late at the wedding or graveyard,
and not know the difference between
newlyweds and mourners . . .

PILING BLOOD

It was powdered blood
in heavy brown paper bags
supposed to be strong enough
to prevent the stuff from escaping
but didn't

We piled it ten feet high
right to the shed roof
working at Arrow Transfer
on Granville Island
The bags weighed 75 pounds
and you had to stand on two
of the bags to pile the top rows
I was six feet three inches
and needed all of it

I forgot to say
the blood was cattle blood
horses sheep and cows
to be used for fertilizer
the foreman said

It was a matter of some delicacy
to plop the bags down softly
as if you were piling dynamite
if you weren't gentle
the stuff would belly out
from bags in brown clouds
settle on your sweating face
cover hands and arms
enter ears and nose
seep inside pants and shirt
reverting back to liquid blood
and you looked like
you'd been scalped
by a tribe of
particularly unfriendly
Indians and forgot to die

We piled glass as well
it came in wooden crates
two of us hoicking them
off trucks into warehouses
every crate
weighing 200 pounds
By late afternoon
my muscles would twitch and throb
in a death-like rhythm
from hundreds of bags of blood
and hundreds of crates of glass

Then at Burns' slaughterhouse
on East Hastings Street
I got a job part time
shouldering sides of frozen beef
hoisting it from steel hooks
staggering to and from
the refrigerated trucks
and eerie freezing rooms
with breath a white vapour
among the dangling corpses

and the sound of bawling animals
screeched down from an upper floor
with their throats cut
and blood gurgling into special drains
for later retrieval

And the blood smell clung to me
clung to clothes and body
sickly and sweet
and I heard the screams
of dying cattle
and I wrote no poems
there were no poems
to exclude the screams
which boarded the streetcar
and travelled with me
till I reached home
turned on the record player
and faintly
in the last century
heard Beethoven weeping

MENELAUS AND HELEN

> *Was this the face that launched a thousand ships,*
> *And burned the topless towers of Ilium?*
> — Christopher Marlowe

Menelaus, the Bear, King of Sparta,
homeward bound with Helen, his runaway wife,
after the death of Priam's fifty sons
– only Aeneas of all the Trojan princelings
surviving the slaughter. Troy running blood,
the marketplace a horror, the people slaves
– beyond the last screams of dying men,
birdsong – at the far limits of both sounds,
meeting at the edges, high notes and low notes,
water over mossy stones, velvet scraping iron.

Menelaus, the Bear, his ships blown south
by Poseidon's wind, oars broken, men discouraged,
three galleys dismasted, the gods unheeding,
beached for a month on a limestone island near Egypt,
where seals slithered like wet black slugs,
making seal sounds of human melancholy –

At Sparta:
to be a king with servants and advisors bowing
and scraping, some of them too nervous to speak,
then meet a woman and yourself be humbled and speechless –
when I first saw Helen it was some time
before I could again breathe naturally.
Even manslayer Achilles was troubled.
I noticed he held his breath for several
seconds in the same air she breathed,
before it occurred to him to think of death
again, and chariots were guttural in his throat.
I couldn't wait to get her into bed.
But it was disappointing, nothing worked out;
she didn't smile at me, she grinned,
as if I'd been boasting about my manhood,
and been caught short. I almost blushed.
But a king must king it. My body servant,
for instance, kept falling asleep
and forgetting to polish my armour
or wipe gravy stains from the tunic.
Grooms need watching, herdsmen are careless
with all that half-wild flesh they tend.
Entranced by Helen, I hardly noticed.
Then – discipline must be maintained, I said,
and flogged them. I will not say
that I grew tired of Helen, but those blue eyes
in which you think to see the sea and see
emptiness, discontent, see the receding
tides of love, deep slumber of the gods –
Besides, she nagged me. Not with words,
just that blue gaze, an azure stillness,

like the sound you hear inside your ears,
before sleep: I was trapped in deafening stillness.
As for Paris? How could I blame Paris?
Of course I said I did, the mandatory
wronged husband's predictable reaction.
No doubt I did look slightly ridiculous,
and Agamemnon, my dear brother, kept saying that:
Menelaus, he said, I think you enjoy it,
I think you enjoy being made a fool.
That did annoy me. And I could see the snickers
twitch on all the faces but Odysseus' face.
Paris: well, she was bathing when he saw her,
and naked her sex blazed like a sunset.
The grin she had for me, visible in darkness,
no doubt became a daylight smile for Paris.
And that Trojan story that nothing at all happened,
whoever tells it chortles inside their soul.
All the sun-leagues to Troy on open decks
of Paris' pleasure-galley: they fucked.
Or, if you will, made love, they merged the words,
fuck-love, love-fuck: the gods alone
can make distinction between those activities,
one physical and employing the excretory
orifices, the other mystical as miracles.
The lovers, bewitched in a green sea-garden,
so young all birthdays were tomorrow;
the old steersman watching, his scrawny body
reflected in water, a scarecrow for fish.
At any rate, my thoughts of Helen changed.
When Troy burned, and we cut the throats
of anyone who looked at us sideways,
I saw the flames mingle with blue in her eyes,
I saw the eager blue run to join crimson.
She stood aloof, with Paris dead somewhere,
his face hacked into a red horror,
she savouring it, enjoying it, as Achilles did
when dragging Hector's body round the walls.
She was goddess then, death and life,

the power bestowing both. I shivered.
Twenty days. I tell you, twenty days
we stopped on that limestone island,
while seals oinked at us. She complained.
She said Paris wouldn't have permitted this.
She said, kill the seals. I saw red flames
from tall Troy towers and mud-brick houses
flicker in her blue eyes. I hate blue eyes.
What colour are Aphrodite's eyes? Blue?
We slaughtered a few seals to please Helen.
I asked an old man what island this was.
There was trouble with the barbarous language
these Egyptians speak. I thought he said Pharos,
Later I was told it was Pharaoh's island,
and Pharaoh is the king of that country.
I would have asked his pleasure and his aid
as one king to another if I had known.
Wind abated, the sea calmed, we hoped
Poseidon had his mind on something else. And sailed.
Home in Sparta, the grooms were still lazy,
my servants half-asleep in daytime,
thieves made off with twenty head of horses.
We caught them next day; I cut their throats.
Helen looked bored. Nothing had changed.
I kept hearing tales of mermaids on Pharos,
and talk of Proteus, the shape-changer,
who does quickly what men do slowly.
Some said I'd asked him for sailing directions,
and forced an answer. Briefly, all was heroic,
Helen a goddess, poets dreamed their nonsense,
ten years under Trojan walls an instant.
I said the mermaids were seals, Helen human.
Nobody listens. I see the young gardener's gaze
on Helen; his breath stutters and catches; her maid,
dressing her, is almost afraid to touch her.
She is 58 years old, and forgets my name;
she dyes her hair yellow. Her eyes are faded;
shortsighted, she sees me as a vague blur,
complains unendingly of bedroom dampness,

totters the parapets to bother my guardsmen
with questions of when the Greeks will rescue her.

Gods, Gods, you have taken my youth for this,
leaving the memory of roaring Agamemnon,
replicas of Odysseus and myself, bursting into Troy
from the belly of a child's plaything,
the children who were us, and murdered Troy.
It keeps happening:
The burning towers of Troy; Helen's faded eyes;
blurred sights she saw along those walls;
the far-heard cries, a windy roar of chariot wheels;
her complaints: "I can't sleep for all the racket."
And this obscures whatever reality is:
seals changing into mermaids, and Helen
slowly into a caricature of a goddess;
myself with hand that trembles on my sword,
an old man the servants ridicule
behind his back. It is all a kind of sleep:
shadows grow to substance, an old fence post
becomes a crouching warrior, some berry bushes
a distant army on which the helmets glisten –
and no one comes this morning with my breakfast.

AT MYCENAE

The dandelions
send up their white balloons
as they have since early time
over the high stone ruins
above the famous citadel
Perhaps a ploughman down below
stopped his horse in wonderment
and sighed a little
to watch the kings and queens go by
when the floating ghosts of flowers
scribbled birthmarks in the sky

in the hot still noon
their white balloons

Ploughmen of the dust
kings and queens at noon
who touched these walls
and their shadows too
dark parallels
the walls still exhale them
whose thoughts were stone
in the broken ruins

Below the citadel
a plain falls away
on earth so known to them
it must have seemed sometimes
that they could never leave
Lighter than air their thoughts
like small white balloons
touching stone and earth
and the floating clouds
anchored to this place
moored like the dandelions
to our drifting earth
where we cannot leave
and where we cannot stay
are stone and earth and clouds
and flesh for just a day

VOLTAIRE

Travelling home to Cirey
with Madame du Châtelet
over the frozen roads of Europe
at night in March 1737:
a wheel came off the carriage
on Voltaire's side and it turned over

piling everything – baggage
the "divine Émilie" and her maid
atop Voltaire with considerable
objection from the great man
– at the same time the two drivers
tumbled headfirst down the roadway
inventing some new cusswords
and horses haunted by ghosts of predators
stampeded inside their harness

When Voltaire was extricated
and servants worked to restore order
quieting the nervous horses
he began to enjoy himself
Cushions were laid on the winter road
Voltaire and his mistress sat on them
laughing together about the accident
until the carriage was repaired
and appreciating the night sky
One of the servants describes it:
"Not a tree, not a house
disturbed the expanse of the horizon.
M. de Voltaire and Madame
du Châtelet were in ecstasies:
wrapped in furs, they discussed
the nature and orbits of the stars
and their destination in space,
while their teeth chattered.
If only they had had a telescope,
their joy would have been complete."

All over Europe
generals marched their armies
the Inquisition tortured heretics
kings sat uneasily on their thrones
sniffing the wine suspiciously

and babies were waiting to be born
while "divine Émilie" and her lover
laughed on the frozen roads of France

Something ridiculous about it
Voltaire and Émilie on that frozen road
like strange children
with their grown-up servants
– you can peer inside their heads
see the litter of toys and games
among the measuring devices of science
and think "Genius is children"
it lives in far Centaurus
and star clusters beyond cold Orion
and sometimes visits earth
when there is no one home

LOST IN THE BADLANDS

We walk into a wound
a torn gash in the earth
where soft fingers of water
grew claws and raged at stone

Of course we have no business
being here at all
in the grim badlands above the Red
Deer River's flood plain
(a big sign where we entered said NO
TRESPASSING UNLESS ACCOMPANIED BY GUIDE)
walking for exercise at 5:30 p.m.
(or amusement and to fend off boredom)
into these immense vistas of time
toward the Upper Cretaceous period
seventy-five million years ago
locked away from the high flickering
blue sky by two stone walls

a canyon leading downward
into the dinosaurs' graveyard
where a movement or an action
begun in the past
is never completed
but continues now
in nerves of my trembling fingers

No vegetation here
but higher on the walls wispy grasses
cling to rust-coloured sandstone
No wind or sound of voices
only this non-silence
a mirage of screaming sound
or an illusion of silence
as if every animal that ever lived
and died was struggling
trying to get your attention
and all the calcium carbonate
in your bones shuffling
its components uneasily

The books tell you something
with names to grasp at nothing
geology zoology palaeontology
and every metre of strata
above me means a million years
but this dinosaur graveyard
400 feet below flat prairie
has no reality in books
– the mirage screaming is omitted
by a typesetting machine
Some learned apeman
with academic degrees
from a dozen universities
overloads your own primitive
computer with excess information
about continental plates
and the Great Death

at the end of the Cretaceous
when three-quarters of all life
on earth died swiftly or slowly
in fact everything larger
than 20 pounds or so
including dinosaurs
– the academic with the degrees
that man didn't feel a thing
in fact left something out
about how the sun went down at 5:30
p.m. one evening and next morning
the Great Dying began
until nothing of any size remained
but some scampering rodents
a few half-assed mammals
still trying to say something
back there at the end of the Cretaceous

I grab at shaley walls ineffectually
trying to keep my difficult balance
touching a coal seam inches thick
(a compressed ten thousand years?
              – of peat swamps)
with furred or scaled forepaws
while my wife with amazon stride
forges businesslike into the past
I try to glimpse in all this shadowy
chronology a narrow band of iridium
in earth strata: placed there
sixty-five million years ago
when an asteroid six miles wide
exploded onto the earth
and smothering dust circled the sky
killing flora and fauna
with a cloudy fist

All these presumed facts
are in fact only presumed
amount to an immense puzzle

about animal origins
in which I can lose myself
and seem to listen mindlessly
hear dozens of volcanoes
exploding west of here
see the sky black with ashes
no sunlight seeps through
becoming vaguely aware
that one of the fossil animals
is saying something to me
my wife yelling at my ear
"Let's get outa here
climb up into the sunlight"
I resist this move conservatively
expecting to lose the argument
and we climb 50 feet or so
– into a dull grey land
of eroded chalky hills
like Satan's nightmare
into another time of being:
thinking of the great lizards
living near the Bearpaw Sea
stretching from the Arctic
to the present Gulf of Mexico
and how we're crossing and recrossing
the paths of tyrannosaurs
and pterodactyls occupying
the same space they occupied
my body coinciding with theirs
knowing those giant heartbeats
knocking on empty air
living so near to them
that a snap of the fingers
or twist of perspective
would make them visible
clomping bone corridors
joining my thoughts of them
their image taking over
the pictures in my brain

In fact they *are* visible
an aperture in my primitive brain
allows their enormous heads
to peer into the mammal mind
with red reptilian mouths

Westward the red sun
dips on a ragged horizon
and clock time emerges
from the shadowy limbic brain
awareness of gathering darkness
causing definite uneasiness
I yammer in my wife's ear
"How in hell we gonna get outa here?
– it's a hall of mirrors
everything looks the same"
She gives me a look
one of those looks you expect
when she thinks you're silly
"If we get lost in this place
we're gonna stay all night
It's damn near night right now
and past the tourist season
nobody even knows we're here
All the park guides are cuddling
their girl friends in Calgary"
(I wonder if every female dinosaur
ate her husband and therefore
the species became extinct?)
We scramble round buttes and hoodoos
my wife leading the way
and me following meekly fearful
in this grey land of lost time
where everything that ever happened
is eerily still happening
every death and every birth
And that red sun tucked into bed
under the horizon is certainly
the same star that sank west of

the Bearpaw Sea in crimson and gold
In all this maze of conjecture
I mean the simultaneity of things
not the false measurement of clocks
but the instant of the dinosaurs
whose instant I am part of
exploding suns and plunging asteroids
iridium jargon and geologic nonsense
which vanish as the brute face
of man lifts cunning from a ledge
of sandstone to sing inside my bones

Emerging from the past
we reach the dangerous present
a dirt track of tourist road:
a studied lack of expression
on my wife's face as she proceeds
to ignore the frightened stranger
at her side a while longer
to prevent conjugal warfare
as we return slowly together
into the wilds of intimacy

IN THE BEGINNING WAS THE WORD

In the Beginning was not *the Word*
– but a Chirrup.

– D.H. Lawrence

We made our speech from moving water
a sound that seems to ache
when there is no pain
whispering faintly in the heart's darkness
– and listening at still pools in the forest
we saw the strangers and fled in fear
from their floating faces
We made our speech from the wind's voice
singing to earth when the moon sleeps

and in weariness after hunting
the red throat of fire the white tongues of rain
We made it from the sound of food
on little pattering feet running
with terrified eyes in the forest
while we watched in ambush
with wet mouths
We made our speech from all things
weaker than us and the sounds moved
when our tongues moved
as if they were alive and they were alive
and our children played with the sounds
until they remembered silence

We made our speech from the beast's growl
the bird's chirp and dumb thunder muttering
and from the ice-spirit at the glacier's edge
desolate voices of the lost ones calling
And we changed the colours of things
into sounds of themselves
for we were the great imitators
and we spoke the strong words that invented men
and became ourselves
And we painted our dead crimson
in order that the blood should remember
in all their voyaging the place they came from

And after the essence of everything
had exchanged itself for words and became
another being and could even be summoned
from far distance we chanted a spell of names
and we said "Mountain be our friend"
and we said "River guard us from enemies"
And we said what it seemed the gods themselves
might say if we had dreamed them and they
had dreamed us from their high places
and they spoke to us in the forest
from the river and the mountain
and the mouths of the ochre-painted dead

had speech again and the waters
spoke and the silence had words

And our children remembered —

SEAL PEOPLE

The big boss bull *harrumphs*
disapproving ten feet from shore
adolescents are darker
drops of moon-water
enclosed in bright sun-water
make little enthusiastic *oinks*
at the tourist visitors
lolloping back and forth
wild with joy
churning the Humboldt Current to froth
One whiskery juvenile is curious about me
snuffs at my extended hand
wants to know
why I can't join the fun
For a moment
I feel an electric jolt
of adult tenderness
as if the inside organs
of my own body had emerged
and were living separately from me
making hoarse little *oink* sounds
— my lungs float in tropic seas
liver a dark shadow remembering water
and the difficult amphibian drag-race
across forgotten sands
kidneys and heart
bob in the salt sea
and I croon some primitive song
while they call me to join them

When it's time to go
I have not retrieved all of myself
and may never

Galapagos Islands

IGUANA

Hunkered on hands and knees
then collapsing sideways
cheek on stony ground
in order to see close-up:
Tyrannosaurus thirty feet high
looming over my head
about to have me for breakfast
My left eye sees separately
seventy million years in the past
but the right eye sees only
a harmless vegetarian
this spring day in 1980
He regards me benevolently
in fact reminds of my Uncle Wilfred
who chewed plug tobacco
and while reading Tennyson
never missed the spittoon
from a distance of at least
fifty years ago

I am travelling of course in time
expect to encounter relations
maybe a mislaid cousin
I didn't like much anyway
across the lava peninsulas
indentured to Polyphemus
maybe a long-dead brother
I wanted to say goodbye to
or kooky aunts and uncles

and clutch my craziness tightly
for fear I might grow sane

However
back near Darwin Station
the black iguanas gather
and they're actually domestic
a trois or dix ménage
the big one old man God
who bullies his female harem
some basic law of the flesh
requires that he demonstrate
requires in the act of creation
that he demonstrate lizard restraint
A separate species
at evolution's stop-light
silent and unaware
that in Mexico for instance
they're regarded as tasty as chicken
here old man God is a sultan
before man a reptile Jehovah
and before Jehovah – what?

With a modicum of trepidation
I touch his back with my foot
expecting iguana explosions
thunder at Darwin Station
at least the earth to open
and my flesh crawls with the effort
But God just sways his head
sways it up and down up down
irritated at this presumption
What can I be but humble
for the reptile and mammal primate
may never touch each other
without fear of opposites
and I feel sad
knowing I will never understand him
nor the races before and after

the starship's rocket landing
understand nothing but now
balanced in the needle's eye
and the impulse to touch God
is as close as I'll ever come

Galapagos Islands

ADAM AND NO EVE

His name is *Geochelone (elephantopus) abingdoni*
a giant yellow-faced tortoise
the last of his species
(call him Lonesome George)
from Abingdon Island
now coddled and cuddled by keepers
the nursemaid scientists
of Darwin Research Station

They have posted reward money
these scientists
ten thousand dollars
for just one female
of Lonesome George's species
but no female has ever been found
Lonesome George's relatives
brothers and sisters and cousins
stern great aunts and harrumphing uncles
are gone from Abingdon Island
and the world

(Summon the bounty hunters:
is there movement somewhere
among the man-high cactus
with four legs instead of two
and neck like a periscope
wandering the 20th century?

– a clumsy shadow blunders
through laboratory glassware
could that be Great Aunt Martha?
– a sudden splash of light
along the mangrove shoreline
could that be Abingdon Annie?)

Man with his symbol-making brain
has said ten thousand dollars
equals one female
but there are millions and billions
of dollars in pockets and banks
and no tortoises in their vaults
or human pockets and wallets
– in fact make it a billion
dollars for one nubile female
the result is exactly the same

Not again shall mud conceive
or the stars bear witness
and lightning flash over chaos
nor any deity of the flesh
send his small amphibians
scuttling onto land for safety
the amino acids are dissolved
their formulas forgotten
– and whatever love may be
weighed and counted and measured
in books and artistic symbols
one female tortoise (shaped
somewhat like an old shoe)
has taken it with her alone
into the darkness

Galapagos Islands

BIRDS AND BEASTS

On the road to Ameliasburg
whippoorwills from nearby woods
sing the very first thought they had
when they first came out of the egg
surprised at being alive
and killdeers run in charcoal dusk
with sparks from the sun's bonfire
while the great black robes of night
slowly lower and lower
Running in front of the car
swerve swerve go little feet
scoot scoot from carbon breath
and roar roar of the Ford beast
home to your nest

Re the whippoorwill:
rumour has it and I would agree
the song actually resembles "More Still"
in the sense of discreet music criticism
instead of the traditional "Poor Will"
whoever that fellow was anyway
i.e. not at all iambic or trochaic
it is like some most enjoyable grief
like the first tears I never let fall
for the first woman I ever loved
when she went away

Poor Newfoundland poor BC and Alberta
they do not go there
mourn ye rugged Newfoundlanders and Albertans
and mourn ye bereft westcoasters likewise
who never hear the bonfire song
the dusk song the heart song of home
And verily be complacent ye effete easterners
for whom the jewelled guts resound
and pour their sorcery in our ears
jug-jug for dirty ears

Nearby they cry "Sleep Well Sleep Well"
to brothers in the woods
and these reply "We Will We Will"
while the little red bonfire dies
and silence   silence falls

DOG SONG 2

Sooner or later
it all comes thronging back
everything that ever happened to you:
suddenly I find myself singing
and I can't sing worth a damn
which doesn't matter anyway
standing on the stony shoreline
of an arctic island watching icebergs
drifting in white night of Cumberland Sound
like ghost ships of lost explorers
trying to find safe passage
thru the ice trying to get home
and without awareness of doing it
I began to hum deep in my throat
then burst out singing with voice cracking
from fever I'd just recovered from –
the actual song-words didn't matter
but for a moment I was prehistoric man
coming out of his cave at night to howl
from sheer self-importance
because he was a damn good hunter
or because a woman had smiled
And the song said: Hello my friends
Hello my friends because we're friends
let's have a drink while we're alive
And the song said: Let's have a drink
for no reason or any reason
and because there's a time in your life
like bacon frying like stars exploding

and you stand on your hind legs and sing
because you're a dreaming animal
trapped in a human body
After a while there was a little echo
the merest whine and whimper and thread
of sound when a sled dog joined me
then another and another
in solemn sadness with a great undertone
of exaltation from weary arctic miles
they had all travelled together
with balls of ice torturing their feet
and whips biting hairy shoulders
and starvation meals of frozen fish
so hard it was like eating fire
they sang the soul's grief of being trapped
and knowing it inside an animal's body
and the dogs mourned

We stopped and there was silence
but not an empty silence
Jonahsie and Leah stood in their doorway
watching me with a peculiar look
but I grinned at them
while the great floating ice castles
swayed by at the edge of the world –

A TYPICAL DAY IN WINNIPEG

My car has a dead battery
on accounta I left the headlights
on in a parking lot
I look around at all the damn snow
provided wholesale for my discomfort
then start walking down the frozen
road in search of a tow
truck: – no use hitchhiking
there's very little traffic besides

Winnipeggers hate pedestrians
especially when it's 20 below
I take a shortcut across a field
which will save me maybe a mile
– snow is shallow near the road
but farther in the stuff is deep
underneath no doubt
rabbits with Quebec heaters
worms wearing parkas
My feet plunge like a spavined horse
until I'm up to my ass
in snow and wheezing badly
knowing a diet of junk food and beer
has unfitted me for athletic endeavours
I pause to seriously consider
a choice of en avant or backwards
then plough another ten feet panting
thinking: this white stuff is beauty
if you got that kinda mind
which I ain't – beauty is shit
here exemplified and made manifest
The shit-snow is up past my navel
and that's kinda alarming
since my navel is higher than most
It occurs to me I could just sit here
and await rescue by helicopter
or maybe a student from Manitoba U.
could arrive with a dogsled
It also occurs to me that death
would be easy in this situation
which seems quite ludicrous
like drowning in a bathtub
I'm half a mile from the road
snow deep deeper and deepest
(Winnipeggers found frozen every spring
clutching Hawaiian travel folders)
At my age I have no pride
any more about backing out of
a fight or not taking a dare and

rejecting other things of like nature
I turn around to go back
with beauty up to my chest by now
wheezing and coughing
tongue stuck to the roof of
my mouth like a shred of dry leather
my left foot reaching with
difficulty and passing my right
foot and vice versa
in panicky weakness
Well obviously the road is reached again
I revert to the trivial
and there's nobody to complain to
but I complain just the same
start toward that service station
which somebody has likely moved
farther away just to annoy me
grumbling softly to myself in transit
shit-snow   shit-beauty   shit-city
thinking of that dead battery
burnt toast for breakfast this morning
and the wife who wouldn't come
west with me to Winnipeg
because she said I needed to
live alone this ice-age winter
on accounta my bad temper whereas
I am renowned for personal
sweetness which I resolve to
curb and arrive at the service
station fairly unfrozen feeling
somehow ennobled and ready to
argue with the mechanic

VANCOUVER

A state of mind of course this city
some geographic quirk
can sparkle in the sauntering eye
or glimmer grey in sullen heart
reflect the moods of trees
– on certain mornings of such clarity
mountains are seen to have moved
stumped on stone legs to Granville Street
– at the traffic light's first green
rose-red spring salmon migrate
the intersection at Hastings & Main

There have been Kitsilano sunsets
that dodge around the glum hotels
a huge red ten-dimensional face
hangs from the horizon's picture
window and never does descend
                              Surprise Surprise
for every tourist corner turned
discover other suns come trundling
from planetary cradles to join
them at the sea's doorway
and finally merge
in one gigantic rose suspended
from a clock tower in the sky

Less lyrical the fog
– mooing tormented voices
of ships whispering in from the Gulf
at Coal Harbour fishing boats
mutter together in the tide slop
There is a lostness even inside buildings
secretaries peer from office windows
wanting to be safe with their lovers
pedestrians walk with hands outstretched
colour-blind in a kind of sleep
in an invasion of the grey flowers

and after a week or ten days of it
the world becomes Biblical
the god of sextant and astrolabe
haunts ships in the harbour

City of the great trees
metropolis of sawdust
and blackberries growing wild
a million black suns
at False Creek mouth
City at the continent's edge
where everyone was born three
hours younger than the grey East
and sometimes light is so luminescent
the air glows glows internally
and nobody breathes for a moment
City of mountains and sea
I have changed much
in my viewpoints and intolerant attitudes
but some things are unchanging
they deserve your love
the fog and the sea and the mountains
the streets of summer

NAMES
for George Galt

Birthing, begetting and dying
– the great hammers of being,
each one thudding against the skull,
each one obliterating the others –

When it was nearly time to die,
Marcus Flavinius, Centurion of
the Second Cohort, Augusta Legion,
by letter to his cousin, Tertullus,
in Rome, concerning rumours of sellouts,

plots, moneygrubbing, treason there:
"When we left our native soil, Tertullus,
we were told we were going to defend
the sacred rights of the empire and
of the people to whom we bring our
protection and civilization. Please tell
me the rumours I hear of this treachery
at home are not true –" Nevertheless,
observed in the bright glare of history,
the rumours were entirely accurate.

When it was nearly time to die,
Oberleutnant Conrad Schmidt, minor
cog in General Erwin Rommel's Afrika
Korps, dying of shrapnel wounds somewhere
between the Quattara Depression and
a little railway station in the Western
Desert called El Alamein – watching blood
drip from his chest in time with the second
hand of his watch onto dirty gravel,
measuring his remaining life by
its quickly decreasing volume:
remembering
persistent rumours of Jewish death camps,
remembering
a dead friend's opinion that Hitler
was a psychotic monster,
and wondering if he, Conrad Schmidt,
his last years spent in the Panzerarmie,
had wasted his life.

How not to waste your life?
– no reliable information available.
One could mention, in passing:
even the last act of death
provides only a few hints.
Earlier, during that mid-life period
when the senses overwhelm the mind,
and the calendar blossoms days,

and nothing has much urgency,
questions about personal integrity
are often regarded as trivial.
It seems to me these particular names
are synonymous with the question itself,
and remember their names:
Marcus Flavinius, Centurion
of the Augusta Legion;
Conrad Schmidt, Oberleutnant
in the Afrika Korps:
two men about to die,
who spent their last few moments
wondering how they could change things
on the earth they were leaving –

THE BLUE CITY

Of such an intense azure
that it seeps into your bones
providing dull earth
with an upsidedown sky
My wife is still sleeping
tired from the long journey
I have awakened very early
and must let her sleep longer
Her face is turned to one wall
of the strange hotel room
not feeling my own excitement
at being here with blood thrumming
and pulse beating a little faster
at the sheer romance of Asia
She turns over and sighs
while I'm standing at the window
trying to glimpse a camel
outside on awakening streets:
a woman is sweeping cobblestones
with some kind of twig broom

charcoal burning in a brazier
much blue ceramic but no camels
It occurs to me that I will remember
this time for its inbetweenness
removed from the continuity of things
and it's as if I'm a long way off
somewhere else and watching myself
watching a woman in bed sleeping
seeing what I see for the second time
the wished-for camel and burning charcoal
a blue city slowly coming awake
the little pulse in my wife's throat
I will be seeing it a second time
or has that second time arrived?
– My wife awakening not exactly
here nor there and aware of oddness
disoriented she keeps looking at me
brown eyes puzzled for a long moment

Samarkand & Ameliasburg

DOUBLE FOCUS

And Timur again set out for the wars –
At this time (late 14th century),
there was not one man in the known world,
from high Pamirs to the Tien Shan Mountains,
who could say his name without trembling.
Timur then was deep in middle-age,
and looked it;
one foot had been lame from birth;
he wore a drooping Mongolian moustache;
no woman would call him handsome.
It may be that power is attractive,
and certainly fear is a factor,
and it may be that age has compensations:
in any event Bibi Khanum loved him.

The Chinese princess watched him go
(beautiful as a roomful of rainbows)
from the blue city of Samarkand:
a long dusty confused line
of horsemen and baggage animals
straggled toward the mountain passes,
short chunky men with faces like boards,
with oxhide shields and bone crossbows
and a leader who would conquer the world.

In 1977,
in the blue city of Samarkand,
a great stone sarcophagus
where Timur is said to be entombed,
waiting to leap out and conquer some more;
red and yellow portraits of Lenin
and Marx cover walls of buildings,
with the inevitable hammer and sickle,
while fleas hop from dust to dust mote.
Stand in a parking lot,
you can see shuddering heat waves
lift and dance across the steppes,
and more distant still the Tien Shan
Mountains and peaks of the high Pamirs,
where armies died of frostbite.
Nothing you can say or think
means very much:
you stand in a sort of trance
for several minutes,
until the dream-movements of a woman,
hanging out washing in the trembling sun,
shatter colour in your unfocused eye,
domestic as dirt.
And thinking: in all this unwashed savagery,
thank god for women.

Samarkand

Beyond Remembering

GONDWANALAND

(Some 200 million years ago – according to geological
theory – there was only one landmass on earth, the
supercontinent called Pangaea, meaning "single land." Then
a large chunk broke away from Pangaea; it has been named
Gondwanaland. The new Gondwanaland split up and
drifted south and west to become Africa, Australia and
South America. The remaining continent, now called
Laurasia, also broke apart, some of it drifting west to
become North America, the remainder Europe and Asia.)

The planet's basic stone
and what they did with it
those old ones:
– stone as art forms
shaped rearranged caressed worshipped
unknown men hammering stone on stone
common stuff from deep within
                              earth's mantle
at Machu Picchu Sacsahuayman Carnac
artisans of the finite

Earlier still
stone islands grating against stone islands
(Gondwanaland dear lost Gondwanaland
and the worm's birthplace Pangaea
when one world self became many
and earth said to earth Goodbye)
when the birds the coloured birds
cried in their sleep for home
and dinosaurs riding stone galleons westward
an inch a year for centuries
lived and died like sailors

And stone as exterior decoration
sliced naked thru road cuts
of the Appalachians
and Precambrian Shield
grey oatmeal-porridge stuff

crisscross tweedy patterns
stone like pink cooked ham
– or diamond speckled bits of light
twinkling on a party dress
across the millennia
in a bring-the-jubilee summons
to a five-billion-year-old
birthday on a one-room planet

(and perhaps two lovers –
their identity doesn't matter
– but maybe you and I are
those puppets caught up
in earth's divine passion
or mere human rut
hands linked in consecration
eyes trustful of each other
that the spell will last forever
– we join the celebration
while time performs its wonders
its carbon miracles)

Sedimentary rock
where a fallen leaf
prints itself on stone
and dies forever
Organic limestone
when skeletons of marine creatures
drifted down floating down in green gloom
each one turning a little in the water
and seeming to nod to each other
as they passed by
until their bones jostled in tiny mimic strugglings
with other bones at the misty graveyard
on the sea bottom

And fossil stone
in which mineral salts
have replaced animal bones:

far in the future a crew of
skeletons replacing living men
under earth's dying sun
crews of fossil mariners
riding ships of floating stone
without meaning or purpose
for there was never any purpose
and there was never any meaning –

Only that we listened to the birds
or saw how the sun coloured the sky
and were thoughtful in quiet moments
Sometimes in these short lives
when our minds drifted off alone
moving in the space vacated by leaves
to allow sunlight to pass thru
at the wind's soft prompting
there was reasonable content
that we were aware of only afterwards
and clapping our hands together like children
we broke the spell

Cairn on an arctic island
blind shape turned seaward
what sails rise there?

VICTORIA, BC

In a depressed blue mood
the day rain-grey
sky nearly weeping
then seeing masses of rhododendrons
a scarlet jubilee in the blood
the flowers half in startled air
and half their petals fallen
– even the ground is cheered up

DEATH OF DHL

Dec. 1929 to Feb. 6, 1930:
Beau Soleil villa, Bandol, France.
A field of yellow narcissus nearby,
blue glints from the distant sea.
A marmalade cat called Mickey,
for whom Lawrence pretended to be a mouse.
Frieda: "Lawrence was such a convincing mouse!"
Mme. Douillet's mother brought two goldfish,
"Pour amuser Monsieur."
They prospered while Lawrence coughed,
spitting his life into porcelain bowls –
Frieda: "Everything flourishes, plants
and cat and goldfish, why can't you?"
Lawrence: "I want to, I want to,
I wish I could –"
The worst time, just before dawn,
in false dawn fits of coughing.
He had said to her, "Come when the sun
rises." She came every day.
The English medico, Dr. Morland, gave
orders: he must not work, read,
have visitors. Visitors: Pino
Orioli, his publisher from Florence;
Norman Douglas, author of *South Wind*.
Earl Brewster, the American painter
friend, who had accompanied Lawrence
to the Etruscan tombs,
massaged his body every morning
with coconut oil: at this time,
his weight 6 stone (84 pounds).
And he worked with Frieda
on a wool embroidery design,
in chain stitch – probably using
old-fashioned wooden crochet
hooks –: an old Etruscan peasant
with a white beard, dancing,
stepping light among spring flowers,

in time to some invisible flute,
his balls jiggling thru eternity;
a blue duck near the old man's head,
a saucy gold-coloured duck
prancing off on duck errands.
And all this time, the letters,
by train, boat, bicycle, horseback,
crisscrossing on the jet streams,
circling the world –
Feb. 6, 1930: Moved from Beau Soleil
to a TB sanatorium called
Ad Astra in Vence (from sun to stars).
The building resembling a resort hotel
in photograph: stucco, wide balconies,
flat roof with two gable promontories,
on which fancy decorative designs
– sun and full moon perhaps?
Lawrence's room with blue walls and
yellow curtains, a Mediterranean view.
Letter to Maria Huxley:
"I am rather worse here.
It's not a good place
– shan't stay long.
When do you think of coming?"
Work on a review of Eric
Gill's *Art Nonsense*, which
interested him. Frieda:
"Then he got tired of writing,
I persuaded him not to go on."
Sculptor Jo Davidson "made a clay
head of me – made me tired."
Visitors: H.G. Wells, the Aga Khan
("I liked him").
Friends arriving, Aldous
and Maria Huxley, Earl and
Achsah Brewster already there.
Frieda sleeping in a cane chair
in the blue room with yellow curtains,
waking to hear Lorenzo cough,

thin blood spattering,
staining his lips in darkness, a chill
wind veering in from the Mediterranean.
Dr. Morland: "I do not think much
of French sanitoria. He does not
seem to be responding to treatment."
Mar. 1, 1930: moved from Ad Astra
to Villa Robermond in Vence,
in a "shaking taxi" bouncing passengers.
Frieda at bedside, singing to him,
old songs they had often sung together.
Mar. 2 (Sunday), DHL to Frieda:
"Don't leave me, don't go away."
After lunch: "I have a temperature,
I am delirious. Give me the thermometer."
Frieda: "I cried, and he said 'Don't cry!'
Then he said, 'Hold me, hold me,
I don't know where I am,
I don't know where my hands are
– where am I?'"
Doctor injects morphine.
Lawrence: "I am better now, if only
I could sweat, I would be better –
I am better now –"
Frieda: "I held his left ankle
from time to time, it felt so full
of life, all my days I shall
hold his ankle in my hand –"
Shortly thereafter: gaps in breathing.
Breathing stops. The informing principle
absent. Slippers beside the bed,
formed in the shape of living feet.

"For me, the vast marvel is to be
alive. For man, or for flowers or
beast and bird, the supreme triumph
is to be most vividly and perfectly
alive. Whatever the unborn and the dead
may know, they cannot know the beauty,

the marvel of being alive in the flesh.
The dead may look after the afterwards.
But the magnificent here and now of
life in the flesh is ours, and ours alone,
and ours only for a time.
I am part of the sun as my eye
is part of me. That I am part of the earth
my feet know perfectly, and my blood
is part of the sea –"

LAWRENCE'S PICTURES

He is in all of them
some element of him
and so is Frieda
– turn your head away
from that stopped "Flight
Back Into Paradise"
and you know there's a
frenzy of action you can't see:
meanwhile back in Eden
Lorenzo is doing the dishes
Frieda watching
they yammer at each other
then start laughing
and pelt Jehovah with rotten apples
At "The Feast of the Radishes"
in Mexico enormous carved radishes
with red vegetable erections
seem to dominate
but weird white eyes peer
from under male sombreros
lost in their own darkness
and the red-bearded man
who is Lawrence
sitting while the others stand
a motionless centre

Only two lovers in the picture
in their rapt expressions
the red manikins disappear
They are a shining tremble
inside the still caught calm
and do not notice Lawrence
– pouring from their eyes
tiny replicas of themselves
In "Resurrection" Lawrence
is Christ turning toward Frieda
and life from the claws of Mabel Luhan
the nail holes in his hands
are healed but still death
lives in his empty eyes
Turn your own eyes away
and you see two white figures
running down a white road
into white distance
far from the rotting Cross
In "Rape of the Sabine Women"
which Lawrence also called
"A Study of Arses"
it is the furor of motion
writhing marble motion
a reverse William Blakeishness
that remains most prominent
the actual rape
is happening elsewhere
under the luminous bodies
And again Lawrence
or some element of him
turns away from the scene
"sex-in-the-head" abandoned
The man Christ-Lawrence
his hand on the woman's breast
she with her hand over his
in the "Holy Family"
a bemused child watching
unable to imagine feeling

the same way and unknowing
it will come to pass
The shepherd in "Boccaccio Story"
fallen asleep with penis exposed
the timorous nuns with balloon skirts
middle-aged and remotely young
who had forsworn such sights
passing in procession to watch
frightened yet attracted
by this pale glimmer of man
with no missing parts
a sun-bright devil
in their dark heaven

Nakedness in all these pictures
as if the stick figures
in Cro-Magnon cave paintings
suddenly achieved flesh
and the several million years
of yesterday when the human
race went forth unclothed
naked and without shame
had arrived again
whatever men and women had been
re-born
time reversed
and all the dead
with a kind of yearning
popping out naked from their graves
and the green world blossoming

BESTIARY [II]
(ABC of P)

Whoever wrote "Tom O'Bedlam,"
the anonymous, the all-of-us,
enduring the pain of everyman,
perched on a throne in the gutter.

Auden for "Lay Your Sleeping –" et cetera,
who was nevertheless anti-romantic,
a nay-saying man, a quiet torturer,
no spontaneity, decidedly magnificent.

Blake – who knew life's central things:
God, money (glory/power) and love.
Nobody can have all three of them:
Blake made two more than enough.

Byron for "So We'll Go No More –"
the glory of loss, the triumph of sorrow,
at Marathon, at Missolonghi:
no excuse given, none needed.

You, Gaius Valerius Catullus
"– here face down beneath the sun":
an absent friend, lost in the centuries' dust
next door, just stepped out for a minute –

Donne, of course, Dean of St. Paul's.
Just the early stuff. That death portrait,
sitting in his shroud, repels me:
the godless lover is alive and warm.

Homer and his characters struggle for control
in the ancient world of Achilles and Hector,
while Cassandra prophesies bloody hell –
You have to remind yourself now and then
                         this is literature.

Housman: aware of a moment coming
when human face and death's skullface
stare directly at each other,
and listened to what they said beforehand.

Jeffers, who was America's Cassandra.
I don't think he ever wrote of flowers,
but glimpsed another reality: dams broken
high in the mountains; after the bombers,
animals returned; earth grown bright –

Keats, the rejected – but rejection wasn't
so bad when you could soar like he did:
with a sadness so unbelievably poignant,
it escapes books and becomes gladness.

Kipling – still unfashionable:
for certain poems that awake the feeling
of woodsmoke in a simpler world,
and whatever poems do that prose can't.

Lawrence! – not for his blustering
Jesus-propheteering: just some delicacy
that stands on one foot and blushes
like a girl, then sticks out its tongue.

A yea-nay-sayer, the political Neruda,
who loved a mythic America
that never was –: in the blue distance
of Machu Picchu, and condors hovering.

Dylan and his childhood Forest of Arden,
whose life paraphrased his death:
as if there were artificial boundaries
between them, with booze in both places.

Yeats for Maud Gonne,
and those little glittering gay eyes

of the Chinese man: and because of him,
a feeling that greatness still lives.

Star painters, lapidaries, and often
poseurs; craftsmen more than artists;
but sometimes, when we had forgotten,
they remembered where the heart is.

MACHINES

The Roll-edge

A hunchback shape
mounted on rails
with clacking jaws
into which you shoved
the mattress edge
with sharp ice pick
lifting it hard
while the needle stitched
a quarter inch distant
from my soft fingers
All day all day
walking backwards
continually pursued
but never quite caught
by a grey hunchback
that seemed to spit at you
because it was steel
and you were flesh

Nobody would teach me
how to run the thing
maybe they worried
they'd lose their own jobs
I practised at coffee break
punched out at noon

snuck back and studied it
the mystic machine
– and decided later
when I was able to think
calmly about it
that learning was like
wrestling someone
someone beyond me
enormously powerful
who could almost
casually
break my back
You could never win
the best to hope for
was not to lose
and $1.50 an hour

The Tufting Machine

A sliding table
also on rails
which held the mattress
You moved the table
to right then left
at spaced intervals
and a foot-long needle
popped buttons in fabric
like spaceships landing
My difficulty was rhythm
I didn't have it
a graceful hip-swing
precise but careless
like a boxer maybe
facing a hard puncher
the boxer with good left
sticking it in front of him
in the other guy's face
and the puncher's wild swings
just missing his chin

and he gets the decision
not really an award
but more personal

The reasons for doing it
learning the machines
never very clear
apart from money
However
an element of excitement
intermittent boredom
then the testing
a little tingle inside
and dubious splendour
You knew they watched you
workmen and foreman
emperor manager
their blank faces
meeting your blank face
carefully noncommittal
betraying nothing
for $1.50 an hour

The Filler

Quite uninteresting
and without problems
or scarcely any
demanding therefore
your ghostly minimum
and therefore allows you
to re-invent yourself
Besides the filler
was not elemental
like primitive roll-edge
which in a moment of
inattention could
break your bones
nor cerebral

like tufting machine
driving you crazy
but only the expected
fulfilling itself

Long after
it might be observed
by morticians or friends
that at a certain angle
the palm of my right hand
is slightly thickened
from using the ice pick
for those five years
a badge or memento
your average millionaire
would surely notice
of $1.50 an hour

MUSEUM PIECE

This boneyard of the dinosaurs
finds me footsore and tired
of all fleamarket history
that sets such store on paperclips
the toilet bric-à-brac of queens
their bowel movements chronicled
by scared astrologers
But ah the dinosaurs they soar
to fifteen twenty thirty metres
(or Biblical cubits if you prefer):
their body sounds of gurglings
rumblings of ancient indigestion
monstrous mooing love complaints
sunk to soft earthworm murmurs

Stand under these bone shadows
of tons of onetime flesh

and the mind harks back
to their heyday in the late
Cretaceous when the Great Death
came and saith: – "All life is mine"
– the red sun stopped its seeming flight
the planet's moon returned to night
when the shapeless shape no man hath seen
walked abroad in its shroud
and Eden gates went clang
shut with no sound

But ah they soared they Soar
this walled space makes no mock
of those with such enormous
appetites they ate the world
When museum cleaners come here
and leave aside their mops and brooms
to climb up teetery stepladders
with rags to wipe the weeklong dust
from fossil craniums they must
tremble a little no matter what
accident insurance rates are
The mind shuffles its feet to think
of that time: – when diplodocus   tyrannosaurus
and the like trumpeted the sky
65 million years ago:
and it occurs to me that our human ancestors
then were small shrew-like creatures
hiding in holes probably nocturnal
– in that instant notice the cleaners
atop their stepladders have all changed
back into small shrew-like creatures
with tragic eyes

MY COUSIN DON

He fought his way up the Italian boot
with the Can. Army and diarrhoea;
came home with something lost,
the "loss" remained with him always.

There are many things you lose
in a lifetime – family, friends,
the stubborn sense of who you are,
which is like living in an empty house.

We all know that "war is hell"
– it's been mentioned often enough;
but life generally flashes a signal,
some brief hint, the birth of something.

Of course:
there were dying men, mud and rain,
screams, cowardice, bravery,
prisoners shot, rape and desertion,
body and mind gone separate ways.

Back on the farm in apple orchards,
with a wife, who often must have said,
"It's over, all over"
                          – but the guns roared,
awake or asleep it never ended.

He left me one drunken night,
staggering, and I went to help him;
he turned with both fists ready to strike;
I bawled hell out of him for that.

I suppose what he lost, finally,
was trust in anything and everything,
including his wife, including me:
and cows shot guns, birds went bang.

Disaster is gradual like the seasons;
when star shells lighted his brain
I never knew: but his wife was gone,
his parents died; booze remained.

Disaster is also swift as a storm:
he had an affair with his best friend's wife:
she sat where train tracks crossed the farm,
when the train came she was cut in half.

– It was a Toonerville Trolley train,
it ran twice a week from the county seat,
it said "God is Love" on the morning milk run:
it killed her, and the gossip started.

Anyway, Don was thrown from his horse,
landed on his head and died later:
"He might better not have lived at all,"
his sister said, and "What was he alive for?"

Maybe she's right, but it's her opinion.
I remember the small boy:
he had grace, whatever grace is,
in an orchard in Prince Edward County

when we were children together,
and Macs, Spies, Tolman Sweets, Russets
– how they plopped rotten on earth,
with pigs crazy to get at them.

But the farm was acutely uncomfortable,
dank house, stern religious parents,
who made hell almost attractive,
and I kept going there again and again.

It was his grin – not cordial but real
– that greeted my visits: it said I'm Don,
I'm me – in that long-ago April
of the twin-conspirators against God.

I insist there was something, a thing of value.
It survived when death came calling
for my friend on an Italian battlefield:
not noble, not heroic, not beautiful –
It escapes my hammering mind,
eludes any deliberate seeking,
and all I can think of
is apples apples apples . . .

THE BOY ACCUSED OF STEALING

What have we to do with childhood?
– no one lives there any more
our replacements are small foreigners
or little dressed up dwarfs

Whenever I went back there
I had to build the buildings up
and recreate the sun and moon
the boy who stepped in every puddle

Sometimes the Airedale dog I loved
would growl to see me coming
this ghost stranger old dog time
he had no memory of

But it was worse to be ignored
although you knew you were real
but pinched yourself to make sure
and kept saying It's me It's me

My friend accused of stealing
I don't want to speak his name
for there would be shame to him
in my knowing what they were saying

I stand in the slightly amber air
of an old yellowing snapshot
which I hold in one hand
with a scratch on my finger

(I was always scratched and bruised)
and slowly another boy appears
out of the developing fluid
between my thumb and forefinger

– and the moment waited waited
and something emerged from our bodies
it stood between us quietly
a ghost that couldn't exist now

– the ghost of one & one are one
We stand among our desolations
which are like sorrows but worse
an exact foreknowledge of loss

a sorrow like death
except that the full electricity
of mile-wide frothing rivers
rages inside the hurt

(Good and evil will change places
many times in our lives
all the adjustable moralities
all the forgivable selves)

We turned away finally
to go on being children
somewhere else awhile longer
beyond Simmons' Drug Store

Now there are not quite duplicates
of ourselves standing where we stood
who never move and never speak
the shadows of old absolutes

THE STRANGERS

It was nowhere that he came to,
away from a war with wife and children,
ox-drawn wagon, axe and rifle.
His thoughts went only two places,
where he had been, where he was now.
In a pine forest: trees so tall
weather was different at top and bottom.
His brain started to work on it
slowly: impossible to fell a whole
forest and burn slash before winter,
but perhaps enough for a garden patch?
How much sunlight does a man need? –
do crops need? – to achieve a sickly
yellow harvest, but still, to grow?
His eye swept the deep green ocean:
here a lean-to, on slightly higher ground,
built for shelter only, water nearby,
a permanent dwelling place later.
And something in him sighed at the thought
of permanence. Hefting the axe he ventured
among ancient giants – all far older
than himself, father and grandfather trees,
felling them a kind of patricide,
however necessary. Here a rotten trunk,
easy to bring down; one that *looks* weaker,
a hunch only – sliced waist high;
there a trunk the size of a man's body;
he blazed it for later; another selected
to join the condemned; and the rest girdled
for slow dying. And since the afternoon sun
was warmer, openings should point westward,
funnel-shaped, allowing light to fan out
among the stumps, shining on their death.
And then, maybe enough light
for rutabagas, potatoes and suchlike?
Maybe, maybe. Walking back through doomed pines,
where the wagon waited, a mourning wind

high overhead in topmost branches.
As much as possible in the green gloom,
he stepped from light to dark in crisscross
shadows that were in no way ominous,
nor hinted at black and white winter.
Almost lighthearted, misgivings hidden
from himself, summer like a spell, the year
a war ended, happiness nearly impossible,
if such a thing was ever possible,
small content only now and then,
the wagon a wooden star ahead in his mind.
They waited, the youngest crying: his wife
making comforting sounds; oxen uneasy,
cropping sparse grass. Pale-haired woman,
her face scratched from underbrush,
thin from loss of nearly everything,
waited. Sons. Jed solid like his name,
an axe-handle boy. Philip a weak thing,
soon to die, he thought with sadness,
a premonition he hoped was wrong.
The girls unsmiling, impatient of course,
one with a white trillium on her dress,
much wilted now, picked along the way.
These were his entire world, here,
and felt tenderness in himself a weakness,
but forced a smile for them, thinking:
what strength there was, the tough fibre
of survival must reside in himself;
and Jed probably; perhaps his wife.
Her innards had not been well tested,
and would be now. Behind him the forest,
ahead the woman waiting, the crying child.

STORY

Thirty years ago
they got married and had children
lived in a town beside the sea
and waves poured in across the sand
in hills beyond the town wind blowing
and sometimes white ships passed by
out at sea as if in someone else's dream

Whatever happiness may be it touched them
with the high seriousness of lovers
who know they are lucky from watching other people:
whose lives rise and fall in peaks and valleys
like the sea waves' constant rise and fall
elated at nothing much and then depressed
because the novelty wears off
and yesterday was just the same as tomorrow

Of course the lovers had that feeling too
since everyone is aware of it more or less
the desolation of vast wastes of time
the monotony of each action so similar
to the last it seems a continual rehearsal
for some great event that never happens
for which many of us get tired of waiting

But our lovers were more fortunate
because they loved or for other reasons
the high emotional peaks and troughs
of despair were levelled to a slight rise and fall
much like the motion of that white ship at sea
whereby no passenger was in any way aware
of underwater mountains and submarine disasters
reflected in their lives

Then they stopped being lucky
the woman ill with cancer
a terminal illness the disease deadly

whether she was aware of this or not
and probably she was
as others have been for thousands of years
whispering goodbye to whoever loved them

Here I intrude myself
to say this story was told me
by the man who was my friend
who saw how the cancer ate her life
and shrank her body down to half
while he kept his surface feelings under control

He slept upstairs and this one morning
in the story came downstairs
naked to visit his wife
naked because he slept that way
and because all of us are part of nature
came down with a large erection dangling
not really a sexual signal
but indication his equipment was in order
the woman seeing it smiled weakly and said
"Sorry love I can't do much about it"

That's most of the story
of course she died and was buried
and in a fairly short time my friend will die too
but it seems worthwhile mentioning all this
as something one would like to feel as well
– not the gruesome part but the tenderness
of someone before being swept out to sea
who says everything to you in a single phrase

The town they lived in is little different
white ships pass far away in sunlight
there are dances at night sometimes no doubt
and another young couple might lean against the rail
of one of those ships
to gulp fresh air and glance toward the land
where vague lights blur in darkness

wind sweeps over hills beyond the town
waves pour in across the sand
and the ship sails on –

THE SON OF SOMEONE LOVED –

If you loved an entire species
it would be similar but simpler
a kind of gooey peanut butter spread
enveloping all tortoises say
because their faces resembled Hebrew prophets
or all elephants because of phallic envy
or all hippos because they're so alien
to Venus emerging from her television bath
and gaze soulfully at herds of them in a zoo
But to love a single member
of any species is the special human lunacy
recipe for wars and nuclear disaster

In this case isolate
your own feelings of affection
for small endearing habits of hers
then transfer and split that affection
for a surrogate kid
– allowing say 10 points or 12
to him for each charming her-extract
add them all up like Gregor Mendel
divide and subtract the sum
with a computer in your head
and damn the nasturtiums

Tear a rainbow's spectrum apart
separate the moon into favourite phases
Beethoven's Fifth into set pieces
of vest-pocket melody
which examples go to prove
originals are not divisible

Include Bruegel's *Fall of Icarus*
as exception
where such logic is umbilical
the boy drowns like a footnote
(notice also that uncanny turning away
from the event which Auden pointed out)
– while the inventor father Daedalus
returned to the laboratory at Knossos
is falling in love with his new mistress
the variable pitch propeller

The sun does not give birth to daughters
nor moon to other moons˜
– but Beethoven to Beethovens?
and Bruegel to Bruegels?
Anyway it was a mistake
it happened in another country
of witches magicians satyrs undines
a negotiated settlement is contemplated

Here all is ordinary
but the mind-flash remains
sun at zenith moon at apogee
Beethoven Bruegel the works
and morning the very early morning
when flowers open and birds begin to sing
a far country
where lawns are emerald
and from each blade of grass
drops of dew sparkle
that have not yet fallen
(This circumstance is recorded severally
in lieu of earth air fire water
– "formerly believed to constitute
                    all physical matter" –
but non-metaphysically
and certainly non-definitive chemically
somewhere between fire and earth
                    add one more)

CHOICES

Small shrines beside Mexican roads
tiny adobe chapels
or mere piles of stones
with artificial flowers sometimes
scissored from coloured plastic
surmounted by the inevitable cross:
where a farm labourer was struck by a car
where a poor paisano died
some ragged Jesus or dimpled Maria
and their relatives and loved ones
erected these small memorials
Above all they are not ostentatious
wealth has nothing to do with it
even a pyramid of six or seven stones
has the same meaning
as the slightly more elaborate adobe chapels
They mark the sadness and grief of being loved
loved so intensely it is like a flame
as if some clotted choked emotion
hovered tangible in air
even after blood is washed away in rain
which is all the living can give the dead
There are never any names
no indication of identity
but there is never any doubt of love
which is so commonplace and rare
that it must be genuine
as well as part of religious protocol
It makes me wonder about myself
and which should I prefer:
a poet's brief undying fame in words
or this love
that shrieks silently beside the highway?
But there is no choice possible
neither my little whispering words
entombed in books and magazines
nor the shrieking stones

Mexico

IN CABBAGETOWN

On cool nights I would creep
from the Cabbagetown house
on Sackville Street to Riverdale
Zoo with hard-beating heart
entering the monkey cage at 2
a.m. with an orange-bitten moon
over one shoulder and wondering:
"Why should the moon taste good
and to whom?"
                    "You you you"
sang the little primates "But
                Quiet Quiet now
the zooman sleeps in his cage of wood
and the wallpaper stars shine thru"
Then they told me about Africa

After the drunks on Parliament Street
released from Winchester pub
like fleas fled fast to their beds
I came
        to the mountain lion's house
in the high dry country of Colorado
at cloud-hung Nimpkish Lake
when the big firs sang the wind
to a silver slurp on Forbidden Plateau
he nuzzled his mother's hairy dugs
that glowed in the dark glowed in the dark
in his head
        He said
           "Tell me why"
the red lights change to green at Queen
& Bay when there's no one about
                  – no one about?"
I couldn't say
but the zooman slept nearby
at Toronto Crematorium Brown
and Mackenzie slept their dead

thoughts stopped at 3 a.m.
At 3 a.m.
        the clocks struck Three
          – Three they said three times

The woman in bed with shoulder bare
and one breast shone like a moon Mare
I left I came
       to the elephant towns
and grey houses on four legs moved
houses the colour of earth rolled by
while Toronto slept and moaned in sleep
the great trunks held me close
And the herd bull said
         "Tell me of India
tell me of snakes and antelopes
the burning ghats where Ganges shines
I was born here and do not know
Speak about jungle heat
when the tiger's whiskers drip sweat
and the monsoon sighs in Cawnpore night
I can't forget I can't forget
what I have never known"
"Four Four Four Four"
said clocks somewhere

The zooman woke in policeman blue
pointing his sixgun finger at me
"Get Out Get Out" and I
fled back to bed on Sackville Street
in Colorado and Nimpkish Lake
and a wind-sung skein of moon
on the Forbidden Plateau lulled me to sleep
in India and Africa dreaming of
what I can't forget
dreams I have never known –

THE TARAHUMARA WOMEN

West by train from Chihuahua
into dry Mexican mountain country
to Creél
        land of the Tarahumaras
Indians so fleet of foot
they run down the running deer
and cause them to die from exhaustion
which isn't very attractive either
but likely mythical
Anyway there we are
my wife and myself
plus an American family of four
in a tourist panel truck from Creél
to visit the Tarahumaras

        – in a cave
cold and smoky and high-vaulted
nature's slum cathedral
nothing like home-sweet-home
the campfire whispering softly
a bucket of maize bubbling
men somewhere else
three women and two kids
one washing her kid's face
and hands with dirty water
one tending the fire
another trying to sell little dolls
that were almost human

        – I hadn't fully realized
(or so I plead to myself)
the difference in their lives from mine
the absence of pride
the absence of everything
except dirt
        – but I'm thankful
for I did not see in their faces

that look of recognition
making each of us vulnerable to the other
that queer knowing
distinguishing us from other animals
there was just dull acceptance
from which I took no comfort
        when I ran away
        when I was ashamed
My wife had already gone
feeling what I did before I did
but instinctively
whereas I had to think about it
And now months later
troubled that I thought more of myself
and my reactions than I did of them
the Tarahumara women
still waiting to see their expressions
change into contempt
or at least anger
for the gringo who bought nothing
and paid for it

THE USES OF HISTORY

Leaving the dry library
and feeling a need for wetness
I settle myself in the Gatsby Lounge
at the nearby Quinte to partake same
and quaff a flagon or six
My books are laid out on the table
beside beer and ready for serious study
while strippers strip on-stage
and deafening music blares
This noisy cultural environment
does not inhibit my scholarly bent:
I read about the 16th century
Hindu kingdom of Vijayanagar

whose courtesans were so beautiful
that looking deeply into their eyes
caused some men to dance like raindrops
on water and others to howl like dogs
These girls were also "great
musicians, acrobats and dancers, very
quick and nimble in their performances"
Now a blonde stripper of outstanding
endowment explodes on centre stage
I gaze at her bemused but not unmoved
while other patrons watch raptly
and sip my beer in chosen solitude
not unlike Thoreau's at Walden Pond
until she dispenses with G-string
Returning to my studies: Mahommedan
raiders swoop down from the north and
besiege the little kingdom of Vijayanagar
the situation desperate whereupon
the king sends all his courtesans
to encourage his deprived army including
one Verynice whose attractions have come
down to us as six of the seven wonders
of antiquity and who was said to be
endlessly inventive and very expensive
beyond reach of bargain-hunters
Virtue of course triumphed
the Mahommedans fled leaving behind
their own considerable troupe of ladies
these inherited by Vijayanagar
and thought by certain sulky wives
to be too much of a good thing
I am again distracted by events
beyond my control: a brunette stripper
similar to the Venus of Willendorf
springs on-stage with appropriate jiggles
as neoclassic music inspires her art
I note detachedly that her acrobatics
are quite beyond my own abilities
(other patrons go into shock

observing her prodigious measurements)
I abandon my books while Verynice
dances in several contrary directions
at once and I fear dislocations
in the space-time continuum as
femur and ulna tangle with my wishbone
mons Veneris glows weirdly in a black
patch of light on-stage
and when she spreads her legs
standing on her devoted head
I can see thru the opening all
the way back to the 16th century
and into the little kingdom of Vijayanagar

A footnote to my scholarly treatise:
when Verynice died
(mourned by countless admirers)
she left a large fortune
some $100,000 in warm cash
(which in those days was a lotta bread)
including lingam and yoni to a favourite aunt
another slightly worn set as
surrogate to a bereaved customer

At the hotel desk after leaving
the Gatsby Lounge I overhear a now
fully dressed stripper and the manager
discussing financial arrangements and
I am struck by the tenderness in her
blue eyes as she contemplates the
timeless virtues of money
far beyond the borders
of the little kingdom of Vijayanagar

IN THE EARLY CRETACEOUS

They came overnight
a hundred million years ago
the first flowers ever
a new thing under the sun
invented by plants
It must have been around 7 a.m.
when a shrew-like mammal stumbled
out of its dark burrow
and peered nearsightedly
at the first flower with
an expression close to amazement
and decided it wasn't dangerous

In the first few centuries later
flowers began to cover the earth
in springtime they glowed
with gleaming iridescence
not just a tiny bouquet
like the colours on a mallard's neck
before mallards existed
or like god's earmuffs
before Genesis was written
and even tho nobody was there
to analyze it
they nevertheless produced a feeling
you couldn't put a name to
which you could only share
like moonlight on running water
          leaf-talk in the forest
the best things right under your nose
and belonging to everyone

And one of the early inhabitants
a comic-looking duck-billed dinosaur
might have lifted his head
with mouth full of dripping herbage
and muttered Great Scott
or something like it

Triceratops gulped a township
of yellow blossoms
diplodocus sampled blue
for several horizons
and thought it was heavenly
and colour became food

It was not a motionless glory
for colours leaped off the earth
they glowed in the sky
when wind blew great yellow fields
danced undulating in sunlight
hundreds of miles of blue flowers
were dark velvet in starlight
and maybe some unnamed creature
stayed awake all night in the
midst of a thousand miles of colour
just to see what it felt like
to have all the blue-purple there was
explode in his brain
and alter both present and future

But no one will ever know
what it was like
that first time on primordial earth
when bees went mad with pollen fever
and seeds flew away from home
on little drifting white parachutes
without a word to their parents
– no one can ever know
even when someone is given
the gift of a single rose
and behind that one rose
are the ancestors of all roses
and all flowers and all the springtimes
for a hundred million years
of summer and for a moment
in her eyes an echo
of the first tenderness

HOW A DOG FEELS TO BE OLD

In old age he slept
on the Mowat doorstep
near Quinte Bay
and kept farting
waking sometimes to snap
at flies and miss often
visiting female dogs
failed to disturb his reverie

Elmer was ancient
for a dog – nearly fifteen
a black and white spaniel
with long floppy ears
and that look of passionate meditation
in reaching the last extremity
preachers have on the toilet seat

Sirius swung on a black
cobweb overhead
cows mooed discontent
and far-distant younger dogs
berated the moon
when Elmer embarked on Quinte
He swam straight outward
toward a dark shore
several miles away
Angus missed him
and rowed after him
called to him coaxingly
helped him into the boat
He was dead next morning

At the hour of departure
there seems to me little
difference between species
and that's as good a way
to leave as any

(Dylan notwithstanding):
swim straight outward
toward a distant shore
with the dog star overhead
and music on the waters

BIRDS HERE AND NOW

Always the gulls
white sails riding
high rivers of the sky
And one morning a dozen
robin clans at breakfast
on our green lawns
with bronze napkins
tucked under chins
heads cocked in wise looks
enquiring at my window
about human migration
"Why so far from home?"
Noisy starlings
jabbering together in
one-syllable language
aah-sounding only
unable to manage
our ghostly consonants
the little stammerers
at words' beginnings
Absurd pelicans
stand on streetcorners
which in this case
means docks and jetties
In the air they lose
any absurdity
– I think of flying
paintings I think
of heavy iron

sculpture become
weightless

Our bird visitors
most of them in
continual transit
voyageurs and sky
travellers elsewhere:
now is here and tomorrow's
country may be Asia
Patagonia Quintana Roo
place mixed together
with time – earthen-time
both see-thruable
    the same
      not the same
  a jump of the mind
    necessary
       for flying
   humanly impossible
        sadly beyond us
– the bird's blue shadow racing
over the earth and our local
heartbeat matching its wingbeat
    in Australia
      tomorrow's Asia
   yesterday's Europe
     in the blood's imagination only
    otherwise
      flightless

HOMER'S POEM

(There's only a hyphen between me and death)

Listen
– we are about to be born
we are soon to become alive
and fear is always alive
when death is near
Listen
– sounds outside the womb
outside are living sounds
of things alive
and they have names
and say their names aloud
but I remember
I have no name
I cannot remember my own name
Listen
to the name of fear
animal fear
for cattle are being slaughtered
it is a great feast day
and there is loud rejoicing
the sounds come to me
as from a far away river
a thunder among the mountains
Listen
I say to him
my brother beside me
waiting as I am waiting
Listen
I say to him
let us stay here
let us not be born
I am afraid of being born
and then whisper to myself
did I say those words
did I say that I was afraid?
– it was only a fever of darkness

only a shred of a dream
Listen
they are making ready the feast-day
there is excitement in their voices
they are celebrating
and the sizzle of cooking meat
comes to me
like the hissing syllables
of words I do not yet know
and saliva in my mouth
is flooding my name
– my name?
what is my name?
but I am not yet born
I have no name
tell me I say to myself
what is my name?
Listen
but there is nothing to hear
there is nothing outside
and we shall be born
into a world of nothing
a world in which there is
nothing to believe in
nothing to hold to
and I think if there was a choice
I would not be born
but there is no choice
Listen
I have remembered my name
and say it to those others
the others around me
who are also about to be born
although not into life
they are being born into death
I say my name to them
my name is Odysseus
in the city of life

which is the city of death
– my name that you may remember
my name is Odysseus

Truva (Troy), April 17, 1986

PURELY INTERNAL MUSIC

Pelicans
their name
becomes the awkward shape
of themselves on land
– patrolling sky shallows
then transformed to ballet
– changing again
to feather bullets
plunged into water
– and all of these three
beings coalesced to one
enter my skull
in cerebral twilight
and I become
inhabited

The blue heron
with clothespin legs
and inhuman patience
on quivering shorelines
of our blue-green planet
– my species and theirs
studying each other
they unable to believe
in our bifurcated oddness
something flawed
in its creation
by the heron god

short-necked and rejected
thrown out of the nest
in pre-Eden mythology

Fog this morning
the world surreal and I
think isn't the world
always surreal?
Never mind
where are my friends
pelican and blue heron
and I know
and can feel them
they are nesting
in my mind

"– GREAT FLOWERS BAR THE ROADS"
for P.K. Page

The motorist stops
in this fabulous country
amazed
at flowers the size of houses
country manors French chateaux
perfumed air surrounding
faint music
that whispers stay
        – the world transparent
            all its feelings showing

Abandon the car
enter the fleshy environs
of something like a giant ear
that soothes anxieties
with Amazonian calm
and lilt of soft waters
in broken rhythm falling

Another
like a monster heart
and its pervasive sound
joins his own heart sounds
as if someone were dancing
a softshoe dance somewhere
under the earth
as if someone
had taken his hand
in something like their hand
and said gently
"Now you are home"

    "In countries where –"
the line is almost remembered
the thought incomplete
and what happens next?
The motorist stays
his car forgotten
as music lulls
until no returning
is ever possible
and time closes over

Or else he goes
and in the arms of Job and Wife
remembers a little
but never wholly
always incomplete
remains haunted they say
by dreams of such potency
fulfillment and discontent
memory enthralls
he wakes to dream
and dreams himself
       into those inner rooms
          one cannot enter waking . . .

ORCHESTRA

Hairs of dead horses torturing dead wood
– the sound remotely equine
reminds me of a dream classroom
of nightmare urchins their fingernails
all at once scraping a blackboard
I listen and go mad
Pigs in a slaughterhouse
scream in unison
when the knife slits their throats
Every instrument
holds a continuous high note
the flute a bubble of blood
balanced on the flutist's throat
violin shrieking hoarsely
the sound of someone trapped in wood
and can't understand their predicament
– the original cry of unsmelted iron ore
before it became piano wire
heard deep within the earth
yearning to be pure

(In desperation
I mention hoarsely to myself
life is a holding pattern
of molecules gathered together
in social intercourse that
briefly delays but does not arrest
decay)

Occurs a twist in the air
occurs change
various sounds coalesce
the shriek of having a baby
joins with its mother's lullaby
the calm spirit meeting death
dissolves in fear of the unknown
Distastefully

aware that I am holding onto
the seat with very sweaty
hands I leave my numbered place
flash around this universe
like a barn swallow
trying to locate the little grace note
I loved in my graceless youth
borne on the air a bubble
of sound dancing
on a jet of nothing:
and I am a child having his hand held
by mother-melodies
conducted into wonder
knowing that in all my lifetime
I will never be able to exceed this
and will never be here again
on this needlepoint that excludes the world
this dance of raindrops on a sundial
this soul-artery that exists
in no human body
I will never exceed this
this being carried forward with a sound
wide-eyed into nowhere
(since where does not exist
until it becomes the past)
I will never be human again
I will be a kind of spirit-seed
floating on black rivers between planets
waiting to be born

YES AND NO

Yes –: I love the word
and hear its long struggle with no –

> – Brendan Kennelly

NO
in its more dramatic aspects
is the warrior with a sword
besieged atop a staircase
in ten thousand old movies
– the shy scholar with incontrovertible
proof that humanity is cosmic fleas
cursing his lousy detractors
– or the girl flat on her back
spitting at an attacker

Heroic examples:
"No I will not yield"
"No I will not retreat"
et cetera
The word has no easiness about it
there's no pussyfooting around
It is not a friend of anyone
it is no help in bad times
it is a hard thing
but it stands up straight
when it says no it means no

No is not a negative
exercise in rhetoric
and reverse self-glorification
– it clears a little space
in the forest where yes may live
blissfully in positive ignorance

No is not a polite "No ma'am"
nor a servile "Yessir"
no is *#&!+=% and 100 per cent
to hell with you

of a man on his deathbed
surrounded by snivelling priests
and refusing to confess
to anyone but their master

Circumstances of course alter cases
in fact alter words' meanings
and no never did struggle with yes
it was no contest
when I looked in your eyes
there was no semantic play of word-games
in this more important arena
where we drown and swim to shore
and have no selves and discover ourselves
and melt in the silences
and our opposites join
and now and then we are happy

THIS FROM HERODOTUS

After the battle for the pass
                    at Thermopylae
after the sea fight at Salamis
Xerxes and remains of the Persian fleet
fled back to the bridge of ships
(shattered by storms) at the Hellespont
– the Greeks sent thank-offerings
to the Oracle at Delphi
and gathered at the altar of Poseidon

The Greek commanders
from Sparta Athens and the rest
voted on which man of all the heroes
most deserved the prize of valour
"for conduct throughout the campaign"
their votes for both first and second place
Every man there placed his own name

at the top of the list but all agreed
in placing Themistocles of Athens second
he was thus first choice for second place

Themistocles of Athens
acclaimed by all of Greece
returned home where a certain Timodemus
(of whom nothing else is known) envied him
claimed he had earned his honours not
by merit but from the fame of Athens itself

The second-place finisher answered well
                              says Herodotus
but after that fraction of time which is
two thousand five hundred years or so
the hatred and envy of Timodemus is
just as much alive as memory of Themistocles
to the latter's eternal annoyance:
two men linked together in time
unable to distinguish the nuances
between first and second place
in death which has no nuances

ON FIRST LOOKING INTO AVISON'S "NEVERNESS"

Inside this squiggly universe
thinking: it's a gloss on eternity
but does eternity go forward or backward
or is it an ambience?
One does run into such characters
tho: lonesome Adam and no Eve
Leeuwenhoek puttering around
absentmindedly with a dog penis
searching for one-celled organisms
                         (orgasms?)
– the "squinting Dutchman" peering

all night into his crude microscope
yawning beside a fish-smelling canal
with green moss at the margins
rubbing his eyes and his feet
stumbling over a thought in his head
that his one-celled Alpha
precedes Adam – precedes – dare
he think it – maybe God?
And Omega a many-celled
mutation after the last Bomb?
And I – like Avison
– "know the lust of omnipresence"
and "thousands merging lost"
live on in these brain tissues?
But my nonplussed Adam
blurs and becomes anyone
becomes one-celled organism
speeding outward past the traffic
lights at far Centaurus
looking for his lost leader
whom he never knew
                    anyway
a man needs something to believe in

Her Adam brightens
– beyond the settlements of God
with Leeuwenhoek in a spare bedroom
puttering around in an attempt
to examine sin under his new
model guaranteed for life
microscope but can't
find a specimen
in sinless heaven thinking
                         anyway
a man has just got to keep busy

HOME THOUGHTS

The lakes I suppose
are not unusual
except in numbers alone
but if you were able to stand on
a great height wherever you are
able to see all that water at once
it would still be difficult to find words
describing anything but quantity:
anyway it's hard to work up much enthusiasm
for large bodies of water
they tend to just lie there being inert

And our mountains are neither higher
nor more beautiful than the mountains
praised and loved by other nations
Moving from east to west the land
rises in successive giant steps
like prairie billiard tables
where players of sufficient stature
can't be found in the immediate vicinity
These mountains however are comparatively recent
in the geological scale altho what distinction
that confers seems quite dubious
But if mountains may be considered
among a nation's most valued possessions
one could say that we are not poverty-stricken

The rivers too are only rivers
taking as much pleasure in their
progress to the salt sea as foreign rivers
but are mostly in no special hurry
giving the freshwater fish plenty
of time to turn back to their homeland

One hears often the lyrical praise
lavished on other nations by their
fortunate citizens – with hands

laid over their hearts for example
attending stirring renditions of the national
anthem with adjectives piled high
paean after paean attaining hallelujah
their valour in war and steadfast practice
of all the arts especially glorious
Sometimes it seems that people of nations
outside my own country's boundaries are dancing
and shouting in the streets for joy
at their great good fortune in being citizens
of whatever it is they are citizens of –
And at other times it seems we are the only
country in the world whose people
do not dance in the streets very much
but sometimes stand looking at each other
in morning or evening as if to see there
something about their neighbours
overlooked by anthropologists
born of the land itself perhaps
what is quietly human and will remain so
when the dancing has ended

ELEGY FOR A GRANDFATHER [1986]

Well, he died I guess. They said he did.
His wide whalebone hips will make a prehistoric barrow
men of the future may find or maybe not:
where this man's relatives ducked their heads
in real and pretended sorrow
for the dearly beloved gone thank Christ to God,
after a bad century, a tough big-bellied Pharaoh,
with a deck of cards in his pocket and a Presbyterian grin –

Maybe he did die, but the boy didn't understand it;
the man knows now and the scandal never grows old
of a happy lumberjack who lived on rotten whiskey,
and died of sin and Quaker oats age 90 or so.

But all he was was too much for any man to be,
a life so full he couldn't include one more thing,
nor tell the same story twice if he'd wanted to,
and didn't and didn't –

Just the same he's dead. A sticky religious voice
folded his century sideways to get it out of sight,
and lowered him into the ground like someone still alive
who had to be handled very carefully,
even after death he made people nervous:
and earth takes him as it takes more beautiful things:
populations of whole countries,
museums and works of art,
and women with such a glow
it makes their background vanish
                    they vanish too,
and Lesbos' singer in her sunny islands
stopped when the sun went down –

No, my grandfather was decidedly unbeautiful,
260 pounds of scarred slag,
barnraiser and backwoods farmer:
become an old man in a one-room apartment
over a drygoods store,
become anonymous as a dead animal
whose chemicals may not be reconstituted.
There is little doubt that I am the sole
repository of his remains: which consist of
these flashing pictures in my mind,
which I can't bequeath to anyone,
which stop here: juice and flavour
of the old ones, whose blood runs thin
in us: mustard, cayenne, ammonia,
brimstone (trace only above his grave)
                    – a dying soup-stained giant
I will never let go of – not yet.
He scared hell out of me sometimes,
but sometimes I caught myself, fascinated,
overhearing him curse God in my own arteries:

even after death I would never dare
admit to loving him, which he'd despise,
and his ghost haunt the poem forever
(which is an exaggeration of course,
but he liked those) –

FOR STEVE McINTYRE
(1912–1984)

He said I was ignorant
and didn't mince words about it
my deficiency was GREAT BOOKS
– so I read Proust Woolf Cervantes
Dostoyevsky Joyce the works
and they were just as boring
as I'd always suspected
– but one night just before sleep
words were suddenly shining in the dark
like false teeth in a glass of water
like the laughter of Australopithecus
mocking other beasts surrounding his tree
like *Thalassa* for Xenophon and the Greeks
like Joshua's trumpet at Jericho
like sunlight under the bedsheets
with her arms around my neck
And I climbed down from the tree
instructed Darwin's non-evoluted
critters to get lost
delighted in the Black Sea with Xenophon
and the Greek Ten Thousand
and stole the wavetips' green diamonds
for my ballpoint –
All because of Steve McIntyre
a dead man who hears nothing
not *Thalassa* nor Joshua's trumpet
not Australopithecus inventing laughter
nor the tenderness I softly withdraw

from my breast in the form of
words that say *Goodbye*
beyond his hearing –

CAESAR AT TROY

Hunting Pompey over land and sea
Caesar stopped there
with his legions
wandering the city ruins
scarcely knowing why
he wasted his middleaged time
but something inside him
that had nothing to do with time
told him it was necessary
The ruins made rough walking
and another Roman general
had fired the place
forty seasons past:
brush grown high since
oak thickets and tall grass
thyme and wild mustard
among blackened stones
earth like whole wheat
bread crumbs mixed with blood
Caesar sweating
in light armor
And someone spoke
"This is the famous river
Xanthus – if you look closely
dead men's blood
still colours the water"
Caesar's nerves jumped
he looked and could see no one
"Who spoke?"
The soldiers stared at him blankly
until a centurion finally answered

"Caesar, we heard nothing"
Stumbling over scattered stones
in advance of his men
he heard the voice again
"Caesar, this is the Scaean Gate
where Paris and Helen passed
mourning the Trojan dead"
Thinking: the voice knows my name
what else does it know about me?
He stepped on a patch of grass
among blackened stones
and someone plucked his sleeve
"Here they brought Hector's body
and Andromache wept for him
her tears shine among the dew
but there is little difference
between tears and dew"
The legions watched
wondering what had got into him
the armies of Imperial Rome
halted at a miserable ruined village
near a dried-up river
while their commander stared witlessly
at something no one else could see
Caesar shrugged
and arranged his face
more suitably for a general
He built a turf altar
burned incense
moved his lips as if in prayer
to gods whose existence
he sometimes considered doubtful
and to ghosts who were
according to reliable testimony
indubitably real
and could speak in tongues
even lay hands on Caesar
which no creature of flesh would dare
without a private invitation

Being a thoughtful man
it occurred to him
standing in the burned ruins
among such veritable proofs
of human mortality
– it occurred to Caesar
that apart from defunct heroes
those nameless ordinary men
who loved and shed their blood
in equal quantity as heroes
and kept their mouths shut
about it – that very probably
their dead bodies supplied
a majority of material
for this turf altar
that kept smoking
and even the dry earth
he was standing on
And sighed thinking
it was not a time for thinking
called in his tribunes
told them his mind
and started off for Egypt
A man with some delicacy
of thought and fastidious habit
and yet a murderer
although more interesting than some
– contemplating mode and method of killing
but able to think
of several other things as well
then returning singlemindedly
to the troublesome matter of Pompey
– like a hound perhaps
nose down on the scent

Truva (Troy)

THE SMELL OF ROTTEN EGGS

The cancer had taken both breasts
and I got the strange impression
that what was left of her
was not really sentient
and wherever cancerous breasts get thrown
two of them mourned their lost body

One almost expected to see
death actually arrive
dressed in sombre medieval garb
or cap and bells like the king's fool
dancing and capering
But there is nothing in books
to match this savagery
the scene in which we are both audience
and players dredged up from a child's
nightmares to achieve instant reality:
on the leading actor's face the clenched rictus
of a slightly amused grin

(You cannot find anything here
in your mind or the hospital room
to make things less unpleasant for you
and must retreat into total selfishness
to avoid suddenly seeing yourself in bed
with the woman's corpse and fucking it)

A survivor of World War I
once told me that before mustard gas
attacks and the creeping yellow clouds
joined you in muddy trenches
there was always the odour of rotten eggs
and death was made *smellable*
before you soaked a handkerchief in piss
and clapped it over your nose
if you didn't have a gas mask
And I smell death in this cancerous room

and clap both hands over my mouth
and start running

I have always tried to avoid unpleasant things
bad smells – death – physical pain
and never been able to
flowers stink beauty rots gods die
we can hardly seize one good instant
of sunlight for ourselves and hold onto it
in our minds before it turns monster
It is no panacea
to describe these various aspects of horror
and no help to name the names of things
nevertheless I name names

PRE-MORTEM

A poem can have a soul
just as a man can
the man's soul of course is unknowable
the poem's soul may be known obliquely
(like the clotted darkness
in the centre of a forest
is the forest soul
whose existence is investigated
nightly by sharp moonlight
swords slicing tatters of shadows)
The poem also ushers the writer
into the presence of cathedrals
mountains rivers continental plates
earth's mantle and the serious
nature of laughter on arrival
at the last days of a man's life
Once said the dying man
"I have never done anything
I was ashamed of –"
while the cancer feeds

and like little lambs in springtime
the heart skips apace
and minor cumulative disorders
make hay at the outer bastions
awaiting the grim reaper
"Virtue" "Merit" "Excellence"
these words replace shame
altho evil must remain in situ
in the poem's beholder eye
and the poem does not condemn
but the writer may

For the dying man
the world's marvellous clichés
fade and revivify
flush into pallor
as the cancer feeds
and like little lambs in springtime
his heart skips apace
A name is spoken in the silence
then only the soul
hears the name which is the poem's
soul and no writer
listens but the poem listens
in a coldness which obtains
at the fire's centre

THE NINETIES

THE PRISON LINES AT LENINGRAD

for Anna Akhmatova

She speaks for them
        – the speechless dead:
the woman in her chill misery
who said, "Could you describe this?"
Akhmatova answering, "Yes."

They led her husband off like a dog,
already emptiness in his heart
– in hers the poems since, a song
that echoes in soundless prison yards.

Number 300 – is she still here,
mourning husband, mourning child?
– the Neva's ice-choked water spares
no swimmer, cannot hear their cries.

The Peterhof in Baltic mist,
and Peter's statue in greenish bronze;
Stalin inside the Kremlin walls
drills unhearing firing squads.

The Tsars arise to cheer themselves,
that's Nicholas who used to wet the bed;
and hand on hip, standing negligently,
a man with ice pick in his head.

Siberia – the name like an anthem,
is requiem for millions dead;
no Mozart here with his last breath
to choir an immense Russian sadness . . .

"Far from your ocean, Leningrad,
I leave my body" – they heard the cry,
those prisoners, their anthem hers:
the dead earth becomes alive.

QUETZAL BIRDS

They exist somewhere between yes and no
that three-foot tail has elements of both
I have not really seen green till now
sea-leaf-emerald dire-jade-jealousy green
so imploded and concentrated one hears
it chunking at the soul's rear window

Only chiefs might wear those tail feathers
not dukes duchesses belted earls
                    just Kings
– in another life on the hot dry plains of Anahuac
I have seen thousands waiting – the commoners
Aztec Mixtec Toltec Mayan unemotional
unquestioning yearning they-know-not-what
faces like scabbards of swords

I knew a guy once would buy a single drop
of perfume worth a trillion bucks
for a girl he knew on the next block
– the quetzal is like that
one glimpse
dipping above the well at Chichen Itza
skimming the sorrowful deserts of Yucatan
and troubled haciendas of Guatemala
this non-Christian-Muslim atheist deity
squeezes the heart

HORSES

– stand beside yourself
your other self
the waiting child
in an imaginary town
and nobody there no one
except the dead

everyone dead
except –

And they'd come
you knew they'd come
out of empty streets
into the sun
my quick steppers my thunder-footed
ones wearing all shades of copper
gold umber satin-covered grey
and black tar babies shining
and me in my plural child's disguise
watching them
in calm sun watching
the wild eye in its rolling heavens

These were the steady cloppers
these were the prancers
going whusp-whusp-whusp all four
feet together like one alone
and I was a witness
in the whispery winter morning
with the shadow beside me
being born over and over
every day outside the warm house
every blink of the eye

Moving to market and slaughter
of ducks and upside-down chickens
in summer the dainty ones
with clover breath
every step a dance step
their feet loved each other
their feet were lovers
before the road was paved
and the great beasts came

(They are of course dog food
and cat feed long since

while the planet cycle
repeats and repeats and vultures over
my head are cancer-stroke-heart disease
but I pay no attention
now is parenthesis
now is going backward)

– and sometimes when I was older
I ran beside them a little
way and they knew they knew
eye blinkers notwithstanding
they knew the small boy
they remembered they remembered
my quick steppers my thunder-footed
ones wearing gold and silver
jewellery brother and sister
to the wind and jingle jingle
in cold weather went the bells
went the years went the child
all the way to the world's edge
all the way home

– and the body-clock ticks on

VOYEUR

Watching "our creek" below the house
(the map shows it but doesn't name it)
this separate slice of wilderness
a green pleat below the pavement
protected salmon-spawning waters
concealed at the city's outer limits
Me an eastern exile
watching the rarity of western snow
and white gets written on quickly
birds scribble signatures
a sleek sea otter from Georgia Strait

swims under the highway culvert
at high tide every morning
– here he is now
romping in from the sea

Farther inland
the creek swirls under two more highways
at Victoria Airport its water-birth
is private and covered over by concrete
a safe distance from runways
and roaring Vancouver arrivals

Under our window
a duck flirts with its water portrait
the otter enjoys being what an otter is
and squirms and rolls over in snow
contorts like a circus performer
unselfconscious
does everything but balance a ball
on its nose and would if he had one
Watching the otter I think of all that joy
in living so rarely seen in people
– downtown faces on Government Street
scrunched with bad temper in snow
people hidden inside their steel boxes
driving home wanting to hurt something

What have we lost
– or did we ever have it?
– the otter's squirming explosion of joy
at being so alive champagne bubbles
pop in his birthday whiskers
But I think: who in his right mind
would want to be an otter?

Upstream
a duck dives for the excellent provender
our creek provides at breakfast
it occurs to me that duck has grown careless

stayed at the same spot too long
and the otter is nowhere in sight
I turn away
remembering the remains of blood banquets
noticed on this tranquil shoreline
a kingfisher watching
a cat from the neighbouring house
turn away while it's still idyllic
make a sandwich for lunch
use the bathroom
watch for blood in the stool

BARN BURNING

Stayed up late
working on a prose piece
around 2 a.m.
when a great light bulged in at the windows
and peered at what I was writing
making it trivial

I drove there
half a mile away
in a kind of anxiety
for I don't know what
maybe fear of the red monster
I parked at a safe distance
while cops prowled around like sleepwalkers
dreaming of arson
with blank expressions
acting like they were needed somewhere else
while the planet burned

It was more than a fire
it was Genesis with a safety match
it was the Destroying Angel with a Bic lighter
– a worm of fear chewed my guts

but I wasn't afraid
it was an exaltation
a shiver at the edge of extinction
a godhead of transience

Meanwhile back at the barn
whiskered whirlwinds climbed the sky
fifty-foot timbers barn-boards steel spikes
and tons of nightmares
became weightless auroras
I stared higher:
the Big Dipper the North Star the
planets dangling like grapes
in a galactic vineyard
and even the home galaxy I'm standing on
all vanished
and words lost their connectives

I suppose it was "important" for me
to keep looking at
everything else diminished
including certainly myself
I went home and slept
and asked my questions in sleep
In the morning words returned
and the sun from a nest of clouds
and little diamonds of dew
sparkled in the pale white light
that filtered into my mind
and the clichés were restful
they made common sense

RED LEAVES

– all over the earth
little fires starting up
especially in Canada
some yellow leaves too
buttercup and dandelion yellow
dancing across the hillside
I say to my wife
"What's the yellowest thing there is?"
"School buses"
a thousand school buses are double-
parked on 401 all at once

I suppose this is the one thing
your average level-headed Martian
or Venusian could not imagine
about Earth:
                    red leaves
and the way humans attach emotion
to one little patch of ground
and continually go back there
in the autumn of our lives
to deal with some of the questions
that have troubled us
on our leapfrog trip thru the Universe
for which there are really no answers
except at this tranquil season
of falling leaves
watching them a kind of jubilation
sometimes mistaken for sadness

ORCHESTRA

They do not know where their bodies are
their flesh has fled
inside the blonde cello
into warm red darkness
of the cherry-coloured violin
– and they are looking for their souls
bent over the crooked instruments
jagged shapes of sound
sheep-gut and horsehair
wire drawn thin as the tingle
of the seeking heart
that says "I want to know you"
See now
they are looking for their souls
and they are outside time
which is to say
their body-clocks have stopped
they have forgotten
wives husbands lovers
the cry of human gender
in one tumescent moment
solemn as eternity's
endless et cetera

None of all this do they know
not consciously
the space between thoughts
expanded to forever
where music is a continuous silence
except for the slight
"ping" sound of the absolute
– and when that other silence
applause begins
bodies are restored
souls unnecessary
doorknobs open doors
manhole covers murmur

buttons enter buttonholes
beasts die at the slaughterers
and the silver hiatus
ends

HERODOTUS OF HALICARNASSUS

This fever in the veins
            this running fire
flickering on the sea
this rumour on the wind
in Ephesus Babylon Persepolis
this whisper in the night
about murdered kings
                – is news?

Belshazzar's overthrow
riding the backs of dolphins
across the sea from Asia
                – is news?

No presses roll
no harried editor snarls
Where? When? Who? How?
                            only
a mild-mannered middle-aged observer
listener rather than talker
quietly deciding what he really thinks
about things other people have
already decided
staring bemused among sleepy herdsmen
near a mountain village at Thurii
wandering the agora at Athens

He fantasizes headlines:
PERICLES IN CROOKED LAND DEAL (No!)
AGAMEMNON A YELLOW COWARD (Very unlikely)
CROESUS CONSULTS DELPHIC ORACLE (True)

XERXES FLOGS HELLESPONT WITH WHIPS
WHEN WATER REFUSES OBEDIENCE
(Informant swears truth of this
on his honour – which may be insufficient)
News of Wars:
Thousands dead on battlefields
Wolves feast on torn bodies
Children die of starvation
The world a desert . . .
Why?

He considers the recent past:
Nicaea   Salamis   Marathon   Thermopylae
Xerxes and the Persians
invading Greece
Headline: WE WIN
(sub-heading)
WE KNOCK HELL OUTA THE PERSIANS
but why – *why* did we win?
Consider some reasons:
– the phalanx?
sterling character of Greek hoplites?
leadership of Leonidas and Themistocles?
But I say the ships
that old man on the docks
muttering to himself
(interview him later)
"Three banks of oars much
superior to double row of oars"
(seems logical)
that doddering old shipwright
who invented triremes
– a new design
paid for with Greek silver
– paid for with death
one always pays for victories

But why Greeks and Persians?
Well now
it's like we got into bad habits

and kept kidnapping each other's women
until someone's husband
got really annoyed
– that might be one Why

A reasonable man
listening to what people say
in the marketplace
at peddlers' stalls
at the docks talking to fishermen
off-shift miners
ploughmen in springtime
taking notes and considering . . .

(For gawd's sake
they're talking about a statue
on the main street
for the old bastard
I mean why?
– that sloppy old man
staring at women's legs
wine-bibber
"old father of lies"
buttonholing everyone
asking the world questions . . .)

Quietly in a vineyard at Thurii
Herodotus
dreams life never ends
– in the Islands of the Blest
of the Western Sea
all his loves waiting
the fair and not so fair
the dark ones with lips like flames
their faces shining on him
their eyes like springs of light
Let it be so!

ON THE FLOOD PLAIN

Midnight:
it's freezing on the lake
and wind whips ice eastward
but most of the water remains open
– and stars visit earth
tumbled about like floating candles
on the black tumulus
then wind extinguishes the silver fire
but more flash down
and even those reflections reflect
on the sides of waves
even the stars' reflections reflect stars

Ice:
far older than earth
primordial as the Big Bang
– cold unmeasured by Celsius and Fahrenheit
quarrelling about it on a Jurassic shingle
– before Pangaea and Gondwanaland
arrive here in the 20th century
born like a baby
under the flashlight beam
Bend down and examine the monster
and freeze for your pains
– tiny oblong crystals
seem to come from nowhere
little transparent piano keys
that go tinkle tinkle tinkle
while the wind screams
– and you feel like some shivering hey
presto god grumbling at his fucked-up weather
hurry indoors hurry indoors to heaven

People have told us we built too near the lake
"The flood plain is dangerous" they said
and no doubt they know more about it than we do
– but here wind pressed down on new-formed ice

trembles it like some just-invented musical instrument
and that shrieking obbligato to winter
sounds like the tension in a stretched worm
when the robin has it hauled halfway out of the lawn
I stand outside
between house and outhouse
feeling my body stiffen in fossilized rigor mortis
and listening
thinking
this is the reason we built on the flood plain
damn right
the seriousness of things beyond your understanding

Whatever I have not discovered and enjoyed
is still waiting for me
and there will be time
but now are these floating stars on the freezing lake
and music fills the darkness
holds me there listening
– it's a matter of separating these instants from others
that have no significance
so that they keep reflecting each other
a way to live and contain eternity
in which the moment is altered and expanded
my consciousness hung like a great silver metronome
suspended between stars
on the dark lake
and time pours itself into my cupped hands shimmering

THE OTHERS

1

We are not alone in the world
our brothers the animals
        our sisters the birds
– at the making day they were late

and the creatures of sea and marsh
remained when We crawled away

With the host on the salt plain's edge
at the giving out of hands
they were chasing each other's tails
or sniffing each other's ass
– when the maker of land and sea
questioned about their souls
there was howling among the trees

When they handed out the blessings
and looked deep in their creatures' eyes
they responded with great unease
and could not meet that gaze

At the naming of things We know
they chirped and hissed and growled
and went with the winds of the world
– when they died their scattered bones
were forbidden the Holy Ground

Ignorant of what they are not
unaware of things that they are
their memory is lost as Eden
their anger the same as fear

   2

To follow a trail through the forest
and not think
        "Have I been here before?"
or remember an odd-shaped stone
that hitchhiked to now with a glacier
from the last Ice Age
a stone reminding them of something else
and triggered a whole series of rememberings
or notice a daisy like the day's eye
déjà vu in the etymological dark

– but how do we *know* that?
Perhaps the caribou with antler antennae
in their hundreds of thousands
have stood on some primordial beach
near Great Bear Lake listening
to music from the Crab Nebula
the debris of a supernova
in a caribou fantasy
– or the arctic wolf searching
his genes all the way back to Genesis
for the Godwolf's terrible face
– at least the deer's soft helpless look
facing death wraps up that moment
for the time when we die ourselves
and the far distant eye from nowhere
peers with instinctive distaste
into our own brief lives

ON THE DEATH OF F.R. SCOTT
(Jan. 31, '85)

The new year continues without him
the Ides of March will pass him by
(no Caesar here important enough for murder)
Easter and its calendar Christ
crucified again on the living-room wall
and all the long hot dog-days
of summer with screaming small boys
tormenting thrilled small girls
pretending boredom
            – he will be absent then

(Now
I hear the customary eulogies
"Invaluable man" – "outstanding accomplishments"
"citizen of the mind's republic"
– but I invented that last one

and feel impatient with myself
because I'm changing from a Scott tribute
the way it started out
and become
another way of saying to myself
"I miss that man")

But the country goes on
content with incompetent leaders
the bland sleepwalkers
                 and glib sellouts of Ottawa
– a man of warm feeling and nobility dies
no flags half-mast on public buildings
citizens remain calm in non-emergencies
for we exist in a special geography
                 of isolation from each other
                         and fear of emotion
prefer to keep a reasonable distance
from one of our number
betraying any signs of intelligence
– but it will not be forgiven us
if a man like this is entirely wasted
another leaf fallen in a maple forest
become humus on the forest floor
and something may grow there

All obsequies are really personal
good taste precludes sackcloth and ashes
but elevators skip the 13th floor
therefore understate the power and glory
delete the Roncarelli case
omit the CCF Manifesto and the like
remember Scott at midnight in North Hatley
when I needed him and his rare
common gift of simple kindness
yes

It will be obvious of course that
I waver between eulogy and the personal

and cannot escape either
and think of Peter Dale Scott
who cannot escape either either
(the father like a hanging judge
the father like a child's idol
            – and such bitterness for both)

At least a dozen Scotts exist
– each a prosecuting attorney somewhere
fighting intolerance anti-Semitism such
blood sports of racists
by which we mark ourselves
as inescapably human
– each a defence witness as well:
include mention of that mysterious
                    phrase "What's right"
all ambiguous crap removed
what's fair and equitable for everyone
What's right?
            Frank Scott knew

I THINK OF JOHN CLARE

When things get miserable for me
and I'm moaning about old age
I think of John Clare escaping
from his madhouse in Epping Forest
tramping home to Northborough
90 miles on the Great North Road
one shoe sole flapping underfoot
gravel inside the other
sleeping anywhere for three nights
no money no food and eating grass
dreaming of his old girlfriend
dead Mary Joyce he didn't know was dead
sick with sunstroke sick with hunger
sick with his own madness

Meeting his wife Patty on the road
she throwing her arms around him
and he pushing her off
not knowing it was Patty of the Vale
believing her a madwoman
– and when I think of all this
I'm a bit ashamed of myself
remembering a rural poet in 1841
John Clare
and his "Meet me in the green glen –"
trudging toward the light

When arthritis is killing me
or a bad hangover
after youth ended with a whimper
I think of D. H. Lawrence
irritated at just about everyone
his reach greater than his grasp
(an 8-inch reach with 6-inch equipment)
escaping from country to country
free from everyone except himself
in search of the sun
spitting a few drops of tubercular
blood in seaports and railway stations
DHL
in a big hurry to know the names of things
in order that his mind might touch
the things themselves
his friends the birds beasts and flowers
– and they have not forgotten him
DHL
turning to look backward
stumbling toward the light

When I'm feeling sorry for myself
(nobody loves me – boo-hoo)
I think of Vincent Van Gogh
searching the faces of the twenty-two
self-portraits he painted in Paris

to discover why all the women
he loved fled in opposite directions
Vincent
searching for the light in Arles
deep in the madness that was his sanity
hauling the moon down with a paintbrush
returning it to the sky transfigured
exploding the stars at St. Rémy
Vincent
with his mutilated ear
hobbling toward the light

I grumble peevishly
(being none of those three)
in the hangover after youth
irritated that I cannot escape myself
irritated in turn at the several
gods and devils with residence inside myself
clamouring for attention
thinking of Clare DHL and Vincent
limping toward the light.

QUESTIONS

What shall we say to Death
you and I
when time is short and breath
scant for you and I?

How can I answer Yes or No
my dear my dear
when we're far away from the cold
but near to each other here?

But what shall we say to Death
when it comes night comes

and there is no cheating it unless
we're blind and deaf and dumb?

What shall we say to Death
with Yes defeated by No
and only the winter of loving left
only the snow?

I have no answer to give you
my dear my dear
only that I *was* always with you
and I am still here

AN ARROGANCE

              – to change the contour
                          of earth itself
bend a small arc of the horizon
to include this unnatural irregularity
a kind of bump
perhaps displeasing to the cultivated eye
I mean build a house
abstract a portion of the sky
place personal boundaries
on nothingness
                  – on nothingness?
– the brain reels and retracts antennae
it's like contemplating eternity or infinity
the mind can't cope
(and no buck-toothed intellectual caveman
in the pause after inventing a skin tent
would tolerate such semantic bullshit either
even before his brain-pan started to fossilize)

              Just the same
when my wife and I built this A-frame
with a pile of second-hand lumber

and used concrete blocks from Belleville
and barn-boards from the country north of –
that's what we did
                    fenced-in the sky
I mean: the sheer grandeur of it!
(it was me what did it God)
a peg on which to hang the ego
while birds and small local animals
apply for new road maps

Occasionally
wandering my rural domain
I notice a hole in the earth
a kind of bump under the horizon
an old house foundation with maybe
rotting timbers old bricks rusty tin cans
and think
                that's what awaits us
it happens to pyramids and mud shanties
and all I can do about it
my small passion for permanence
is to stand outside at night
(conceding probability to the "Big Bang")
in the full rush and flow of worlds
dancing the firefly dance of the universe
stand on my local planet and
neighbourhood galaxy
beside my crumbling little house
inside my treacherous disappearing body
while the dear world vanishes
and say weakly
                I don't like it
                I don't like it

      – to no one who could possibly be listening

FOR MARGARET

We argued about things
whether you should seek experience
or just let it happen to you
(me the former and she the latter)
and the merits of St. Paul
as against his attitude to women
(she admired him despite chauvinism)
But what pitifully few things
we remember about another person:
me sitting at her typewriter
at Elm Cottage in England
and translating her short story
"A Bird in the House" into a radio play
directly from the book manuscript
in just two or three days
(produced by J. Frank Willis
on CBC his last production)
and being so proud of my expertise
Then going away to hunt books
while my wife recuperated
from an operation
Returning to find the play finished
Margaret had taken about three hours
to turn my rough draft
into a playable acting version
fingers like fireflies on the typewriter
and grinning at me delightedly
while my "expertise" went down the drain
And the huge cans of English ale she bought
Jocelyn called "Al-size-ale"
and the people coming over one night
to sing the songs in *The Diviners*
(for which I gave faint praise)
And the books she admired –
Joyce Cary's *The Horse's Mouth*
Alec Guinness as Gulley Jimson a Valkyrie
riding the Thames on a garbage barge

– how Graham Greene knew so much
that she both loved and cussed him
for anticipating her before she got there
and marked up my copy of his essays
These are the lost minutiae
of a person's life
things real enough to be trivia
and trivial enough to have some permanence
because they recur and recur – with small
differences of course – in all our lives
and the poignance finally strikes home
that poignance is ordinary
Anyway how strange to be writing about her
as if she were not here
but somewhere else on earth
– or not on earth
given her religious convictions
Just in case it does happen
I'd like to be there when she meets St. Paul
and watch his expression change
from smugness to slight apprehension
while she considers him as a minor character
in a future celestial non-fiction novel
And this silly irrelevance of mine
is a refusal to think of her dead
(only parenthetically DEAD)
remembering how alive
she lit up the rooms she occupied
like flowers do sometimes and the sun always
in a way visible only to friends
and she had nothing else

LAWRENCE TO LAURENCE

On my workroom wall an original letter
from DHL that reads
            "Dear M,
                    I send you
by this post, registered M.S.,
an article I did on the Indians
and the Bursum Bill" et cetera
I think he used a steel nib pen
and dipped it in ink when dry
and you can see where the nib ran
short of ink and faded the words
in his letter like *"and the"* above
Reading DHL's handwriting hypnotizes
me as Mabel Sterne and Walter Lippman
and Scofield Thayer flit past and are dead
and the New York *World* of the letter
died long ago of financial malnutrition
I read the letter and my hand reaches
for ghost ink that isn't there
just the way he did
and stop to think about this poem
I'm writing (trivial): and from
the other side of the letter
I can see its continuation there
visible thru the Taos NM notepaper:
"from the other side" I say
And this is what obsession does
you read meanings into nothingness
or perhaps into very little
And remember a remark by Margaret Laurence
"I expect to grow old raising
cats and roses –" (but she didn't)
When you dismiss the groping metaphysics
what all this means is a patented
method of jumping from Lawrence
to Laurence and I mourn both
from steel nib pen & ink to cats & roses
Goodbye –

THE WOMAN ON THE SHORE

A music no Heifetz or Paganini knew
it never occurred to them there could be
– at night when man-sounds fade
and shadows pretend to be shadows
the lake is trying to decide about itself
whether it is better to be ice or water
and can't make up its mind
it yearns toward both of them
And little two-inch tubular crystals form
phantoms in the water
– when the merest hint of wind comes
they *sing*
they sing like nothing here on earth
nothing here on earth resembles this
this inhuman yearning for something other
sighing between the planets

On earth
I have manoeuvred myself near them
my face close to the crystal hexagons
kneeling uncomfortably
on this rocky shoreline near Ameliasburg
temperature 32 degrees Fahrenheit
shining my flashlight on them
trying to observe the exact instant
water stops being water
becomes uncertain about what it is
trembling
it shivers and questions itself until
until the ice-amoeba in the world's veins
sings in midnight silence

I can't stand the cold
run back into the house to escape it
you watching at the window
questioning me:
"What happened out there?"

– kneeling on the rocky headland
remembering something left behind
shivering a little in the bedroom
my cold hexagons and your warm flesh
refusing to come together
and the cry of one lost animal
wandering the frozen shoreline
wanting to be everything
and silence
and sleep

SPRINGTIME
(after Housman)

All the springs unite with this one
both the first one and the last
when the birds are winged flowers
and the flowers are singing birds

Every sunup's like a birthday
every sundown promised more
there are candles lit for noonday
and the darkness shines with stars

As for dying – when it's over
there'll be time to make a fuss
– but for now there's love and laughter
and the springtime is for us

YELLOW PRIMAVERA IN MEXICO

Tasting with both your eyes
hearing with all your blood
as if you'd been listening
a very long time in fact

for some hundred million years
when flowers first arrived
in the waste places of earth
the bright trumpets of April
announcing themselves to God

In some misty Cretaceous valley
dinosaurs glopped around
suddenly caught the scent
snuffling stupid not knowing
they had only thirty-five
million more years to live
Mammals chattered excitedly
forgetting opal and vair
of the sun's heraldic birth
then rushed to tell their wives
how intelligent they were
And everyone who was still
undecided about being born
changed their minds fast
and materialized from nothing
as all miracles do

In a cold Cretaceous valley
all that long ago winter
the little hairy mammals
huddled together for warmth
waiting to become human
stared hopelessly at each other
while earth prepared that summer
for an additional miracle
this time a coloured one
as if a child had clapped his hands
for yellow yellow yellow

THE GOSSAMER ENDING

Each generation keeps trying
to explain to the next generation
how terrified we all are
of something that can't be explained
and keep talking and talking around –
as if talking will delay indefinitely
whatever it is we are afraid of

The closest you can get
is that the explanation involves being human
which of itself cannot be adequately explained
except to say that as human beings
having a beginning and middle and end
we are born we live and we die

In the beginning
we don't know where we came from
apart from our most recent ancestors that is
and in the end
after a million years or so of being dust
we don't know where we're going to
only in the middle
do we have some control over things

Walking a tightrope over Niagara Falls say
the beginning middle and end of the rope
are all present simultaneously
except that the middle and end are interchangeable
in that context
                and looking down
instead of my drowned and crushed body
I see a fine mist floating upward
holding in its greyness a faint rainbow
rising from the gorge to meet my ancient dust

In the middle of things my future dust
hears itself make a small cry

and after a million years or so
when your own dust may be listening
the ghost decibels sound their chimes
and a planet of inconceivable heaviness
moves fractionally to make this possible
and a small rain like tears
that can only be imagined by lovers
who do not yet exist
is falling somewhere

OVER THE SIERRA MAESTRAS

Riding the back of a bucking jeep
thru the Sierra Maestra Mountains
holding onto the canvas hoping
we don't leave the earth altogether
and red dust of Cuba
seeps into clothes and hands and faces
– like riding thru an earth sunset
and lights in the dust are people's eyes
Pigs asleep on the road run squealing
chameleon lizards by the roadside
palm-thatched huts in heat haze
and the sea a thin line of blue lace
white-edged perhaps 25 miles away
The jeep driver must be a madman
we just miss a team of oxen
once we nearly hit a truck
our small red cloud and its big sunset
join like dusty diarrhoea
with scarlet Spanish curses
and the jeep blushes

Pilon on the sea coast
dusty small town like a movie set where
man and boy clop past on a Hollywood nag
and hitchposts all over the place

We stand in dust and wait for Gary Cooper
who turns out to be the sugar mill manager
and shows us the damaged buildings
where a sea raider opened up two days
back with shellfire wounding a pig and
hitting a woman in the buttocks with splinters
destroying the sugar warehouse
making a million dollar bonfire
of mountainous slag sugar

       Now a tall gold-
toothed black with a longshoreman's
hook climbs over the slag heaps grinning
and the sun breaks his face into pieces
of light

The road back:
rain falling in the mountains
a hot rain making pockmarks in mooncountry
or it would be except for soaring royal palms
the live smell of red earth rising
to your nostrils like animal urine
decayed flowers and tidal marshes
the not unpleasant smell of Cuba
so rank and fertile you think the jeep
might sprout roots if you ever stopped
if you ever stopped
and your arms are tired rubbery tentacles
holding onto the reeling bucking planet
as the insomniac jeep
plunging thru wheel ruts
takes you back where you came from

Pilon, Cuba

ULYSSES ALONE

No way of knowing where we went
on those long journeys
Sometimes there was a whiteness
as of snow that obscured everything
but it wasn't snow
Sometimes it seemed we left a campfire
and looking for it again
couldn't even find the burned place
blundering into the trees and buildings
but then nothing
has ever confused me as much as light
Sometimes we arrived back separately
but still seemed inside the borders
we crossed by accident
and want to be there if we think it real
but we do not think it real
There is one memory
of you smiling in the darkness
and the smile has shaped the air
                    around your face
someone you met in dream
has dreamed you waking

GROSSE ISLE

> *Look, stranger, at this island now*
> *The leaping light for your delight discovers*
>   – W.H. Auden

Look stranger
a diseased whale in the St. Lawrence
this other island than Auden's
dull grey when the weather is dull grey
and an east wind brings rain
this Appalachian outcrop
a stone ship foundered in the river estuary

now in the care and keeping of Parks Canada
– a silence here like no mainland silence
at Cholera Bay where the dead bodies
awaited high tide and the rough kindness
of waves sweeping them into the dark –

Look stranger
at this other island
weedgrown graves in the three cemeteries
be careful your clothes don't get hooked
by wild raspberry canes and avoid the poison ivy
– here children went mad with cholera fever
and raging with thirst they ran into the river
their parents following a little way
before they died themselves
– and don't stumble over the rusted tricycle
somehow overlooked at the last big cleanup
or perhaps left where it is for the tourists?

Look stranger
where the sea wind sweeps westward
down the estuary
this way the other strangers came
potato-famine Irish and Scotch crofters
refugees from the Highland clearances
and sailing ships waited here
to remove their corpses
and four million immigrants passed through
– now there's talk of a Health Spa and Casino
we could situate our billboard
right under the granite cross by the river:
                 UNLIMITED INVESTMENT OPPORTUNITIES

Look stranger
see your own face reflected in the river
stumble up from the stinking hold
blinded by sunlight and into the leaky dinghy
only half-hearing the sailors taunting you
                 "Shanty Irish! Shanty Irish!"

gulp the freshening wind and pinch yourself
trying to understand if the world is a real place
stumble again and fall when you reach the shore
and bless this poisoned earth
but stranger no longer
for this is home

HOME

Dreaming is living backwards:
in the mind's reverse gear
I ride the same freight trains
I rode long ago in Saskatchewan:

Saskatchewan –
the name produces ripples in the mind
travelling through a lost childhood
and ride those crooning syllables
to where all dreams begin
and climb the sky-steps to Alberta
and BC mountains like stone seeds
sprout alpine flowers
inside my neolithic skull
they jam into the bedroom
I squash them flat
and spread them out
to make a mountain blanket
I wrap around the world

Ontario is trees
the kind that meet from both
sides of the road
and make a continual whisper
and nothing begins or ends
but cities are aberration
do not exist in my mind
are green mirage in the land-sea

in which people drift by
and forget where they were going
Quebec is a long grey sidewalk
going nowhere and people cry out
where is nowhere?
and I don't know what to tell them
In the Maritimes
all those provinces heave and lift
as if there were land-tides
where a girl swims up to me
and demands a fish
I tell her I don't have a fish
sorry
would a jackhammer do?
but I don't have one of those either
and we weep for jackhammers

Back among the crooning syllables
Saskatchewan
the name becomes
quadruplet sisters
I ask them all to marry me
just so their name can mingle with mine
forever and forever yesterday
and Alberta you marry me too
and we'll forget your maternal parent
and live in geographic polygamy
Manitoba you are stern and silent
which is just as well
your winters are spirit-glaciers
Portage & Main is an Ice Age
with a white blossom of frost
decorating the sun's face

On the Pacific I have kidnapped an island
from a rich dog-salmon
and take it home with me
park it beside the bed
and now I dream of islands

in a spring of wild roses
and write another poem
in this enchanted country

NAKED WITH SUMMER IN YOUR MOUTH

Riding the mountain ridges
where the avalanche waits in winter
to spill its full moon torrents
onto the trembling ski trails –

But summer
perched atop the boxcars
hugging myself in morning cold
then drinking the sun's white whiskey
and beginning to realize
there is no past and no future
you're born at this precise moment
in the high mountains
the roots have climbed your summit

Well – that's all very dramatic
I hear someone say to myself
and it's me saying it:
a very long time later
the margins and edges of time
and place have widened for me
euphoria in the blood stream
yeast in the *gluteus maximus*
and an obvious senility
send me back into summer
climbing the switchback highways
reversing again into winter
in Arcturus and the Pleiades
Orion and his dog in the sky
where time has lost its boundaries
and space jumpstarts to infinity

I return to the mountains
my roots have climbed your summit

CHAC MOOL AT CHICHEN ITZA

Five hundred years of sun and rain
have pounded Yucatan limestone
to dust then back to stone again
– I am a stranger here to this god
with the broken face
and scarcely worthy of his notice
where he lies with sacrificial bowl
extended before him
and manages a recumbent arrogance

A country the colour of an old brown dog
where men have gone mad staring
at a sky clamped down on their heads
or remained so terribly sane
they mocked at heathen gods

I sit at the pool's edge
a sweating tourist
where priests sacrificed to the sun
the same sun as this morning
                the same water
and I wait for the resplendent quetzal bird
– he comes when my mind is empty of things
and the jungle silent
the bird a scarcely believable rainbow
a sunset with wings
posing for its own photograph
then gone
and an old brown dog wanders by in the dust

Slowly back on a stone pathway
winding around the pyramids

the sky darkens to grey
and the grey god in his temple waits
the god with a broken face
his head turned sideways to look at me
his head with holes for eyes:
You who refuse to believe in gods
shall find nothing else to believe in —

WOMAN

— and some whose home is the wind
that lifts the curtains at night
when you wake up and don't know why
and she is there too and unprovable
as the sun on the other side of the world

— and now there is only myself here
in this cage of bones kept prisoner
forever and cannot be free
to hover and hover as a moth
hovers around its beloved light
beloved light

IN THE DESERT
for Milton Acorn

My friends die off one by one:
and far away in the desert
caravans are plodding thru the sand
I can see them at the horizon's edge
the young on their many roads to Mecca
but I have been there often
and returned again

My friends die off:
far distant in waste places
the living move in many directions
I could run after them shouting
across the desert "Wait for me –"
And sometimes I have done that
but things went badly for me
and rushing to meet those people
excited and panting
their faces change into someone else
their faces change . . .

This morning
wandering the grey desert
looking for a cactus flower
in the wrong season
with caravans moving in the distance
sinking under grey horizons
I noticed someone moving in the shadows
coming toward me at a great pace
and they cried out as I had done
"Wait for me –"

A single figure
and impossible to say
whether male or female
crossing the sand dunes shouting
arriving where I stand waiting
in a great flurry of dust and sand:
it was someone I did not know
and very young
I was about to say in a neutral voice
"You had better go back –"

But looking into that eager face
and hopeful eyes –: I glimpsed the flux
of what exists and does not yet exist
a wavering between disappointment and joy
and knew there was only a moment left

before the little gap in time healed itself
I said welcome
and knew this messenger from the desert
was someone I had been waiting for
and clasped them in my arms
the stranger

EARLE BIRNEY IN HOSPITAL

He knows me and does not
know me and the fatal
facility for transposing
myself into another someone
ends with me peering out
from his eyes into my eyes
and dizzily thinking
My God! My God!
I have stopped being Me!

But calmer now:
he knows me and does not
know me and I am a coloured
shadow in sunlight
his brow furrowed and puzzled
with the effort of not knowing
poems he's written and not written
yet that will never be
and he smiles in memory
what might be memory
of whatever smiling was
and it is somehow left for me
to write them remembering pain
of not writing beyond
this grey land of nowhere
forgetting the pain before
beautiful verb and handsome noun
agreed to live together

for better or worse somehow
and kicked their heels
in the printed word
while the shadow stranger waits
the strange shadow
watching and ill at ease
and a little afraid:

as he questions himself
asks himself: *Who is this guy?*
Why is he here?

At that very moment
when the puzzlement is greatest
I smile at him
and the *why* and the smile together
glow just beyond the poem
and shine on his face and his face shines
and for that one moment
my friend remembers
among the multiple choices
of his lost remembering
he chooses
and the poem blossoms

YEATS

To his sister when Swinburne died in 1909:
"Now I am the King of the Cats"

What docs one say of a man
who believed in fairies
– and swooned metrically all his life
for a strident female patriot
– who was accused of being Fascist
with perhaps some reason
– and subscribed to the beliefs of Madame Blavatsky
whose name might be spelled "charlatan"

– and in old age contemplated
an operation to restore sexual vigour
– what does one say?

– at a conservative estimate
fifty thousand people
in a dozen different countries
                    all over the world
will stop whatever they're doing
several times a year
and a thought wrapped up
in a few commonplace words
will sing in their minds like summer
– for them the sound of traffic ends
a man will pull his car off the road
and sit there motionless
a woman with a wet dinner plate in her hand
will stand there holding onto it
in the sudden silence of her mind
while the sun and the sky and the clouds
and the sea
are quivering in otherwhere
and time does not look back
at the man beside the road
or the woman washing dishes
for whom nothing is important
but something they can't describe
or even talk about
except to quote another man's words
that moment in your lifetime
when the body and mind
have joined themselves to another mind
– and there is an improbable glimmer
of fairies in the twilight
and patriotism seems very necessary
and mysticism quite feasible
and sexual vigour admirable
and silence
thunders into a continuing silence

THE FREEZING MUSIC

Lake water sings into ice
– the mysterious everyday stuff
you can drink or drown in
can't be depended on and
now is changing before my eyes

I shine my flashlight along
this shoreline searching for
the moment the exact instant
of hey-presto creation
– and the *materia medica* of chemistry
whereby the process is possible
and physics of matter and energy
mean nothing before my intense curiosity
that shuts out everything else
– hurting my knees on sharp rocks
peering into dark changing water
wanting to feel as water feels
as the werewolf feels
in its last human moment
nothing large or dramatic
just this hangnail curiosity
while my mind empties itself
and the instant wavers
and the lake blossoms
a silver rose of pure sound

my flashlight picks them out
the new-born baby ice cubes
tiny jellyfish jostling together
for cold comfort
their hydrogen-oxygen mother
penetrated by a dark stranger

I kneel on the rocks and shiver
designated oddball to my neighbours
once again being ridiculous

and thereby cut off from any company
but the loon crying in darkness
and dead writers in silent books
the woman waiting in a warm house
who does not know she is waiting
while ice sings its small music
and the cold comes
from far away on Baffin and Ellesmere
glaciers inch perceptibly closer
and I'm not dressed for this
blood-sugar low
(whatever that means)
and now I'm overwhelmed by sadness
anticlimax
post-parturition and coitus
interruptus blues
detumescence of curiosity

Dissatisfied with myself
I wander back to the house
peer out the kitchen window
remembering the birth-cry of ice
while the world behind glass
is changing into winter

FLIGHT OF THE ATLANTIS

At Cape Canaveral the spaceship
rises on a diarrhoea of fire
explosions rock the earth
the earth mantle shudders
dishes and cutlery gyrate on shelves
old bones in graves dance
outside a strange daylight holds
each leaf flower blade of grass
stands in shimmering detachment
and achieve their most-possible selves

At sea
the dark components of light
and silent components of sound
weave ghostly murals in the sky
on land
armadillos stop in their tracks
suddenly naked
with all the planets staring at them
– rattlesnake jaws fall open
stars glitter on their fangs
– pelicans – the grey costume jewellery
of earth – wait for taxidermists
and continue their dream of serenity

Cities principalities powers –
we have forgotten
whatever is important
except "marvellous" science
clichés abounding
we recede backwards from womb to womb
in the flash photography of eternity
at least relinquishing everything
at most only remembering
the sound of summer voices

BITS AND PIECES

the exact moment
not the incident or entire happening
a shapeless bulk in the mind
but the instant
the needle's point
when time divides
into before and after
leaving behind
a clown's face
at the beginning of things:

When she leaned forward
I could see the white ghosts of breasts
shape themselves to reality
an inclination of my head
and a pink nipple like a wild raspberry
melted in my mouth
– and she turned toward me
caught my eye
and knew

I had stolen a handful of silver
from my grandfather's coin hoard
while he was in the john
returning he said
"How much did you steal"
voice stripped of anything
his face hung there in sepia light
of 1924
while I groped for love

In the mind's eye
seeing myself dead
collapsed on the kitchen floor
peering upward sightlessly
expression indicating curiosity
as if the mind was continuing active
speculating
about the reception elsewhere
– but I've failed
and realize now
escape is nearly impossible

When the phone said "Tom is dead"
and I yelled NO
at the mouthpiece
the moment folded and repeated itself
possessed duration
and became pain
the world blanked out

I was alone
watching the expanding universe
a white scarf of the Milky Way
flung round creation
and a moment later
the sense of nothingness
so overpowering reality wavered
in a world of
diminished certainties

The woman standing naked beside a bed
telephoning
pulling back from light in the doorway
almost as if she was recoiling from
Phidias' chisel on the Athenian Acropolis
if it wasn't for that telephone
– so enchanting in her hinterlands
as the dimples undulate

a fox a fox a red fox
running in front of my headlights
near the farm in Little Ireland
his tail a red hot poker
streamed in the wind of his passage
– and it seemed like this was forever
we had been running together forever
at least from Monday to Friday
and I was a child in a story
and he was the friend I included
we were both on our way to nowhere
in a dream from my long ago childhood
when I was pursued by bad men
or wolf wolf wolf
– then I slowed and he vanished forever
and ran to include me in his story
for his friends to listen and marvel
how he was pursued by a monster
and I wonder I wonder
                    do foxes dream?

Riding a bicycle into the country
with another kid named Bernard Campbell
when I was 12 or 13 years old:
seeing a woman come racing out of
a miserable shack made of bits
and pieces of scrap lumber
she trying to climb a wire fence
before a man wearing overalls caught
her and started to beat her to death
the woman screaming and screaming
and the sound of that scream
slicing off bits and pieces
of my youth moment by moment until
I stand at the bathroom mirror
watching a shapeless gasping face
that tries to escape being human
a monkey that doesn't want to be either

PROCNE INTO SWALLOW

I am dive-bombed by swallows
nesting in our garage
and all my assurances of goodwill
have no effect whatever
– and their lovely swooping flight
sun tangled in bodies
breast dull orange
bearing down on my head
like bullets with tail feathers
is not very reassuring
Still it does occur to me
that one of them might be Procne
who once picked the wrong husband
and now lives in our cold country
yearning for Athens
and the Isles of Greece

Itys into Goldfinch

Procne's son in our front yard?
– looping-the-loop at Roblin lake
going "yip yip" like a cowboy
dressed all in yellow
riding an invisible bronco
In the unlikely event
that heaven actually does exist
the goldfinch must be there
homesick for earth

INSOMNIA

I wake up dammit at six and five
and four a.m. all spring and summer
the noisy birds haunt my sleep
lecture me about early rising
expound the benefits of foreign travel
and how tourism sublimates sex:

Robin just back from Guatemala
                    and the Indies
goes "cheerily-cheerily"
in my cedars and wants to know
what's new in Canada?
Oriole from Colombia and Mexico
whistles romantically "truly-truly"
like he's proposing or something
and I hope the lady refused him
Bobolink home from the Amazon
strums his banjo at Ameliasburg
and his mate cusses humans
("Damn that plate glass window!")
– nearly whapped herself last week
when she saw her own spittin image
flying toward her singing and

wants those people to post warnings)
Now the mourning dove
        goes "oh-Woe-Woe-WOE"
with which sentiments I heartily agree
since I can't sleep any more
– then unexpectedly sleep comes
I sleep and dream again
dream ahead to autumn
and wake in winter
of my old age whispering
to the little wanderers
      "Oh take me with you
               wherever you're going –"

CONCERNING MS. ATWOOD

There is Margaret Atwood
– she is meeting Premier Peterson
in the Ontario Legislative Buildings
he is congratulating her
for being Margaret Atwood

There is Margaret Atwood
– she is swinging a champagne bottle
against the bow of a super icebreaker
it winces noticeably from the blow
and escapes into the water
muttering
"My name is Henry Larson"

There is Margaret Atwood
– she is accepting the Nobel Prize
and reporters are crowding around
with tears in their eyes
asking why she is so marvellous
she replies simply and modestly
"I am Margaret Atwood"

There is Margaret Atwood
– sitting in an unmanned spaceship
waiting for blast-off her lovely
eyes slightly dilated from a sleeping
drug administered by flight surgeons
She wakes at the edge of the universe
where someone says "Hello
Pleased to meet you Ms. Atwood
My name is God" She smiles
and writes the name down promptly
in her little notebook to prevent
forgetfulness

There is Margaret Atwood
– at the edge of the universe
speaking to the First Cause at last
he is slightly ill at ease and says
"Did you have a nice trip"
"Reasonably so – and I'm glad to see
there are no autograph hunters around
(he had been about to ask for hers)
But where do we go from here?"

Beyond the solemn hinterlands of nothingness
beyond the last lonesome uninhabited galaxy
("There are rooms for rent in the outer planets" –
                    Travel Brochure)
in the calm green meadowlands of heaven
being interviewed by the neutered blessed seraphim
concerning the relative importance of YIN and yang
– there is Margaret Atwood

PROCNE INTO ROBIN

To dance like that in firelight
with music playing
and throw off all your clothes
around midnight
is no ordinary woman's way
with a man and no
you are no ordinary
woman but a bird
I have just made this discovery
– not the Greek bird Procne
                nor her sister Philomela
not swallow or nightingale
as the gods changed them to –
not exactly your namesake either
for she is much too red-breasted
and you're white all over or nearly

I have made another discovery
those short dainty steps of yours
are the shore-birds dance steps
on a storm-battered beach
after the rough waves recede
stitching the world back together
And when you hover over me
I am already at your feet
unable to say anything
only murmur as men do
and wait
when they know the little dancer
from the sky must rest sometimes
must rest soon
with folded wings
and wait

ON MY WORKROOM WALL

Photo of Gabrielle Roy with her much-lived-
in face a relief map with all the wrinkles
like badges of honour
her face a banner in the wind
Two of Margaret Laurence whom I loved dearly
one looking bored the other alight with amusement
Don Coles' poem which says so much about the
lost "Forests of the Medieval World" it loses
me in places I've never been
Harold Ballard on the cover of *Saturday Night*
his cane spanking the world in geriatric rage
My sister-in-law at age twenty-two
so beautiful the photo sizzles despairingly
knowing this one chance was lost
Acorn of course
who dreamed himself into otherwhere
and never found his way home
Me pissing behind the Owen Roblin tombstone
only the stream of piss visible in photo
presaging dry centuries
Poster of Atwood's breasts surmounted by
her Proteus-face which she objected to
or would cancel the reading
Tiff Findley's verse from Euripides
which says "never that which is shall die"
pollyanna stuff but I like it
Eurithe as a fifty-year-old child in water-
colour pretending she isn't there
but she always has been
Xerox of Milosz with cigar looking cynical
Gary Snyder poet-smug and Wm. Everson a dead prophet
Ben Johnson beating Carl Lewis in Rome
grinning back at him like a little boy
saying "Haw-Haw-Haw" without stopping
MacLeish's "You, Andrew Marvell"
– and I too follow shadows around the world
at Petra and Ecbatan and Sumer and Palmyra

and sleep in those ruined cities still
Two original Lawrence letters
both so alive he can't be dead
Three Kipling poems I like much
megaphones into silence
Colour photo: on rock slopes of Nimrud Dag
in Turkey: wrecked stone heads of kings
whose makers placed this glory
atop the mountain
I sit in my rotating office chair and marvel
and wonder that thought itself
could body forth such shapes and forms

I have gathered them all together
like a casual group of strangers
at this meeting place under my roof
who will never meet again
their only relationship supplied by me
who told them to come here
to wait and be silent on my wall
while I contemplate
not their nature but my own
and know as much about myself
by proxy as from looking deep
into the mirror of what I am

It is very puzzling
this flow of self outward
and silent reception in return
and being pinned to a wall
and being what passes for human
and looking again outward
to see myself
a shadow in the sunlight

Beyond Remembering

GARY: SELF-PORTRAIT

I still have it at Ameliasburg
the painting he discarded as a failure
and project it on the mind-screen:
dark hair growing low on his forehead
skin the colour of old ivory
slender aristocratic nose
and an extremely snooty look
with which he viewed himself
as if he were intruding without
permission on his own privacy

At Chemery in central France
painting in the luminous
                    fading of the light
rushing colour onto canvas
– brain tissue and uncanny earthlight
and first early stars
all coinciding
before the light failed entirely
giving his picture an unearthly dimension
despite its subject
the brown colours of an old cowshed

Every evening at the same time
he'd try to make transience permanent
and three precise furrows growing
transversely on his forehead
denoted the days and weeks passing
while I stood watching
him spend youth on a nuance
of light

Only later
studying Turner Renoir Sisley Monet
Degas Pissaro and all the others
as well as our own Seven
when I began to think of

life itself as a kind of Impressionism
in the traverse of fading light
only later
in the interstices of the moment
provided by Gary
who never achieved anything very much
except perhaps a brief local celebrity
catching a glimpse of his face
in the forehead museum
to which fame alone
does not ensure entry

PNEUMONIA

1

I wake from a fever dream and find
square-assed Sairey Gamp
double-parked beside my bed:
"Have you had your nice bowel movement today?"
(I tell her half a dozen)
– and thermometers get shoved into my face
pills like cartwheels
jostle thru my innards
needles like glassy vampires
plunge into my arms
gallons and gallons of antibiotics
flood my veins
from a kinda coathanger on wheels
– a raging battle going on inside me
where all my blood pours down
in crimson cataracts
– but are the good guys winning?
I don't even know who the good guys are
holding tight with both hands
to Sairey Gamp's umbrella
which turns out to be her own gentle hand

2

Shakespeare's old cliché:
"To be or not to be?"
– but I never thought the question
applied to me
being me I was immune
being me I was exempt from dying
and never doubted this eternity
of instants would continue
the hard unbroken carapace of self
has barred all intruders
from my private places except
that disgraceful little manikin
slouching in the brain's hallways
puffing a cigarette or maybe
marijuana the little bastard
now nowhere to be found tho
probably playing billiards
around the *medulla oblongata*
later maybe footsie
with the talent that's available
– unexpectedly he speaks to me:
"Of course you're gonna
die but not just yet"
like an organ obbligato
"– not just yet"

3

Pain has entered me
under my fingernails
and through all my orifices
it screams at me to die
I am so aware of pain
the world all around me
is completely unreal
I feel myself panting
like a huge extinct beast

a sack of grey flesh panting for air
trying to breathe all the air
in the world at once
swallowing curtains furniture all
then shrinking to a bag of empty skin
eyes popping from my head
fingers become claws
– the toilet mirror
I cannot bear to see myself
whatever me that I once was
has abandoned the body here
never to see myself again
no other visit my bedside
until I feel their eyes
I cannot bear their eyes
and lie still under the earth
and sleep alone under the earth
alone in the earth

     4

Grab anything
hold onto anything
whatever made life good
whatever made life real
feeling your brain actually touch
whatever you were looking for
before you knew what that was:
until you become at least
partially that other thing
And Blake's "What is it in men that women
do require? The lineaments of gratified desire"
– those moments certainly
moments of silence when nothing could be added
to life and nothing taken away
and the moment was everything
when it seemed your face
had surrounded me like the sun
and your body surrounded me

like the living moon
and I was bathed in you
and I was drowned in you
– in the hallway someone tries the door

5

Some time in the night
my brain had darkened
I found myself far distant from earth
lost in high nothingness
and it is a question now
whether I shall return to earth
and the doppelgänger in the hospital bed
will keep on pretending it's me –
All my loves on distant earth
seem imaginary now
my feelings for them like a story
written by another writer
– at my elbow that Other
like a friend – like a friend?
and yet someone you don't know
but someone who looks familiar
I try to see his face more clearly
but darkness swirls around his face
like fog except that it is darkness
and his clothes are the same non-colour
I want to speak to him about my indecision
whether I wish to return to that confusion
on earth with everyone rushing about
and nothing very important
and nothing that can't wait until tomorrow
and the loves that once seemed all in all
changed from moment to moment and become
only a vague discontent with myself
But nothingness? And lose everything?
– the entire world coiled tightly in my brain
the obstreperous inhabitants of this ball of mud
and all the lovely women

I ask again the question: is there no one?
– and of course my loves are there
but scattered at different points in time
almost different stars and different planets
none extend beyond their small perch in time
except as I have given them reality
But netted in my brain I draw them in
with some surprise I do feel something for them
in some surprise notice they are nearly everyone
and feel myself maudlin silly stupid
for not having realized my own feelings
except in this extremity
but there it is: I don't want to leave earth
at least not until I look once more
into their eyes and reach beyond indifference
into their hearts and minds and impossible souls
till I have remembered them beyond forgetting
– the Other turns away as if I had spoken
and darkness swirling round him scatters
the unreadable expression on his face
he nods to me and goes

Sweating I lie in the narrow bed at Saanichton
fever aches in me
antibiotics in little plastic bags
going glug-glug-glug like bad table manners
and I am standing up precariously in a small boat
in the midst of all the beer I ever drank
and cheering loudly for I don't know what
and cannot see the shore

6

This is the earth of Lawrence
who could not bear to leave the place
and even in death his feet danced on the earth
– and do not forget those others
it's also the earth of Yeats & García Márquez
of Sakharov & Frank Scott & Margaret Laurence

Sairey Gamp and MacDiarmid's Audh
asleep in Iceland
in her resting place of stones
How could you bear to leave them here
and go where there is no remembrance?
– and all your friends those very few
you retained long enough to deserve the name
and this earth where your evolving mind
made little leaps and jumps and sideways hops
uncertain of intent or compass or direction
and reaching out from islands in time
overtook your different self like markers
pointing where you'd never been before
– how can you bear to leave them
all your selves
and never know what they might have done
or been or seemed or lost themselves in being
in your own absence in their own loneliness?

– like an organ obbligato
"not just yet –"

ON BEING HUMAN

When my mother went to hospital
after a fall alone in her bedroom
I was eighteen miles away
trying to build a house

I visited her later
and something in my face made her say
"I thought you'd feel terrible"
and she meant that I'd be devastated
by what had happened to her
– I wasn't feeling anything very much
at the time and I guess it showed
just thinking I'd have to travel
those eighteen miles every day

to visit her and grumbling to myself
At that moment
she had seen behind the shutters
normally drawn across the human face
and suddenly realized
there wasn't much if any
affection for her in my face
and that knowledge
was worse than her injuries

But there is no going back in time
to do anything about it now
if something wasn't done then
and nothing was
She died not much later
her mind disoriented
forgetting what happened to her
but I remember those last words
list them first
among the things I'm ashamed of
as intolerable as realizing
your whole life has been wasted
– remembering my cousin's words
about her drunken brother:
"It would have been better
if he'd never lived at all"

I remember those last words
before the fever took her mind
and the only good thing now
is thinking about those words
and she is instantly
restored to life
in my mind
and repeats the same words
"I thought you'd feel terrible"
again and again and again
                    and I am still ashamed
                    and I am still alive

SEASONS

Winter
in our thoughts of each other
and I remember
the way another woman looked
at me as if I were the most
least thing on earth
and I was somehow I was
my own existence ended
and summer gradually coming on
to fill my vacuum in her mind
In late winter
before the melting time
the crocus stirred preparing
underground for its spring entrance
I lessened and grew more:
all least things affect me in season
all those remnants of memory
wind-worn and transparent
seen from the other side of now
as if I were looking at you
across some kind of curtain
and you were looking at me
from another curtain
as all things lessened
and grew more

Summer was very late that year
the birds seemed bewildered
questioning each other about snow
which some had never seen before
Ice rimed the shorelines
and made small tinkling sounds
as if to say welcome
but wind blew colder
and they sent messages
to relatives farther
south and said "Don't come"

It made no difference
the weasel's red eye glittered
foxes hunted and the human hunters
blew on their hands shivering
We shrugged close to the heater
and didn't speak
I would have said
"Why do you hate me?"
but it was useless
we grunted with our eyes

Let me be quite forgotten
and come to think of it
I want to be
anonymous as a raindrop
slightly off course and falling
away from the sun maybe
finding the slim wingbones
of a bird among the cedars
a bird who may have thought
"oh dear – oh dear – oh dear"
before dying
let me be quite forgotten
as snow falls from the red sun
like a thousand thousand flowers
until our tracks are covered

DO RABBITS –?

Rabbits running
an inch ahead of slavering dogs
do they experience intensity equivalent
to Gounod's *Faust* say
in its closing passages
as the dog's teeth click together
and the rabbit comic strip ends
in real-life death?

Our romantic human orgasm
has been likened to
the fall of Troy:
"A shudder in the loins
engenders there
The broken wall,
the burning roof and tower
And Agamemnon dead"
– Yeats lousing up
both Freud and Homer
Which is all very well
but in this small enquiry
is there a rabbit equivalent
to hitting high C
in operatic performance
the vision splendid
of a rodent future
during rabbit orgasm?

But leave off the grandiose:
is there an artistic equivalent
(apart from D.H. Lawrence)
for the tortoise's slow dance
of tumescence and detumescence
into personal oblivion
Beethoven's such-and-such concerto
sounding like tortoise nonsense
at a beach-front casino?

All great imaginings
prefigured by the word "all":
a streak of blood
in the yolk of a chicken's egg
the violin's grating nerves
shrieking in a dog's bones
warmth of heat and light
transferred to music and literature
the painter's passion
interchangeable with nerve endings

of fish and fur and fowl
of course deity
would experience all this too
wakeful on his/her golden throne
and to imagine it is also
to hear the soundless bellow
of eternity
chipping away at a china teacup
and the rabbit's cry . . .

ATOMIC LULLABY

No second spring again
for you and I my love
our half life is thirty years
there is no second coming

We stood on Mount Moriah
counting from one to ten
and slowly we stopped our caring
or pretending we ever did

Say love when the ice gnaws deeper
say love when the fire eats down
could we waste a thought on each other
have we time for romance then

Our myth is the cherished nonsense
that somewhere something survives
and the minds in our dying bodies
glow deep in a stranger's eyes

Sleep – would that have been better?
It is so – it becomes the same
when stars rush out at evening
my dust forgets your name

To pass on the street without knowing
well that won't happen to us
but the most we can be to each other
is someone who looks like someone

We were flesh but our hearts were shadows
we sent them off on their own
to a place where the stones are strangers
but bone speaketh to bone

DEITY

In grey weather along the Ionian coast
we found a god near Bodrum
– it had no body only a stone head
smothered in grass by a ruined temple
and picking off this tangled blindfold
uncovered a face momentarily uncertain
of its own identity in the absence of believers
– then the eyes seemed to find us
standing knee-deep in grass
bending over whatever it was

The Greeks were long-vanished when we
came here and for centuries
our newly discovered god was forgotten
but now our eyes are compelled
by those other eyes
as if we turned to see a grey fire
burning along the Aegean littoral
and dancing figures in the grey light
and cannot look into that burning long
and yet having awakened the god
we cannot turn away

Turkey

COUNTRY LIVING

Spring with Pablo Neruda
and I peering out the bathroom
window at some imaginary
female and he sez to her
"I want to do to you what
spring does to the cherry trees"
whereat I am so jealous of
his metaphors I point out that
no imaginary human female could
behave like a cherry tree does
which shuts him up just briefly
and I draw his attention to two
bushtits nestbuilding in our lilac
bush with a rufous hummingbird the
size of a gold thumbnail watching
domestic activities avidly then
he starts to spin round and round
inside that lilac bush like a
small rotor or prayerwheel for
midgets going
zing-zing-zing soundless as
a cardinal picking his nose
with a gold thumbnail and
bragging at the same time
"Can you do this? Canyoucanyoucanyou?"
Obviously no this great corpus of
unwritten poems can't even
circumnavigate a toilet bowl
without my wife's astrolabe
and my astonishment at this goofy
bird explodes out of the bathroom
window in full view of all and
sundry whereupon
hummingbirds bushtits and Pablo
are shocked out of existence and
repair to the heights of
Machu Picchu searching for
some mislaid condor eggs

WANDERING THROUGH TROY

To actually be there
hover between myth and reality
earth chemicals identical
with Ameliasburg or nearly
same time stream
various co-ordinates checking
ticking off the list of names
the way he thought/the way I think
my imagination churning away
and pleased with myself
Sure it's kinda silly
but you feel it
the Troy-Homer-Achilles deal
the sweat and the watchers on either hand
a great roar of chariots
without axle grease
Priam and Agamemnon
with death-botched reflexes
death two huge eyes
watching you indifferently
whispering soon enough Soon Enough
and Achilles
waking up in his tent
scratching himself
trying to remember
if he'd killed anyone
since yesterday

And stumble from city to city
all nine of them
all the different levels
jammed into each other
and you almost expect
to find human leftovers
from the instant between
one town and another
– arriving here bewildered

a little girl from the Iron Age
hugging her doll
and heat waves rising
among the broken stone

WANTING

I wanted to say wait
when you were looking back at me
when time stopped for that moment
and I kept looking at you forever
I wanted to say wait

I wanted to hear your voice again
on the phone you sounded happy
but the party line was crowded
prairie and mountain were listening
when I wanted to hear your voice

I wanted to write a letter
in which I would say everything
but it seemed as though the empty continent
was soaking up all my unsaid things

I wanted to remember
the you that was so entirely you
that I could never be mistaken
seeing you a thousand miles away
but it was someone else

And I wanted to re-live the moment
that owed nothing to before and after
the you that blotted out me
and yet did not lessen me
I wanted to
but I have forgotten how

GLACIER SPELL

Ice – islands archipelagos continents
worlds of ice
stretching north and holding the sea prisoner
wriggling uneasily in the moon's hypnosis
– and meltwater drains at the glacier's south
where a smaller sea reflects its monster parent
east and west a blue witch-light
spreads into darkness
And year by year the ice recedes
an inch or a foot on the sun's yardstick
yielding entombed creatures thawing slowly
till ice unlocks them
and they tumble from the shoulder-breech
with earth regained they tremble and shudder
appear to take a step then sink to their knees
suffering a double life and a double death
while the ice rings with a dumb chanting

As the sun strengthens a slender line of green
paints itself crookedly at the glacier's foot
and plant faces turn away from the cold
– when rains come a hundred miles of ice
and a thousand miles of sky join in
the roar of drainage to a southbound river
a sound heard by no one
– only a wandering hunter
outcast from his tribe
a man with demons in his heart
unexpectedly not at home
in the great sky rooms of earth

Time speeds and slows
moves in the altering shapes of stillness
speeding to plant a forest
slowing to welcome a bird
waiting for the first beast
while the glacier pretends it isn't there

but shitting lateral moraines
– a brown man and a brown woman
day eyes peering at night eyes
of animals outside
the fire's cave of red light
through the black and white door
where fear waits

Do not touch words to what has no name
or feel the place of wandering stones with eyes
the beast we hunt must not be said
its smell rides under the wind
its face remembers our faces

THE FARM IN LITTLE IRELAND
– *Renfrew County*

All the big wild emotions
that ramp and roar in the bloodstream
love hate fear jealousy
and those feelings that evoke
Hobbes' "sudden glory" of laughter
          they seem faded here
but there remains a sullenness
like ground mist
rising . . .

The 40 acres old Wannamaker
and his sons cleared
on the 200-acre farm
are grown up with brushwood
even humpback piles of rocks
horses dragged here on stone boats
have green hats
          the old log house
with asphalt siding rots slowly
porcupines chew at the backhouse

hungry for salt
inside the house pine steps
to upper bedrooms are worn
thin by dead feet
only the raised tough knots
in boards resist time

Impossible there shouldn't be
some resentment at new owners
who bought with money
the lifelong sweat and pain
of old Wannamaker and his sons
and must have made them feel useless
even to themselves
– but am I inventing such emotions
to survive when flesh is dust
and dust here is everywhere?

– grey ghosts in overalls
meander through house and meadows
where the bent grass
a bear slept on last night
is slowly springing upright
hair prickling at the back of my neck
from this excited melodrama
– an ancient rag doll in the stairwell
reminds me of vanished children
but one eye is missing from the doll
and the other button eye
blames me for the lost one

TO –

To the you that has been given some twenty
pounds of added flesh
– I have made room for this added you in my mind
and love that too

To the throat and neck that were once a column
of light holding up the moon
has been added little noughts and crosses of webbing
like to an earth pattern during the long hot days
before the end of summer
– and the clear luminous mirror of the sky
that was your face has been examined by God
and all the gods and given shadows
here and there that the sons of men
may look upon you and not lose their vision

And the mind that is both fearful of nothing
and fearless of everything has grown and become
lovely and earthly and yet beyond our soiled planet
its innocence the wisdom of things newborn
before corruption has entered their minds and bodies
and directed them to walk toward their death

– to see everything and to realize the best and worst
of everything
is to love and not forget

FRAGMENTS

I loved being alive
to stand between earth and sky
in springtime
a great organ playing in your bones
when earth moves
under your feet
over the long Sundays of our lives

– to feel your insides changing
                    and writhe from loss
and knowing the loss has added
to you and what you are

and clinging to life
that makes such gifts

– to feel
that your own absence may be counted
a continual presence
an onward movement
to change the future
where you are entirely unknown

– to feel your brain
lifting to stand on tip-toe
your feet pushing against the clouds

– to climb the steps of your own writing
and fall off at the highest point
and know that in falling far enough
discover what you were climbing for
and fall short of the sun

– to feel your body crumble
as the high places of earth crumble
the Athenian Acropolis and Machu Picchu
and join them as an idea
springing to life
in flesh and stone

LAMENT FOR BUKOWSKI

It isn't only the Great Bards
who "perne in a gyre"
believe in "the dark gods"
and court the Muse
wearing condoms:
it's also a guy
in his undershirt scoffing
a hot dog and 6-pack

in a crummy LA bedroom
betting a $350 horse
losing on a hundred dollar whore
and watching "the golden men
who push the buttons
of our burning universe"
and writing it all down

Well Buk
sometimes at least
you wrote like God with a toothache
cursing the whores cursing the horses
cursing the world
and blessing
something you rarely mentioned
hovering behind the scenes
there by indirection
your exact opposite:
Mozart dying alone in Vienna
quicklime over his body
snowflakes falling gently on Franklin's men
the frozen world so beautiful
there was nothing else in life
except what they dreamed was death
the King of the Jews on his cross
composing dirty limericks for Pop
– Bukowski in his coffin
dead as hell
but reaching hard for a last beer
and just about making it

TO PARIS NEVER AGAIN

Looking for Sartre
and Simone de Beauvoir
at the Café Deux Magots
looking for Voltaire

in bookstalls along the Seine
looking for Van Gogh
to say I loved him
finding only fleas
racing round my midsection
stomach upset from the water
turning over and over
every half hour
drinking only wine

Rounding a corner suddenly
to confront Audrey Hepburn
(which is nice confronting)
and her new husband Mel Ferrer
I had read in English papers
they were on their honeymoon
and had a kind of glow
that marks some newlyweds
it was like finding a story
on the Paris sidewalk

At the Louvre
moving from painting to painting
I began to lose the sense of reality
from these larger-than-life
people and places
expecting to see Pierre Bonnard
sneaking in to retouch his paintings
when the guard wasn't looking
and me acting suspiciously

Before you speak to someone
they look at you knowingly
betrayed without a word
into being a foreigner
and thought American
– at least half of Paris
sitting somewhere
in front of street cafes

old men playing chess
other old men
searching for cigarette butts
old men wise as encyclopedias
old women who once knew Casanova

I want so much to be in love here
but no one to be in love with
and finding an emotion
shimmering like a pearl
lost near the Arc de Triomphe
by a despairing lover
it's copyright and belongs
to someone else
I left it there
in the gutter shimmering

A room near the Metro
with the noise of trains
a vibration in your bones
of such an intensity
it sucks you out of bed
dreaming of Marie Antoinette
and Eleanor of Aquitaine
in a castle the size of Alberta
joining the other scared passengers
clutching their transfers
and wake up sleepwalking

Before leaving Canada
I'd stayed with Irving Layton
a man so positive of himself
he'd exposed all my negatives
and in this most glamorous city
in the world I wandered
around not knowing who I was
tramping the Rue Pigalle
and Montmartre
at the Tuilleries and Odeon

making notes for poems
pretending to be a writer
then returning to London
back to Canada
– and after a long time
finally beginning to understand
the man in my head was me

AFTER THE WAR

Late in the Bronze Age:
guardsmen lounging at the Lion Gate
discussing Helen's sexual preferences
what happened to Priam's family
laughing about the Wooden Horse
scratching their fleas
– in his marble bath
Agamemnon King of Mycenae
washing off the dust of travel
on his return from Troy
and mulling over his confrontation
in the Troad with mankiller Achilles
an argument over some slave girls
and gazing into those uncanny eyes
his own fear and the difficulty
of continuing to stand there
pretending to be King Agamemnon
the idea of himself wavering
– then noticed an odd reflection
in the water – it seemed like
a sunbeam dancing on the water
then became a flashing sword
hovering at his shoulder
his wife and her lover
– then one long moment passed
a moment filled with centuries
while the Furies buzzed

about the bloody bathwater
like fruit flies

A JOB IN WINNIPEG

That summer we hated each other
the gender wars ablaze
brief gunfire then silence
she left me to stay with friends her face
twitching fiercely

– summer's end
maple sumac poplar yellow and red
sunrise and sunset leaped at the sky
joined at the navel like a huge
McDonald's hamburgers logo
above the house we built together
I moped from room to room and mourned
the broken marriage and my own mistakes
all things seemed to say goodbye
and I enjoyed my own mournfulness
– outside
muskrats pushed the lake ahead of them
with their noses like marathon swimmers
black squirrels were permanent voyeurs
at screens and windows until
I began to feel like a black squirrel a little
and a naked woman smiled at me her body
covered with red sores like blossoms
I kept dreaming about her
in the cedar-scented night
        in pine-smelling evenings
she prowled through my veins
        like a diseased goddess
and I
Homo Erectus in the woodshed

– afternoons
I wandered Norris Whitney's woods
thumbing my nose at him
and the shotgun he had for trespassers
trying not to enjoy the autumn colours
for that would mean my marriage wasn't serious
but it was by God it was
and I am completely bewildered by myself
by my own ruses to avoid pain
and the syllogism I'd figured out
about life had only two parts
and "therefore"
went wandering alone in the desert
trying to complete a *ménage à trois*

– the great pike have sunk into deep water
rabbits search for underground apartments
butterflies decamped for Mexico
birds likewise
and the son of man hath nowhere
        to lay his head
except Winnipeg where there's a job waiting
and if I set my mind to it
I can do without Winnipeg
– I think there must be a spell laid on me
by some god or other
and I've got to stop this facetious voice
hysteric metrics
that I hear going on and on
destroying everything that's important
genuine feeling and emotions
I'm hurt and laughing about it
which is silly
for I know the pain is real
which might mean that I am not real
at which the trees and moon and sky
waver and fade waver and fade
and maybe Winnipeg wavers too
right before my eyes and I pass my hand

completely through
what I thought was a tree
and swear it's a tree
but I'm standing on the planet
which is myself
seeing only my shadow self
dancing on a cave wall
in a kind of semaphore ·
visible to no one

DEPARTURES

I was unable to join them
in that unknown country
where people were made of glass
and you saw their hearts beating
in the mirror of memory
and I have invented
imaginary souls for them
that kept on living when they died
and think their thoughts for them

There was Enid
once when I asked for ketchup
to use on a delicate recipe of hers
she was so angry with me
I was delighted and loved her for it
– she told me a story about an Irish tinker
and another about an aristocrat in Ireland
who lost a wager over a thoroughbred horse
and rather than relinquish the beautiful animal
he killed it
a different kind of creature
it couldn't realize what being owned meant
– and Enid wept a moment
          in the hot afternoon
          of southern Florida

four thousand miles from Ireland
And Tom
years ago when he was especially boring
and I was taking pride in my bad manners
I told him so and he said
"I hope that won't make any difference
to our friendship"
which till then I hadn't known existed
but after that it did
– one of those people partly invisible
and after you understand
about the missing parts of them
you begin to see the others
where they hadn't been noticed before
And Hilda
a warmth about her
and yet so contained in herself
you could know only about sixty percent
she consented that you know
– on a holiday back in Germany
at her relatives' party
she showed up in a clown suit
red nose white cheeks blue chin
a stranger to all her relations
they wondered where she came from
and didn't know the clown
and Bill
who left a note for me in a book that said
I'll wait for you in the west
Till your sun comes down for its setting
And the world has become darker now
And Milton
who was not content in life
in earth he has forgotten
the earth
and that being there might be happiness
if he had known what it was
– then please tell me someone
"What is happiness

that is gone before you remember?"

all these and more

– go where the wandering waters go
all the way home

BRUEGEL'S *ICARUS*

– a ten-year-old boy
escapee from the island of Crete
with a child's delight in having wings
exploring the endless blue sky
argonaut of Cirrus and Cumulus
brave as Jason and Theseus
in a discovery of eagles
flying over Samos Delos and Paros
over drowned valleys of rivers
and seas like upside-down skies
then bewildered by the sun
navigation all screwed-up
heading west by mistake
and down in the sea
off Bruegel's Flanders
"a boy falling out of the sky"
in Auden's poem drowning far
from home: in the painting
the ploughman with eyes only
for keeping a straight furrow
and the "expensive delicate ship" with
perishable cargo too busy to launch
a lifeboat goes about its business
making more profits for investors
– and Daedalus the boy's father
giving up the search as hopeless
turns east for Sicily

– off to one side of the painting
a dead body in nearby woods
which everyone managed to ignore
and one wonders why since dead bodies
left in woodlots are generally those
of murdered men or raped women
and cops very scarce

(– a school text footnote
supplies this dead body info
some black squiggles on paper
repeated in other books
a print run of ten thousand say
and I therefore deceive myself
into thinking I've made a discovery
not mentioned by Auden
the result of this self-deception being
like a flower in my mind
the footnote blossoms)

– questions:
did someone in authority say
"Round up the usual suspects"?
and where did the victim come from
and who knocked him off
and where did the killer get to
and were the equivalents of Sam Spade
and Philip Marlowe in charge of the case?
– one can't help feeling
Bruegel had someone special in mind
for victim in that painting
and the body wasn't just his invention
a man who didn't show up
for breakfast and lunch next day
one of those "Hunters in the Snow"
trudging wearily homeward
gun slung across his shoulders
or a cook in his "Peasant Wedding"
mixing up a nice batch of poison

– or has the murderer escaped
sneaking off with bloody fingers
just beyond the painting's edge
entering a different reality
his genetic inheritors
named Bernardo and Clifford Olson
or maybe an unknown someone
sitting next to you on Air Canada
(more than one myth operating here)
walking behind you late at night
the sound of his steps echoing
pursuer and pursued
and which are you?

– but another image
persists in my mind:
just before drowning
a scared little boy
a long way from home
crying for his mother

THE GODS OF NIMRUD DAG

On my workroom wall: a large colour photograph
from an English Sunday paper: stone heads of gods
on top of a Turkish mountain called Nimrud Dag.
It gives me a weird feeling to glance at it,
and find blank stone eyes staring back at me.
These heads have a majesty that surpasses their
non-existence in any other form than sculpture.
One of them, ten feet tall and facing the camera,
has an expression that might be indifference;
or it might be an emotion entirely unknown
to humans. You look and begin to understand
now the way the old ones felt then,
when a graven image belched fire,
and a spirit presence touched your face.

These were the gods of our fathers:
they are not to be dismissed from our own lives,
even if we worship no longer at their shrines
– an unused part of the brain knows them,
when the priests' chanting dies
and the moon silent on the silent mountain.

MARIUS BARBEAU: 1883–1969

In 1968
a little old man dancing
at home near downtown Ottawa
demonstrating western Indian dances
out of courtesy to a visitor –:

wearing a feathered headdress
and beaded buckskin jacket
ducking his head and beating a drum
chanting *HI-yah HI-yah HI-yah*
the sound part animal part human
circling the dark dinner table
and old-fashioned sideboard
his feet tremulous
age too much for him
– then something happened
something invisible to me
and he seemed to gather strength
perhaps remembering Rocher de Boule
the mountain at the end of the sky
his body weaving among shadow totems
of Kitwanga and Kitwankool
gathering to himself and of himself
Tsimsyan and Gitksan people
villages of the mountains
and rivers of the valleys
Skeena and Nass flowing swiftly
past legs of the dining room table

– his face a tranced dream face
having forgotten his visitor
chanting and beating the drum,
he danced himself into silence

Remembering that time
I was slightly embarrassed for him
now I'm embarrassed that I was embarrassed
and faintly in my own lifetime
have glimpsed the shining mountains

LISTENING TO MYSELF

see myself staggering through deep snow
lugging blocks of wood yesterday
an old man
almost falling from bodily weakness
– look down on myself from above
then front and both sides
white hair – wrinkled face and hands
it's really not very surprising
that love spoken by my voice
should be when I am listening
ridiculous
yet there it is
a foolish old man with brain on fire
stumbling through the snow

– the loss of love
that comes to mean more
than the love itself
and how explain that?
– a still pool in the forest
that has ceased to reflect anything
except the past
– remains a sort of half-love
that is akin to kindness

and I am angry remembering
remembering the song of flesh
to flesh and bone to bone
the loss is better

MACHU PICHU
– in the Peruvian Andes

Like being surrounded
by menacing picture postcards
standing on end
an overwhelmingness of stone
a thunder in the vision
– ghosts of Incas so absent here
and I so aware of them
their absence a negative-plus
– and next morning the neighbouring
mountain Birney once climbed
completely mist-obscured
and perhaps he is still climbing
from his Toronto hospital room
and if I yell "Hi Earle"
I'll hear his Andean bellow
"Come on up Al"
– only one thing to do
in a place like thunder and lightning
stand and rejoice
that you're alive in the mountains
for as long as may be
and to have all these things
fizz in your head like cheap booze
is using up all your quota
of inexhaustible delight
– that life should bring such gifts
and wrap them in clouds and stars

UNTITLED

I am waiting for time to come
holding the many days' sameness inside me
fold on fold of invisible stuff
that you can't see and yet piles up
secretly in the mind like nothing at all
an unseen dust
– then I ask myself what I'm talking about
and can't answer that either:
a quantity of something I can't describe
or measure or prove or disprove

– but there is something
that keeps me from madness:
for the astronomers have told us
about an unexplained "wobble"
an eccentricity of movement
in the orbits of certain stars
which predicates the existence
of an invisible something
some kind of spatial presence
which can be measured and calibrated
and they attempt to describe it

– this stuttering little story of mine
has nothing to do with science
except make an inadequate parallel:
my own blood leaps sometimes
in its arterial voyaging
its circular journey to nowhere
when the spirit seen by no human
makes its presence known
and I can't describe its "wobble"
other than to say there is a loveliness
my heart knows

MINOR INCIDENT IN ASIA MINOR

It's a worrisome matter
every day in my workshop
I think about it
during the back and forth
motion of the handsaw
crosscutting timber
the grating sound
making my ears ache
– in silence at the tavern
everyone talking at once
until I enter the place
I glance at them
they turn away from me
and whisper to each other
my anger bubbling
– stopping work this morning
in a rare calm moment
to contemplate the shrinkage
in width of a green board
and the puzzle of relative
non-shrinkage in its length
invisibly in the night
the thing happens
which every carpenter
who ever lived
must be aware of
– then throw down my hammer
wander onto the barren plain
of Esdraelon at noonday
for a breath of air
a bird calling somewhere

Then the voices return
in tavern and street
the voices like raindrops
like poisoned rain
I hear them continually

around the corner
somebody talking
just beyond hearing
somebody saying things
I don't want to know
and cannot escape:
my young wife a virgin
but pregnant yes pregnant
a word that offends me
but I cannot escape it
and supernaturally pregnant
by some other "person"
and not by her husband?
– by a god then
by a goddamned god

The wine-bibbers watch me
for a sign that I know
what they think they know
that she is no longer a virgin
I watch her belly day by day
for some hint or clue
eager yet apprehensive
of what she may bring forth
Yesterday one of the village
ne'er-do-wells taunted me
about the rumours
stood in my face and said
Cuckold Cuckold
and a great rage came over me
I leaped for him
left him on his back pleading
he didn't mean anything
then went home and drank wine

I cannot ask her for the truth
maybe she does not know the truth
a young girl still and innocent
even when she is not innocent

and what does that mean?
– that she dreams reality
and cannot tell the difference
I have taken a fresh pine board
and laid it gently on her lap
and I say to her:

"The width of this board will shrink
and change but its length
is as it is and will remain
– so tell me then
is a god responsible for
the board's shrinkage the same
by whom it is said you are pregnant?
Or is that some other god?
And I who am your husband
the drunks mock me and call me
cuckold when I pass on the street
and will you leave me to go
with this god who has no name but god?
Who am I then in truth
that you should forsake me
for a god you have never seen
who comes to you only in darkness
and leaves at the first light
of whom you say 'I am chosen'?
Who am I then in the darkness
no man can escape
who am I when daylight comes?"

HER ILLNESS

Since Eurithe became ill
(more like damn sick)
she's growing more and more distant
from me at first it was
only in the next town

where somebody phoned to check
if I knew anyone with an odd name
when I arrived to pick her up
she was gone again this time
reported in Sutton Hoo
site of a Viking ship-burial
gazing contemplatively
at the excavation
getting farther away
in the festering heat of Africa
where Kurtz had been sighted
during the full moon
then it was made known to me
in a dream that she had arrived
on the ghostly companion of Sirius
and might have gone undetected
for centuries and I was alarmed
on accounta air is a bit thin there
then a faint wailing cry
like a bereavement of witches
(but she is notably undemonstrative)
coming from Betelgeuse
in the constellation Orion
and she is frightened
for bedbugs and dung-beetles there
engage in endless warfare

– this is what illness does
and I think from her expression
that she will never return to me

134 FRONT ST., TRENTON, ONT

Entering my mother's house
six years after her death
when the will is finally probated –

The family portraits stare
all haunted by each other's likenesses
the parlour become a museum
and serious
for being dead is a serious matter
faces frozen for the camera
expressions fixed and unforgiving
as if they agreed with the trust company
that prevented settlement of the will
– under their eyes
I shrivel to a small boy again
awaiting my long-delayed punishment
it takes sunshine for my spirits to recover

Outside
the old red barn
in the backyard is gone
– when I was 12 or 13
I built a sailboat in that barn
it had a monster wooden keel
that I secured with steel shelf brackets
it wouldn't tack into the wind
and turned over near the town bridge
I had to be towed back to Bronson's dock
with people watching from the bridge
– that red barn
somebody on the town council
must have decided the world
was just as well off without a red barn
– there were ring bolts on the wall
from the time when horses lived there
a few wisps of ancient hay
stuck between boards
and strands of coarse hair
remaining when some impatient animal
switched its tail in small unhappiness

The maple tree in front is gone too
and once I thought that tree

was as old as the world
and came to believe
there was another country
hidden among its high branches
and I called from my bedroom window
to another kid in that green sky
and he became my friend
– my mother thought I was talking in my sleep
when she came into the bedroom
I snored a little

Upstairs
opening an old chest full of wool blankets
a cloud of moths explodes at me
like biblical locusts
thanking me for self-determination
and looking for something else to eat
– they would have dismayed my mother
so would the missing red barn
and vanished maple tree
standing bewildered in the doorway
"Everything looks so different" she would say
"Don't things look different to you dear?"
Yes they do
but I can't tell her the reason

BECOMING

. . . yeast in the mud-pie
or was it a lightning
and ammonia cocktail
with maybe a *soupçon*
of spectral sunshine
to trigger chemicals
into one-celled creatures
tyrannosaurus monsters
and shrew-like mammals

then *Homo Erectus*
Leapfrogging continents
Africa to Asia
Asia to Europe
the wandering primate
early man
searching the hemispheres
to find a woman
deep as a well
then a long pause
of millions of lifetimes
between the rivers
Tigris and Euphrates
to create cuneiform
writing and mud houses
then the Ubaid period
(pale green pottery
with black designs)
Uruk and onward
the Sumer king-list
Gilgamesh et cetera
part man and part god
and things got interesting
with heroes and suchlike
philosophic questions
that remain unanswered
long after humans
inventing laughter
inventing God
invented themselves
and looked into a mirror . . .

. . . a knowledge strikes home sometimes
full realization of the invisibly obvious:
we're all related to those people
potters and priests and farmers
scribes and armorers
          craftsmen and kings
all of us every one

and in rare moments of meditation
when I am naked to myself
it has seemed to me
that I have entered their craniums
my oneness become twoness and threeness
joining those long ago people
lodged in their multiple brains
immured there
unable to speak words
only see and listen
and sometimes understand
hidden in their brains' pulsing chambers
witness
in uncanny rose-coloured light
to the slow-evolving machinery
of human existence
moving from dim room to dim room
in whispering stillness
my own blood leaping
in the weirs and valves of their bodies
in the falls and rapids of their blood streams
                        and theirs in mine
early in the human adventure
proceeding in zigzag disorderly fashion
from the impossible to the inevitable
from the Lascaux masters to Rilke
        then quite suddenly
        over the long millennia
quite suddenly
I become

. . . an apprentice in Kiangsi province
lying down to sleep in kiln dust
with a few snowflakes falling
thinking
    not of Chang Ch'ien sailing
    a log down the Milky Way
    or himself plunging into the fire
    to make a red bowl for

some emperor
being only an apprentice
homesick for the wet green
of Kiangsi province
lying down to sleep in the hot dust . . .

THE NAMES THE NAMES

I'm scared "they flee from me
that sometime did me seeke"
– George Margaret Milt John
Gus Tom – and suddenly
old age grabs cruel tight
I have to look em up in letters
to remember their names
then forget all over again
I think of the old farmer
who fondled his land
who loved what he thought it was
then both thought and reality
were taken from him
as my names are gone
I pursue them into darkness
follow the remembered faces
I've conjured in my head
by an act of will
they have no names attached
but light up when they see me
they smile with recognition
and depend on me for something
for something vital to all of us
our faces our faces but names
the names of my life are gone
and what am I but what I remember?
Well I remember Van Gogh's painting
the one with bursting stars
and whirling constellations at night

and a little provincial restaurant
at night in Van Gogh's head
the artist's head full of them
crowded with bursting stars
and think of my own lost skull
hairless skinless and yellowish
tucked away in some deserted
lonely unnoticed place
but full of Van Gogh's bursting lights
shining inside the empty abandoned thing
and full of those names the lost ones
the lost names returned at last to me

and the worms rejoice

ON THE BEACH
for Patrick Lane

On the beach at Galilee
mending nets with Cousin Nathan
when this young fellow comes by
trailed by a bunch of other guys
"Nathan" I say "what you done
that they sent the cops for you?"
And the young fellow says to us
"Follow me follow me
and I will make you fishers of men –"
Now I've seen guys like this before
quite a few times before
and they was generally on the make
"Well what about it?" he says
"What about what?" I answer back
and it's a stalemate
"Are you coming with me?"
"Nope"
"What do you mean 'Nope'?"
"Whaddaya think I mean?"

That was a few months back
and the news just come from Jerusalem
how the Romans killed him
me wondering now why I said no
but the man is very dead
which is a very good reason
Other reasons as well:
he was a criminal of some kind
a thief of souls they say
and I would have lost myself
or some part of myself
it would have been taken from me

On the great lake of Galilee
at night I have studied the water
and stars that were the likeness of stars
shining on the water's surface
and thinking – am I a man
that I follow another man
as a sheep might follow
– a man in another man's likeness?
The rumour is he was more than a man
but many have that pretense
as if being what you are
is never enough

Well he is gone
and the sun still shines
by day on Galilee
at night the stars look down
and stars in the likeness of stars
shine on the water
I wish him well this man
who died
this man in the likeness of a god

HOUSE PARTY - 1000 BC
after Rilke

A god standing in the doorway
and looking like everyone else
another late arrival at the party
until he speaks to King Admetus:
"You must die within the hour"
– no question of belief
or disbelief from anyone
the god could not be doubted

It was like Icarus falling
from the sky
when his wax wings melted
screaming all the way down
Admetus falling from his couch
screaming on the floor

"Unless" the god said looking
at the writhing body with distaste
"unless someone willingly dies
in your place –"
"willingly?" "instead of me?"
My friend Creon? Parents?
Wife? Alcestis?
Alcestis

The king's features collapsed
inward on themselves
like bubbles in hot soup
nose mouth eyes ears moved
from their places in his face
rearranging themselves
and twitching horribly
twitching
he became completely
a stranger to himself
and completely mad

The woman – really only a girl
her face becomes a screen
with pictures for thoughts
in which another self lived
a life within her life
so that all the house guests
she looked upon were dead long ago
and her thoughts were a grief for them
then changed from grief to sadness
the sadness of remembering
what her friends were like
and what her husband was like
when you can't feel any longer
and love for her husband was the ache
of not feeling love any longer
the ache of knowing what love had once been
knowing now only the imitation feeling
occupying the same place
remembering what it felt like
from the imitation inside herself
but not remembering very well
And now to die?
But the child?
What child?
– the child who does not yet exist
with doorways opening and closing somewhere
arrivals and departures
memento of herself in another body
the residue of a self gone elsewhere

All this time the god
has lingered in the doorway
his face changing and changing
– the parents bewildered
clinging to each other
in the way of old people
"What's going on here?"
affixed to their faces
Creon in deathly fear and hiding

behind a candelabra's silver flowers
Alcestis moves toward the god
who has joined the other guests
but they keep some distance away
and now remember his name
the messenger of the gods
Alcestis stops in puzzlement
something important was happening
and just one moment ago
she can't remember what it was
– the child – ah yes – the child
who cannot yet exist
but cries within her body to exist
Glancing back at her husband
and then at the god's changing face
which calls her to him
– so beautiful a face it is
that speaks of generations
in the far future
but nothing earthly added to itself
nothing earthly
so beautiful she thinks it is
and after that
the shining

Admetus watches them
the god and his wife who was
they are vanishing in light
rushing away from his guests
and from his own life
seeing them fade and give birth to light
and it is suddenly yesterday
then tomorrow
and none of these things happened
between yesterday and tomorrow
and now it is much too late
for anything but weeping
and he weeps
Admetus weeps

IN TURKEY

Crossing on the ferry from Rhodes
arriving bewildered without Turkish money
I brandish travellers cheques to a cop
in dumb show hoping he'll translate this
to money money money
he grins and points and we grin back
and catch a minibus north
with several other passengers including
14 hens two goats and a pregnant lady
and a large basket holding maybe a cobra
judging by the slithering internal noises
also a dozen women chattering in Sanskrit
so we grin at them our universal grin
which means everything and nothing
in high country fit only for mountain goats
I hope the driver drinks nothing but milk
and his helper shrieks for new passengers
at every small town and village firing
A-E-I-O-U like semantic rockets
so I guess Turkish is nothing but vowels
back on the coastal littoral
passing real camels on the highway
"Lookit a real camel" I say
"You ever see an unreal one?" she sez
witheringly to which I say no humbly
and it's spring and all the veiled women
labour in farm fields at one place
we pass 15 mysterious Turkish behinds
planting seeds bending over their furrows
all pointing toward Mecca
at the three-bucks-a-night hotel we find
the toilet is raised footprints and a hole
and no door where I stand guard
when necessary and down the street
passes a wedding or a funeral
I guess the latter the corpse on
a wooden platform kept warm with a blanket

and the bearers bum's rush the dead man
quick into his grave before he can say no

When I can slow down the mind fever
and calm the strangeness to a kind of peace
the place still feels like being on Mars
or maybe Saturn or something and me so foreign
and stupid it's like returning alone
again to earth and alone together
we lie in an uncomfortable bed
and talk to each other comfortingly
and hug each other to sleep

HERSELF

"Sometimes I can feel myself
tossed about in the swirling
currents of your mind
and then-"

"Write that down dear"

– and then sneak around one corner
of the *medulla oblongata*
and leaning against the central
nucleus of the thalamus
you again
But how did all this begin?
– back in a cave somewhere
I regarded your rather pendulous
lower lip and slightly crossed
eyes with unmitigated longing –
How's that again?
Far back in the Pre-Cholesterol
Period of the Mid-Colonic
Age your psyche asserted
itself as a genetic modification

in my scrotum's brain cage
and now
my brain is up to its ass
in social anthropology
and such tenderness as
I have I can never feel
without wondering whether
I should write it down first
or explore this inward melting
feeling that stops just short
of weeping
(pulse rate 75 per minute)

– and now far into old age
with its inevitable conclusion
I am deeply troubled
a profound literary sadness
of knowing I am using death
too much in poems
but turn about
is fair play I guess and
I expect to have it use me
soon for its own purposes
whatever those might be
and it won't be for poems

MY GRANDFATHER'S COUNTRY
Upper Hastings County, Ontario

Highway 62
in red October
where the Canadian Shield hikes north
with southern birds gone now
thru towns named for an English novel
a battle in Scotland and Raleigh's dream of gold
– Ivanhoe   Bannockburn   El Dorado
with "Prepare to Meet Thy God" on granite billboards

– light thru the car window
drapes the seat with silken yard goods
and over rock hills in my grandfather's country
where poplar   birch   and elm trees
are yellow as blazing lemons
the maple and oak are red as red
as a thousand thousand sunsets
refusing darkness entry
to the world

Of course other things are also marvellous
sunsets happen if the atmospheric conditions are right
and the same goes for a blue sky
– there are deserts like great yellow beds of flowers
where a man can walk and walk into identical distance
like an arrow lost in its own target
and a woman scream and a grain of sand will fall
on the other side of the yellow bowl a thousand miles away
and all day long like a wedge of obstinate silver
the moon is tempered and forged in yellow fire
it hangs beside a yellow sun and will not go down

And there are seas in the north so blue
the small bones of the brain take on that same blue glow
like unto a fallen sky
they speak of the illimitable
those immense spaces of nothing and nowhere
the mind can scarcely comprehend
so far beyond human touch we must rely
on impersonal science
to tell us of shimmering violet meadows
and comets visiting earth and returning
                          at such measured intervals
the ancient rememberers were long since dust
and we cry our name to the stars and the stars
do not remember

But the hill-colours are not like that
with no such violence of endings

and earth would appear like a warm red glow
to casual eyes of travellers in space
the woods are alive
and gentle as well as cruel
unlike sand and sea
and if I must commit myself to love
for any one thing
it will be here in this marginal country
where failed farms sink back into earth
the clearings join and fences no longer divide
where the running animals gather their bodies together
and pour themselves upward
into the tips of falling leaves
with mindless faith that presumes a future
Earth that has discarded so much so long
over the absentminded centuries
has remembered the protein formula
from the invincible mould
the chemicals that after selection select themselves
the muscles that kill and the nerves that twitch and rage
the mind-light assigned no definite meaning
but self-regarding and product of the brain
an inside room where the files are kept
and a little lamp of intelligence burns sometimes
with flickering irritation that it exists at all
that occasionally conceives what it cannot conceive
itself and the function of itself:
the purpose we dreamed in another age and time
an end just beyond the limits of vision
some god in ourselves buried deep in the dying flesh
that clutches at life and will not let go

Day ends quickly as if someone had closed their eyes
or a blind photographer was thinking of something else
it's suddenly night
the red glow fades and there is no one here
but myself and I am here only briefly
and yet I am not alone
Leaves fall in my grandfather's country

and mine too for that matter
– later the day will return horizontal and gloomy
among the trees and leaves falling
in the rain-coloured light
exposing for ornithologists here and there
in the future
some empty waiting birds' nests

OUR WILDERNESS

A yellow splash in the green
hill across the water is flowers
and this morning a white plume
of mist floated down from nowhere
inserting itself in the emerald
– our house crouches beside water
a tuck in the landscape
wilderness in miniature
beside a protected salmon stream
and there such marvels appear:
below the kitchen window
sea otters were born
they return recur and reappear
are exiles away from here
and sometimes actually seem
to change into beads of water
and play on the far shore
like circus acrobats
appear to be moving
in all directions at once
whiskered faces comically serious
then all stop as if at a signal
waiting to be interviewed
by imaginary reporters
and ducks kingfishers herons
sometimes raccoon families
switch on our sensor lights at dusk

and caught in the act
they traipse past the windows
like nosey neighbours
on their way to the movies
(and I suppose
in all that nearby underbrush
their babies die sometimes
as human babies do
little burglar faces
twisted in agony
their mothers beside them
in an equivalent of weeping)

Beyond our trees that belong
to themselves the highway
traffic's sullen sounds
a quietness in our bones
we scarcely notice the cars
and underground here
small furred nations
raise their flag in tunnels
below ground
sing anthems at dusk
and we are the aliens here
but at least there is peace
and time's slow passage
the sun a gold coin
from lost Byzantium

IN CANNAKKALE
Turkey

On the third floor
of the Hotel Anafartalar
beside the Hellespont:
– at midnight a Soviet destroyer
parades by with blazing lights

reflecting in our windows
– close to the hotel site
Leander swam the Hellespont
to meet his girl friend
Hero a priestess of Aphrodite
on the other side
and one stormy night Leander drowned
well within sight of our Hotel
Anafartalar
if we'd been watching
from the window then
– also near here
Xerxes built his bridge of ships
on his way to conquer Greece
in 480 BC
but Greece refused to be conquered
– if we'd been drinking beer at the time
suspended in air in our third floor
room that didn't exist till much later
Xerxes was right under our noses
– and Xenophon passed by as well
around 401 BC
with what was left of his Ten Thousand
bad-tempered and needing a bath
– and Byron dogpaddled across
from Abydos to Sestos in 1810
and made sure everyone heard about it
– 20 miles from here
a dozen cities of Troy
all piled on top of each other
dreaming of Paris and Helen
– but I arrived too late
to do anything
but sit beside the Hellespont
and dream about old battles
and book a flight home
quarrelling with my wife
about the date of departure
and whether or not women
are actually the dominant sex

FOR HER IN SUNLIGHT

Didn't turn my head
kept absolutely still
for seven seconds stayed
my fractional life
in this skin tent
until an unpredictable
you has joined me
with river and rain song
and your long quietness
a cloak of invisibility
around both of us
your brown-gold head
turned toward me
and white places
on your hips
are silver
birches on them
       we swing

And this is the way it was:
friends and relations dropped away
the cities blinked out
one by one
and left nothing in their place
but a vagueness
the landscape was dim background
we could see only each other
on the tiny island of us
standing in sunlight
and it was enough
it was enough
– then after a while
the people began to appear again
and they seemed strange to us

we heard the news of the world
and that was strange to us as well
and we glimpsed in each of us
hundreds of dozens of others
in different times and places
                    and mirrors
and glimpse among us
a discovery of strangers and lovers
a collected self

These are life's gifts
and in the loopholes and catacombs of time
travel glance back
to see far-distant replicas of ourselves
perched on a mirage
waving to us
surprised to find us still alive
as if both had imagined the other
as the seed imagines the flower
beyond death
                    the idea we are used to
                    like a far-away train wreck

IN MEXICO

– driving south always south
three or four hundred mile leaps
like a motorized grasshopper
over plains and mountains
skirting cities and crossing rivers
leaves long fled from roadside trees
dead brown grass in meadows
dull sun hung low on a forlorn landscape
storms brewing high in a dirty sky
and south south south
motel to motel to motel
morning frost on motel blacktop

the prone ghost of Canada
and sometimes we looked at each other sadly
who are you?   who am I?
– until finally the pale sun turned golden
the summer solstice double-crossed winter
our cold bones danced into springtime
and orange trees bloomed at the Mexican border

– the hacienda south of Victoria
in Tamaulipas
where we stopped overnight
with suits of armour in the halls
expecting to see Hernando Cortes
in his winter underwear
peering from stone doorways

– driving a ridge road
on the razor edge of mountains
still in Tamaulipas
and fog like grey midnight
all morning
nothing between us and death
a thousand feet down
except the crumbling gravel road-edge
rationally knowing the road *was there*
but the knowledge uncomforting
just guessing your way ahead
nerves popping
the world condensed
to a car-size tin box
and no god available
for rescue purposes

– on every road and highway
road-killed animals
some quite large
even occasional horses
awaiting the carrion-eaters
and where people died
run down by cars and trucks

shrines beside the road
with flowers for the dead
from relatives and lovers
there may even have been
shrines for pet dogs and cats
for all we knew
and it made the highways
into warm human places
except that over everything
circling the sky ceiling
something watching
and if you stopped there
by the road for anything
anything at all
there was a pause
in your own breathing
and high above you
something leaned out

– we had no Spanish
except a few words
for use in stores and markets
and therefore we felt
the peculiar sensation
of not being really there
in other people's eyes
we saw "gringos"
printed on their retinas
as if something vital
had been removed from us
we became abstractions
labelled strangers
possible enemies
beyond friendship
on the human littoral

– noise of feeding in restaurants
each kind of Mexican food
making its own special sound
in the frontal orifice

a protein orchestra
dance of the carbohydrates
and after a while you could identify
tortillas (dry shushing sound)
huevos rancheros   enchiladas
tacos   pimientos   frijoles
chili   (muy caliente)
jalapeños   even more so
– and names the names alone
if pronounced correctly
ignite inside your mouth
– but *cerveza* marvellous *cerveza* (beer)
helados   (ice cream)   dripping from
every inch of a kid's grin
mangos on a stick
flashing yellow signals at the sun

– climbing a steep curving hill
in the Sierra Madres
following a heavy transport
a stake truck rushing down
on us with failed brakes
missing us narrowly
its wheels striking sparks
from the road's stone curb
and faces inside
inside the cab white faces
desperate with knowledge
caught in the act of dying
tumbling end over end
thousands of feet
down the mountainside
– we sat there stricken
with second-hand death
then remembering
cops throw you in jail
for even witnessing accidents
we drove around the transport
and were on our way again

all afternoon
stunned into silence

– in Mexico City
at the high castle
of Chapultepec
where the boy cadets
leaped to their deaths
in 1847
rather than surrender
to the invading Americans
under Gen. Winfield Scott
– I think of the 960 Jews
fighting their last fight
long ago in 73 AD
who leaped to their own deaths
from the hill fortress of Masada
rather than surrender
to the other Romans

– not just poor people
on the streets here
but hungry starving people
beggars in rags
scratching for a living
at the cold concrete
and sometimes nearby
staring vacantly
at absolutely nothing
faces devoid of thought
and after a while
you start to blame them
for having made you feel
so damned uncomfortable
and somehow you owe them
but neither they nor you
know what it is you owe
except that you must take
full responsibility

in your own mind
for not being them

– thinking of Graham Greene
who disliked Mexico
and Waugh who felt much the same
then a bell rings inside me
when I remember the lottery seller
on the Avenida Reforma
face wrinkled as dead leaves
and another ancient in Chapala market
selling iguanas like trussed chickens
old women
they too are Mexico
indomitable as potatoes

– shown over Lawrence's house
near the lake in Chapala
all one hot afternoon
by a real estate salesman
and the estate owner
– transported back to the 1920s
while Lawrence searched for his *Ra-na-nim*
the great good place
where friends would live in harmony
and everybody be happy
Lorenzo an irritable saint
lungs dissolving and death nearby
but triumphant anyway
in ways impossible to explain

– monster Olmec heads
each of them
taller than a man
on the way to Yucatan
carved by artisans
of a vanished race at La Venta
and they stare at you
from half-closed eyes

indifferently
as if to say
we have seen you
many times before
and will see you again
and all will be the same

– at Acayucan we stopped
"to water the engine's horses"
and passing the local prison
dozens of hands reaching out
from dungeon windows
begging us for money
in order to buy food
and stay alive a little longer
– that night at the motel
rain thundering down
even running under the door
and our electric frypan
blew the motel fuses
and looking outside our doorway
we saw only silver
daggers of falling rain
pounding the drowned world

– stopping at a quiet place
of palm trees and silence
where it seemed human beings
had never been heard of
and being suddenly presented
with the flat blue plate
of the Gulf – such a blue
as jarred the teeth in your head
such a blue

– in Yucatan listening to Babs
from Toronto's Rosedale district
telling a story about
her dead relative being cremated

other relatives taking the ashes
somewhere in deep winter
but getting stuck in the snow
spinning the wheels
          spinning the wheels
finally using their relative
under the car tires
and roaring away
leaving their loved one's
ashes in the silent snow
silent snow

– meeting people from time to time
and sensing that they hated you
and twice somebody saying so
not because you were you
but for being *Norte Americano*
thinking you American
– and to be hated
for no personal reasons
gives one a very odd feeling

– at Chichen Itza
a great city in the past
its long-dead people almost
alive in the present reality of stone
where we are ghostly visitors
– climbing the Toltec pyramid
91 steps to the crowning temple
Eurithe and I holding onto each other
clutching precariously
little jerks of movement
edging toward eternity
("If one of us falls
will it be burial or cremation?")
– seeing the landscape widen
the Mayan-Toltec city
jumps into sunlight
scummy sacrificial pool

emerald jungle beyond
where quetzal birds
fly to their own music
– into a tunnel leading downward
to the Toltec sanctuary
and sprawled at the doorway
a reclining god
Chac Mool
who governs the rain
and a throne shaped like a jaguar
with jewelled eyes
and green jade jaguar spots
– and I think Eurithe and I
I think we feel like children
visiting the future
when we emerge into daylight
to play with our toys
a 1967 Ford Custom
with various travel equipment
in the trunk and some books
parked across the road
from the deserted city
– we look at each other
on our return from the past
"Were we lovers back then?"

– the island of Father Morelos
in Lake Pátzcuaro
muleskinner-turned-priest
turned leader of the people
in the Mexican War
of Independence from Spain
executed in 1815
– his statue stands atop the island
130 feet tall with arm upraised
signalling the future
like any ordinary hero
– when we climb the volcano-shaped
island (several hundred feet)

we're much too exhausted
to climb the statue stairs as well
from legs to guts and belly button
heart and head and soul of Father Morelos
dust long ago and far from where
we sit beneath his effigy
and pant for breath
watch fishermen on the lake
below with butterfly nets
and dugout canoes   earning their bread
as their fathers and fathers'
fathers had done
long before Gen. Winfield Scott
long before Hernando Cortes
and the Romans knew they were Romans

– visiting "the place of the hummingbirds"
called TZINTZUNTZAN
onomatopoeia
for darting whirling rainbows
of birds sailing over the town gardens
like tiny coloured angels

– on the Day of the Dead
Nov. 1 and 2
people visit the cemetery
with food and drink and gifts
for their dead relatives
and we huddle around our fireplace
hiding from ghosts in the cold motel
7000 feet higher than the sea
and in the first light of early morn
so difficult to distinguish with
any accuracy the dead
from the living
– but there's such a richness here
that makes you twice alive
that sends you singing silently
Tzin-TZUN-Tzan

and I see clouds of hummingbirds
circling round my dopey head
and Father Morelos blesses me
(an act he'd regret
        if he knew me better)
and during the Night of the Dead
someone leaves two loaves of bread
at our motel room door and "Hey"
I yell after him "we're alive"
but he grins and goes and morning
is a cluster of green and red and gold
and the island of Father Morelos
glows deep crimson and the world
is cleansed and newborn
and we are enthroned
in eternity for now
for this one moment only

– wandering Mexico for ten years
seasonal visitors
beginning to love the country
for reasons one can't believe
are believable
for someone who hasn't lived here
– endless deserts of tree-cactus
many of them
15 or 20 feet tall
with multiple threatening arms
you half expect they'll uproot themselves
and chase you down the highway
and snow-capped volcanoes
shimmering against the sky
cities sweltering in the heat
the sun burning into your head
and then the low moan of rain
(once in Merida in Yucatan
it rained hail like golf balls
we took refuge in a toilet factory
and watched wooden two-by-fours

racing down rivers of rain
in the middle of the street)
and the jungle the Jungle
green that pours into your head
washing over your brain
and the brown people
multitudes of brown people
living in such screaming poverty
you wonder how they can remain silent
and not run around cursing the world
of course they're resilient
but to live and love without hope
of anything better
– or does the same amount of hope
reside in all of us
and you use a small bit of it every day?

– somewhere along the line
in Mexico you think:
is happiness measurable
the same amount available
for all of us?
and your delight in accomplishment
writing a poem you like – say
is that comparable to finding
a crust of mouldy bread
in somebody's garbage can
the same delight?
– is it possible
for one of these *paisanos*
with slack jaw and vacant eye
to be standing alone somewhere
and slowly starting to smile
as I have done myself
all alone and smiling like a fool
knowing how marvellous it is
to be alive?

– sadly there seems no answer

no real answer to anything
only the sea and the land
the beauty of the morning
terror of the night
and a brief residence
here on earth
there is no other place

IN THE RAIN

– approaching a bridge over the Murray Canal
I am seized with a feeling of incompleteness
the desolation of being the last man on earth
and yearning to such a degree that it becomes
a physical illness
yearning like a potato or turnip yearns
or maybe a tall tree in the forest yearns
listening to the silence between raindrops
for a voice to speak in my mind
knowing quite well that I am ridiculous
and stop the car and rush into a phone booth
listening to the ringing sound far from here
listening to the bells ringing far from here

– those few moments waiting
for the receiver to be picked up
rest on a needle point of time
and I will never be here again
but everything I do and say is permanent
unerasable on the blackboard of the instant
on the slate of what was and is and will be
and the word "Hello" in my ears
is a paean an overture and jubilate in the blood
and I hang up without a word

I will sleep my way into death
searching for an instant in dreams

to find that moment again
for that face reconstituted and intact again
with all past ages echoing
from microscopic amoeba to Rilke
culminating in that moment again
on a plastic electronic device
for a rented instant
for a rented instant –

THE STONE BIRD

Lady
      with the very modern illness
      agoraphobia
      but ancient as fear
      in a Greek marketplace
Lady
      I have seen your face
crumple and break in ecstasy
of terror of horror of being
alive in this sewer world
feeling alien thoughts beating
at your mind an office desk
protruding from one ear
a subway train from the other
bells clanging gongs shouting
while you're washing the dishes
terror
      of the marketplace
                and falling
falling into that white place
without shadows
      where the rivers are milk
and Lethe dreams
and nothingness has no horizon

        Lady

I do not say
that underworld is not a good place to be
the land of forgetfulness
where the truly mad with wolf faces
cannot follow
past our floating speck of life on the oceans
from which we emerged bewildered
                              and wet
behind the ears
this earth which is a graveyard
built on dead bodies and decayed matter
of all those before us
                  animal and vegetable
– but now is the question
                  is Lethe better
                  tell me Lady?

                  – once on an arctic island
of the Kikastan group in Cumberland Sound
in a moment of desolation
I laid my head flat against island stone
a mountaintop of gneiss and granite
ice floes silent nearby
where I was lost
in the crevices of existence
and I heard the world's heart beating
                  inside the silence
all else an illusion
I heard the singing sound
                  of a stone bird
that flies through the centre of the earth
and I listened

I hear it still
among the nickel-and-dimes people
I know it in the agora
I feel it waiting for that moment
of grace in the unexpected word
the instant that transfigures things

when all your weakness falls away
and your body floats in light

          Lady listen
to sun-song wind-song and song
of the sweeping planets
and the song of the corner grocer
an earth song I heard in the darkness
on an arctic island
from the stone bird flying
through the centre of the earth
          – listen Lady

TRANSVESTITE

Going out naked into the snow
late at night
most unnaturally
    I mean why so silly?
I bet you never did that Julie
          or even in the rain
                    women don't
they must wear G-strings
and minimal make-up
because of the Apostle Paul
out there watching
But I'm trying to say why
I do things
          think like that
I can't
only there is an earth-power
in the lazy plunge and swirl of falling things
I don't know what it's for
and somewhere across the neighbourhood lake
a campfire rests against the curve of earth
and touching it the drifting snowflakes
make tiny spitting tasting sounds

and the small furred creatures of the night
        lie under the snow
listening for their enemies

Outside at midnight
in the bright strange air
I have lost and gained myself
rendered invisible
– it's as if I were never here
        had never been at all
        nobody saw me
        tended my wounds
and I did prove I was never here finally
inside the sea inside the silent earth
separate and contained exploding inwardly
the body-clock ticks on
– going outside without
clothes into branching white
coral forests under a sky
surface so many miles over me
the Sky Huntsmen don't know
I'm here and snowflakes falling
back to me are feathers
are cold butterflies
dancing on my shoulders
fused to my broken heartbeat

– so I regained this white plumage

NEW POEMS

SAY THE NAMES

– say the names say the names
and listen to yourself
an echo in the mountains
Tulameen   Tulameen
say them like your soul
was listening and overhearing
and you dreamed you dreamed
you were a river
and you were a river
Tulameen   Tulameen
– not the flat borrowed imitations
of foreign names
not Brighton Windsor Trenton
but names that ride the wind
Spillimacheen and Nahanni
Kleena Kleene and Horsefly
Illecillewaet and Whachamacallit
Lillooet and Kluane
Head-Smashed-In Buffalo Jump
and the whole sky falling
when the buffalo went down
Similkameen and Nahanni
say them say them remember
if ever you wander elsewhere
"the North as a deed and forever"
Kleena Kleene   Nahanni
Osoyoos and Similkameen
say the names
as if they were your soul
lost among the mountains
a soul you mislaid
and found again rejoicing
Tulameen   Tulameen
till the heart stops beating

say the names

THE LAST PICTURE IN THE WORLD

A hunched grey shape
framed by leaves
with lake water behind
standing on our
little point of land
like a small monk
in a green monastery
meditating
        almost sculpture
except that it's alive
brooding immobile permanent
for half an hour
a blue heron
and it occurs to me
that if I were to die at this moment
that picture would accompany me
wherever I am going
for part of the way

FOR ANN MORE
1584–1617

No pictures exist of the seventeen-year-old
girl who had so many kids
                she died of them
which I suppose isn't exactly true
altho kids were the end result of
that "shudder in the loins"
which must have racked her soul
and made happiness an agony
of childbearing

A genius doesn't often look like one
unless you can stand back
                and see true

it's much too much to know if you're not
                    one yourself
– or maybe when you're in his arms
nothing matters but what you feel
and can't say
            and maybe nobody can

Look back on Ann – 400 years ago
when something in her genes
began to scatter into the future
along with John's
– but that isn't exactly so either
who knows what happens
            in that sky-touching moment?
I vision her as a girl so tender
and heartbreaking in the way she was
you couldn't look at her without tears
and I can't write about her
            without a peculiar kind of love

How far do the elements of lovers go
slingshot as far as the new millennium?
her body trembling among the outer planets
when he touched her
remained on earth among her dying children
But that isn't it either:
                you say her name – Ann More
and both of them
                Ann and her lover
                John Donne
flash quicksilver in the mind mirror
– her madman her iconoclast her "genius"
with microscope brain
and the girl who might have suspected all this
but knew it didn't matter much
beside the tenderness and laughter
a kind of formula we humans have
for making whole our broken lives

THE GIRL AT SCARA BRAE
Orkney Islands

Not a girl any longer
since she's five thousand years old
and something anthropologists puzzled over
her forehead indented from
what was probably a feather strap
marking her bare skull deeply
and the pressure of days and months and years
speak in that indentation
of lugging a basket full of nearly everything
somebody else could think of

– and what does a skull think of?
eternity is endless and immeasureable
there can be no return ever again
to knowing the green earth with the hot hands
of the sun on your face and body
5,000 years
you could maybe tick them off one by one
on your bare bony fingers
with small hope of being alive again
staring into the waters of Scapa Flow
and strange rocks of the Old Man of Hoy
feeling yourself most alive
on day one one day day one of your death
your face new born as a skull
a baby's bare skull
gone back to sleep for another 5,000 years
wrapped round at first in a cocoon
of hair and fingernails still growing
waiting for graves around you to open
tick off the lost days
the faint tick of 5,000 years of days
and instants and hours you got tangled with
here on earth
how could there be any sadness left on earth
for her just one girl after so many millions died

when all the demons and angels and witches and warlocks
and Milton and Dante sitting around on their hands warming
themselves at God's Quebec heater
while the Carbon 14 slowly leaped from her bones
how could there be any sadness in rocks of the Old Man of Hoy
but there was sadness in the dark earth at Scara Brae
that remains unexplained

FRIEND

for George Woodcock

– at convivial times
the talk had ranged everywhere
with hints on far voyaging
to Machu Picchu   India   Tibet
and flying to Cuzco
in a non-pressurized plane
where I would be travelling soon
– once listening to him chatting
with a clever young play-director
using a verbal concept beyond me
past my understanding
I wanted to hear it again
feeling both annoyed and enraged
that the idea escaped me
then slightly amazed when he glanced at me
and I knew he knew what I was thinking
– and now I am saying it
the last goodbye
and can feel my eyes smart
when he says "congestive heart failure"
meaning no hope at all
– always before there was hope
in all our lives
now there is none in his
only that he leaves behind
something of himself

and a feeling
which is indescribable
and dates back before the time
we humans began to employ words
to label things with
the time of the early hominids
(cloudy grey outlines of thought:
when anger was the mind's lightning
flashing in bone-dark
and happiness a warm confusion
of safety and sex and food
and joy the sun's white heat
caressing hairy flesh
with sorrow's demented shapes
nosing into human sleep)
– now that we have words
something something is lost
there are still no answers
only sorrow
and remembrance of love
but stronger
pain that is outside time
and lives in a secret place

turn your mind over a little
so you can find where the entrance is

IN ETRUSCAN TOMBS

At Cerveteri the mossy stones
scare hell outa my unbroken legs
teetering along narrow masonry
or scrambling down dark tunnels
then back into sunlight
to escape the long sleep of the dead

(– and at this point

I cuss out D.H. Lawrence some more
the guy who got me into all this
on accounta my DHL obsession
and I'll send him a hospital bill
from the Etruscan Underworld
if I can just get his home address)

– and wondering if the Etruscans
were really the gentle souls
Lawrence fancied they were
while the ominous tombs surround us
buried bones and ornaments and stuff
still undiscovered by tomb robbers
or vanished into museums waiting
for us in Tarquinia and Volterra
room after room and sarcophagus
after sarcophagus each with stone
sculptures of their one-time
occupants leaning negligently
and invariably on their left elbows
in the customary eating position
when the stone was alive
all of them focusing blank eyes
in unison at gaping tourists
as if they cast uncanny spells
and forced visitors to join them
prisoners in glass cases

– but the tombs the dark tombs
tumbled heaps of earth and stone
and my fixation with Lawrence
propelling me onward
– thinking of the small dark men
who fought the Romans and lost
they left so little of themselves behind
except their blood in Tuscany
a great tide of blood
from a vanished race
flowing now in living veins

making everyone here slightly different
giving them a yearning feeling
in their hearts for what they can't remember
– and to understand that much
about them is very close
to having a million people
in my arms and hugging them

– clambering over the mossy stones
from sunlight into darkness
my own imagination so vivid
I half expect to encounter a little man
with red hair and bright blue eyes
wearing a slightly snappish expression
when I inquire about his latest book
he is continually re-writing
and together
we scramble out of the tombs
to follow the well-marked trail
leading back the way we came from
the way we came from

FOR CURT LANG

O Lydia, Lydia, why are you sound asleep
while all night long I suffer in the alley?

– Horace

How awful to spend the night in an alley
trapped in a little English Prefect
wide-awake and dreaming sexual dreams
at age 17 in 1952
beer-drunk and comically romantic
forbidden to love delicious Norma
afflicted with a permanent erection
condemned to this dreadful fate
by your hard-boiled friend Purdy
thus allowing Norma a good night's sleep

Yah

Ah yes the parallel to Lydia's boyfriend
is obvious – but skip from Rome to Canada
Curt died of cancer in Vancouver
two months back and I am now 80
unfit for all but literary endeavours

Well I remember going out to the Prefect
again to see if Curt had killed himself
for love or lust or both
and thinking "migawd the poor guy"
his pale face at the car window
imploring the night piteously
"Oh Norma, Norma, why are you sound asleep?"
and will you hate me forever Curt?
– but now it's 1999 and he's dead

Talking to Norma on my return
to the house – she quite agitated
and possibly aroused
but wanting her beauty sleep
and that is the way it was?

But Norma has forgotten the incident
as she grows old and me older
the new millennium around the corner
which makes such things trivial
but think how lucky I've been:
this lifetime of writing excitement
and itching torment to *get it right*
a double reward for being alive
like a rolling Niagara of what I am
thus reversing the flow of time's river
stand confronting that Greek mountain
(yah Parnassus)
admiring but without envy
of all the dead great masters
reversing time to meet myself there

with the same feeling of
                    triumphant discontent
I've always had and thinking
                    poor Norma poor Curt
entombed in a verse that may last
at most fifty or a hundred years
and poor Lydia deep in Roman earth
asleep for two thousand years
and Horace the master of us all

HER GATES BOTH EAST AND WEST

Wanderings in Canada in the century
before the Millennium . . .

This is where I came to
when my body left its body
and my spirit stayed
in its spirit home

Beside the seething Fundy waters
my friend sleeps
and wrote this message for me
"I'll wait for you in the west
Till your sun comes down for its setting"
That grand summer in Newfoundland
when we feasted on wild raspberries
bakeapples Screech and salmon
walked four miles in the rain
(you blamed me for) to L'Anse aux Meadows
where Helge Ingstad and Anne Stine
were digging up Leif the Lucky's ruins
talked to them an hour
while I watched the Viking ship
and horned heads leaping ashore
reflected in Ingstad's blue eyes
On Baffin Island

north of summer and summer
comes again with every flower
a river where I slept a moment's hour
to dream and plucked white blossoms
and sent them searching for you
from that island of lost memory
are the flowers still searching?
Quebec was summer in Montreal
Côte des Neiges and St. Joseph's
with Brother André's heart
pickled in alcohol
where I climbed the steps in winter
"the lame and the halt and the blind"
climbed in summer
in search of Brother André's miracle
and threw away their crutches
On a green Island in Ontario
I learned about being human
built a house and found the woman
and we shall be there forever
building a house that is never finished
Camped by the South Saskatchewan
all day we listened to voices
we heard inside ourselves
the river like a blue bracelet
where the Métis fought their last battle
Dumont Letendre and old Ouellette
their ghosts came to us in sleep
as white mist moved over our bodies
the river flowed into the sky
In the Alberta prairie badlands
camped by the vanished Bearpaw Sea
in Dinosaur Provincial Park
after the campground closed in fall
we wander NO TRESPASSING badlands
– the white light suddenly changes
to brown sepia twilight
we're 75 million years back in time
beasts like bad dreams ramp around us

with bodies we can see through
transparent in the sepia sun
and Canada becomes a very old country
the Rocky Mountains fold themselves upward
giants rising slowly
and we are children again
Through the Crow's Nest mountains
at age 17
the freight train a black caterpillar
climbing climbing climbing
vertebrae chattering up the mountains
red coal cinders blackening my face
riding the high catwalks riding the empties
like bugs like dwarfs like boys pretending
they're men halfway high as the mountains go
below us valleys bathed in sunlight
glowing enchanted valleys
and I came to believe we were beloved there
beloved in a land fortunate of itself
beneath black cinders on our faces
we glowed in turn from the soul's well-being
while I tried to explain myself to myself
the simple earth and sky-searching mountains
were things I never could explain
Flying north and following the Mackenzie
River long after the Scots explorer
endless forest then endless empty land
we seemed to hang between earth and sky
then a monster hand with a hundred fingers
spreading itself over the river delta
and a permafrost town still Canada
the Beaufort Sea beyond
where the world was blue forever

– comes the millennium into our brief lives

I suppose it's like a kid growing up
to see the parts of your own country
like a jigsaw that suddenly comes together

and turns into a complete picture
you've touched nearly all the parts
you've become a certain kind of adult
and the ordinary places become endearments
that slip into your mind and grow there
and you change into what you already are
in a country you can wear like an old overcoat
Joseph's coat of many colours

The millennium really makes little difference
except as a kind of unsubtle reminder of
the puzzle that is yourself and always changing
the country that you wandered like a stranger
but stranger no longer
yourself become undeniable to yourself
wearing the lakes and rivers towns and cities
a country that no man can comprehend
Joseph's coat turned inside out
now indistinguishable from your own innards
– a country that no man may comprehend
asking the same questions as in ages past
time measurable by the tick-tock of millenniums
and if by chance we are not alone
some traveller on another planet
may catch a glimpse of us sometimes
looking outward into the night sky

TO SEE THE SHORE

To all the many thousands of poets who have been, who are now (and those who will be), poets bad, good, or indifferent – I'm grateful. The same bug that bit those others also took a chunk out of me, infecting all of us with this habit, craft, art, or whatever it is. As a result, I've experienced tremendous feelings of euphoria when writing what I've thought was a good poem. Even at the worst of times, writing poems has been joyous and rewarding.

Travelling has almost been a way of life for this poet, especially in the last few years. Strange landscapes and foreign climes have produced a feeling of renewal, the earth itself has given me a sense of history, the stimulus of the original events carrying over in time and entering my own brain. Mircea Eliade, a kind of social anthropologist, has some interesting theories about myth and legend: primitive peoples re-enact original events in ritual repetitions, and each time becomes for them the first time. And thus they negate huge areas of time itself.

I know what Eliade means, or think I do. And travelling in Peru, the Soviet Union, South Africa, the Galapagos Islands, Greece, Mexico, etc., has evoked excitement in me that is like a small stain of colour derived from some original event. And so one lives many lives, all condensed like a compacted millennium, waiting to spring outward at the trigger-moment in your mind.

I spent most of the summer of 1965 on Baffin Island. After flying from Montreal to Frobisher Bay by Nordair, I hitched a ride on a mining company charter to Pangnirtung off Cumberland Sound. The regional administrator at Pang arranged for me to go along with an Eskimo family, travelling by canoe to their home base in the Kikastan Islands.

I was completely equipped with what the well-dressed Arctic explorer should wear: parka, heavy clothing, tent, sleeping bag, Coleman stove, and groceries. The Kikastan Islands' location had been pointed out to me on the map. Jonahsie, my personal Eskimo hunter, was a crack shot and highly regarded by the administration at Pang. But Jonahsie had no English, and I knew about two words of Eskimo. When we landed at a big humpbacked rock in Cumberland Sound in late afternoon, I knew this was not one of the Kikastan Islands. But I couldn't ask Jonahsie what the hell was happening to our travel schedule. It made me a little nervous: was I being kidnapped and forced to read William Blake to a northern audience, the way Evelyn Waugh's hero read Dickens in *A Handful of Dust*?

There was a blind dog in our canoe. I helped Leah, Jonahsie's wife, get the dog onto the beach. Several other canoes were there already, their owners farther inland on the hilly island. Rancid pieces of fat, gnawed bones, and dogshit littered the gravel beach. The sea surrounding our island was like the concentrated essence of all the blue that ever was; I could feel that blue seep into me, and all my innards changed colour. And the icebergs! They were shimmery lace and white brocade, and they became my standard for the word beauty. How could one ever think that a malignant relative of theirs once sank the *Titanic*?

All through early evening the hilltop hunters fired their guns at seals far below in the flaming blue water. During lulls in cannonading, other hunters in canoes picked up the bodies. I had thought dead seals were supposed to sink, but apparently not. Even when rifles stopped firing, weird echoes bounced back from mainland mountains. Close to midnight the sun balanced on the horizon like a crimson egg; light turned grey, changing the landscape to skull-like desolation.

I was curled up in a sleeping bag, feeling lost at the world's edge, bereft of family and friends. As the tide went out, icebergs were left stranded on the beach. With the water's support removed, they collapsed on themselves with a crash whose echoes kept repeating themselves. A dog would howl, and others join in, a bedlam chorus. Old Squaw ducks moaned about how awful life was, an *OUW-OUW-OUW* dirge for the living. And all these sounds repeated themselves, as if some mad god were howling from distant mountains.

Somewhere in my head a poem began. One of the lines was about those ducks, the loneliness and defeat the birds signified: "I think to the other side of that sound": I think to a place where uncertainty and loneliness are ended, to a happier time. But, I say to myself now, think again: I was never really happier than when I was lying in a sleeping bag on an Arctic island, listening to those noisy ducks at the top of the world and writing a poem.

Next day we reached the certified actual Kikastan Islands, Jonahsie's home stomping grounds. I set up my tent, and wrote more poems.

I was lucky on those islands; sometimes poems do not get written so easily. Inner recesses of the mind are not at your beck and call. Perhaps there are small elves in the head, privileged guests living there and continually busy with their own affairs. The only connection the conscious mind has with them is when they permit a collaboration, which perhaps neither the conscious nor the unconscious was capable of alone.

Quite a few years ago, I wrote a poem called "Necropsy of Love." I'd been working on it in late evening. After going to bed I'd think of still another line or phrase, get up and write it down, then go back to bed. My wife, predictably, did not appreciate cold nocturnal drafts in the bedclothes, or the risings and fallings of bedsprings at unpredictable intervals. Especially she did not appreciate my enthusiastic renderings of poem-fragments that kept jumping out of my brain.

Earlier that evening the television set had blatted out a commercial about Success Wax, and how "it shines like a good wax should shine day after day after day." And that commercial kept running through my head along with the poem; Success Wax mixing with the absolutes of love and death. My conscious mind had to tell my unconscious mind sternly: stay the hell out of my poem. Or was it vice versa?

My elves were never more or less present and unaccounted for than when I was in Hiroshima, Japan, in the early 1970s. I landed in Tokyo, took the wrong train to Hiroshima, got into the wrong car on the wrong train for the trip, bumped my head on both exit and entrance of the train. But I drank Japanese beer with a Japanese passenger and joked with him, neither of us knowing the other's language. I wandered the city that was bombed nearly out of existence in 1945; developed sign language and facial expressions to the point where an anthropoid ape would have thought me insane; watched television, drank beer, and cooked food in my hotel room.

I didn't fit the country physically. Too tall. I kept hitting my head on something or other. The jarring and pounding must have been terrible for my resident elves (I didn't like it much either), because after I wrote an unspecified number of poems, they stopped collaborating. No more poems got written despite all my efforts. Or perhaps it wasn't the bumping and jarring by themselves: for when I was asleep the ghostly shape of a mushroom cloud hovered over my head. My collaborators must have seen it too. It frightened them, and no one does his best when he is frightened.

You watch them, those little elves who are your guests. You try to familiarize yourself with their habits, and how your own actions will affect them, how your own thoughts might meld with theirs. You say of them: they prefer strange things, they like high drama and soul-stirring events – then find that something quite trivial means more to them than wars and headlines. You try to predict their thoughts during the sun by day and the moon by night, then discover they have their own internal moons and suns.

Their appearance I can only imagine, but I believe they love to dress in odd costumes; I think they look at themselves in a mirror sometimes and admire what they see. Of course, they are very old. I think it's probable that they have been around since human time began and even before that. I'm sure they were hiding somewhere in the heads of those small shrew-like mammals who preceded humans.

For all my efforts, midnight searchings and dawn questions, I know little more about them than when I first decided they actually existed. And it's only when I forget about them entirely that they gently intrude into my thoughts. Gently, but with something sardonic about their attitude to this human with the ludicrous pretensions in whose head they reside.

A "collected poems" is either a gravestone or a testimonial to survival. When you remember all the early deaths among writers, survival can be considered a little out of the ordinary. And, if considered only as a metaphor for gravestone and the end of a writer's life, a "collected poems" will be seen to have just enough validity to make it meaningless.

This volume does not contain every poem I've ever written. However, it does contain the ones I like best. Some of my stuff is simply too awful to include and there seemed no great urgency about other omitted poems.

As a writer, I've always felt like an eternal amateur. Even after writing poems all my life, I'm never entirely confident that the next poem will find its way into being. And then I find myself writing one, without knowing exactly how I got there.

In my lifetime, there have been many other writers whose work I've admired and absorbed. They are constantly nudging me somewhere in my unconscious mind. If I had to name two of the most important influences, D.H. Lawrence and Irving Layton would qualify. As examples, not tutors. And perhaps Milton Acorn gets in there somewhere as well; I learned from him both how to write and how not to write. (Very few people can teach you opposite things at the same time.) I think I've learned from everyone I've read, on some level, though I've digested their writing in ways that make it impossible for me to recognize it in my own work. All of us who write are indebted to everyone else who writes for our enthusiasms and craft (or sullen art).

I have enjoyed being alive and writing a great deal, being ashamed and prideful, making mistakes and stumbling on answers before I knew the questions existed. In a world so abundant with both good and bad things, in which my own unique lighted space of human consciousness burns and flickers, at this moment when the past and future converge to pinpoint now, at an age when the body says, "Slow down, you silly bugger," there are still important things in my life, and still poems I want to write.

Which is a very long sentence: it makes me thirsty for a beer or two. And it occurs to me that if I were aboard a rowboat floating in the middle of all the beer I've drunk in a lifetime, I'd never be able to see the shore.

At which point the high gods of serious things throw up their hands in horror.

AL PURDY
Ameliasburg, March 1986

EDITOR'S NOTE

Beyond Remembering contains the poems that Al Purdy considered his best work, the ones, in other words, that he wanted to be remembered for and on which he wanted his critical reputation to rest. They are taken from *On the Bearpaw Sea* (1974, 1994), *In Search of Owen Roblin* (1974), *The Collected Poems of Al Purdy* (1986), *The Woman on the Shore* (1990), *Naked with Summer in Your Mouth* (1994), *To Paris Never Again* (1997) and his recent uncollected work. They are arranged chronologically with the exception of a handful of early poems republished in heavily revised versions in the last three collections; these have been placed with the poems from the later volumes. Thus, although "Transvestite" originally appeared in *Sundance at Dusk* (1976), the revised version is placed with the poems selected from *To Paris Never Again*. Poems that were only slightly revised for *Rooms for Rent in the Outer Planets: Selected Poems 1962–1996* have been placed among the poems with which they were originally published. Thus "Spring Song," though touched up in the 1990s, is with the poems selected from *Poems for All the Annettes* (1962). The poems that appeared in the 1986 collected edition are reprinted in the same order as in that volume. The only exceptions are "Homer's Song" and "The Dead Poet," that book's first and last poems; they have been restored to their proper chronological places. Though some of the early poems later incorporated into *In Search of Owen Roblin*, such as "Elegy for a Grandfather," were rewritten in the 1980s and 1990s, Al Purdy has chosen to reprint that volume as it originally appeared in 1974. *On the Bearpaw Sea* was published in a slightly enlarged and revised version in 1994, but appears, with revisions, in its original chronological place.

Despite Al's trust in my editorial judgment, I have been reluctant to make many changes simply in order to make the poems conform to a house style. I have silently corrected errors from the earlier editions (*pissoir* for *pissoire*, Xanthus for Zanthus, cooperage for copperage, Regency for regency, Noboddady for nobodaddy etc.), but have left in both plowed and ploughed because of the possibility that in some cases the poet liked the look of one (there are other "w"s in the line) and in some cases the other. In "My '48 Pontiac" only the Pontiac is capitalized because I suspect that Purdy wanted the car emphasized typographically as well as thematically. I have, however, attempted to make uniform italicized words and phrases from foreign languages by italicizing only those that are not relatively common in English; thus déjà vu but *Rananim* and *pissoir*. I have also been reluctant to add or remove hyphens. Since Al always saw the books through the press, the final versions of the poems have his approval.

Though Al Purdy did not live to see this volume through the press, he and I had completed the final selection and arrangement several months before his death on April 21, 2000. We were helped by the tacit collaboration of Russell Brown, the editor of the first *Collected Poems of Al Purdy*, the "ur-text" for this one, and Dennis Lee who helped shape some of the earlier collections. Our thanks to both of them.

My thanks to Eurithe Purdy, to Howard and Silas White and the staff at Harbour Publishing, and to the staffs of the libraries at the University of Saskatchewan and Queen's University for their help with research in the Purdy Archives. And finally, a warm note of gratitude to André Solecki, Vanessa Solecki Nelson, Ursula Solecki, Lydia Powers and Susan Addario for their encouragement and for keeping the candle burning in the darkness.

SAM SOLECKI
University College
University of Toronto

INDEX OF TITLES

Beyond Remembering

Beyond Remembering